Healing
for a
Bitter
Heart

Releasing The Power Of Forgiveness

Charles R. Gerber

COLLEGE PRESS PUBLISHING COMPANY • JOPLIN, MISSOURI

Copyright © 1996, Charles R. Gerber
Second printing 2001
No portion of this book may be reproduced in any form,
except for brief quotations in reviews,
without written permission from the author

Printed and Bound in the United States of America
All Rights Reserved

Cover design by Mark A. Cole

All Scripture quotations, unless indicated, are taken from
THE HOLY BIBLE: NEW INTERNATIONAL VERSION®.
Copyright © 1973, 1978, 1984 by International Bible Society.
Used by permission of Zondervan Publishing House.
All rights reserved.

Library of Congress Cataloging-in-Publication Data

Gerber, Charles R. (Charles Richard), 1958–   .
   Healing for a bitter heart: releasing the power of forgiveness /
Charles R. Gerber.
     p.   cm.
   Includes bibliographical references.
   ISBN 0-89900-787-2 (pbk.)
    1. Forgiveness—Religious aspects—Christianity. I. Title.
BV4647/F55G47 1997
234'.5—dc21   97-20400
                                                 CIP

Foreword

What happens when anger turns to bitterness? What are the effects of bitterness and how can our counselees get free of its grip? Would a perusal of Amazon.com point to books to help us find answers to these questions?

Apparently not. Despite the prevalence of bitterness, there are few books dealing with the topic. Put aside those dealing with bitter foods, bitterness in politics or international affairs, and only a few general books remain. Maybe half are written by Christians; few appear to be helpful.

American Association of Christian Counselors member, Charles Gerber, produced an exception. His 300-plus page book looks at the causes and crippling effects of bitterness. It gives helpful and interesting profiles of bitter people in the Bible, describes how bitterness affects Christians, and presents biblically-based steps for getting free of bitterness. Almost half the book deals with forgiveness, the ultimate answer to bitterness. It starts with a chapter on "the hardest person to forgive." You can guess who that might be.

This is a refreshing book, written by a Christian counselor who knows his psychology but is not bashful about

Healing for a Bitter Heart

bringing a lot of biblical information into his work. If you deal with bitter people, as we all do, or are bitter yourself, consider finding and reading this book. Healing from the grip of bitterness may occur.

Dr. Gary Collins

Preface

The truths presented in this manual form the foundational cornerstones that provide the biblical, spiritual and counseling theory of Christian Counseling Services. It is my hope that this book becomes a best-seller; not because of design, but because of need and its healing potential.

Many people have helped in the writing of this book. There have been many people who have encouraged me during the eight years of this project. This book is dedicated to my wife, Janelle. She has heard me speak on this topic for the past eight years. She has put up with the late nights and hours of research.

It is also dedicated to: Will Walls, who has been my example of the Christian life; Pat Rivest, the minister at University Christian Church; and the elders and the members of University Christian Church of Muncie, Indiana who have been a great source of encouragement and strength. I especially want to thank Tom Lesh for doing so much editing on this project. His suggestions and dedication helped make this project a reality. I also want to thank Matt Stafford for helping me with the Greek used in this book.

To the staff at Christ In Youth in Joplin, Missouri, I want to thank you for the dedication you have shown to *Healing for a Bitter Heart* and Christian Counseling Services. Thank you all for the love, support and encouragement you have given me during the past several years. You have allowed me to speak on this topic and many others. You are friends and family to my wife, my two kids and me. Thank you for allowing me to teach "forgiveness therapy" across the nation. Without you I don't know if this project would have been completed.

I also want to thank the Board of Directors of Christian Counseling Services and the supporting Churches and individuals. Many of you have been with me since the beginning of this ministry back in 1985. You have been very supportive with this whole project. You have been the backbone and the motivation for this ministry. Without your love and support, I could not be doing what I am doing for the kingdom of God!

Table of Contents

Introduction

Forgiveness is the most important aspect of Christianity. It is what separates Christianity from other major world religions. If you pull forgiveness away from Christianity, what do you have? You have an eastern religion; a new age religion. You have a list of worldly religious rules, but not salvation and heaven. Can a person believe in God, Jesus and Christianity and not believe in forgiveness? No! These four things go hand in hand.

The book you are about to read is dangerous. Satan knows it, and he did not want it written. In the past year, during the final editing, I have had three computers break down and a monitor go out. It is my hope that this is because Satan is afraid of the power and purpose of this book.

It is my prayer that this book will release people from one of Satan's strongest oppressions — bitterness. I have written this book because I believe that a solution to bitterness is needed in our society. Bitterness has become epidemic. It is everywhere.

In the writing of this book one thing became very obvious to me: in every broken relationship bitterness could be at the root (Ps 69:20; Heb 12:15). In my Bible reading I began to see parables that dealt with bitterness. Bible stories I had known all my life took on new meaning. Cain and Abel, and Jacob and Esau, began to be seen as stories that dealt with bitterness. I realized the book of Jonah dealt not with a poor evangelist, but with how God makes those who are bitter confront the things embittering them. Even *Time* magazine said on its October 28, 1996 cover "And God said... Betrayal. Jealousy. Careerism. They're all in the Bible's first book. Now there's a spirited new debate over the meaning of Genesis."

I was beginning to think I had a one-track mind. Or was I actually on to something? Is bitterness that common of a problem in our society? The newspapers show this to be true. Is bitterness the cause of a lot of pain people face? Does it cause illness and disease? Consider the following quote, "For me, the physical symptoms (physical illness and its symptoms) are often an indication that bitterness might be operating in a person's life."[1] Medical science has done much research on physical illness and emotions. Bitterness has been linked to cancer.

This book was written for those who have been physically and sexually abused. It was written for victims of divorce, adultery, rape, robbery and incest. This book was written to promote healing and help people regain what bitterness and past events have stolen; and help them to lead healthy, productive lives.

Warning: This book may cause pain for a while. It may expose areas in your life where bitterness resides. It may explain what has been going on in your life for years! This material can easily be misused to cause harm for people. But, if used properly, it will show you how to get rid of bitterness and how to forgive.

Even though I may have been the one who put this book together, the author of it is the Lord. As you go on this journey in understanding forgiveness, it is my hope you learn what forgiveness is. The teacher of forgiveness is Jesus. Jesus said he wants us to learn from him (Matt 11:28-30). It is important to learn about and understand forgiveness for two reasons:

1. So you can forgive those people who have hurt you, as well as forgive yourself. This will get rid of bitterness.
2. So you can teach forgiveness to a hurting and dying world, which needs to accept forgiveness from Jesus and be saved.

I am constantly asked why I have included so many references to Scripture in this book. The reason is found in Isaiah 55:10-11:

> As the rain and the snow come down from heaven, and do not return to it without watering the earth and making it bud and flourish, so that it yields seed for the sower and bread for the eater, so is my word that goes out from my mouth: It will not return to me empty, but will accomplish what I desire and achieve the purpose for which I sent it. You will go out in joy and be led forth in peace; the mountains and hills will burst into song before you, and all the trees of the field will clap their hands.

The reason I have used so many Scripture resources is because God promises it will produce a crop of healing and deliverance (Ps 107:20). It is also because the Word of the Lord stands forever (Isa 40:8). The Bible contains the wisdom of the Lord and this wisdom leads to healing (Isa 28:29). I believe that this book gives the truthful words of God, his teachings to help bitter people (Isa 28:26; 45:19; Ps 73:24; 119:24). In a very real sense, I plagiarized this book, but God won't mind because I am one of His ambassadors.

You are about to go on an adventure through the Bible dealing with aspects of forgiveness. I have put in many biblical references with the hope you will look them up and commit some of them to memory. In doing this you will learn about forgiveness. This will not be an easy task, but it will be one that reaps a reward.

The word "heal" is used in the title of this book because healing requires that the cause of the injury be identified and treated. This book will identify three of the most common reasons for bitterness. This book will stress that healing is the process of reclaiming something that was lost or wounded. Bitterness is such a pervasive human condition that just about all of us need some healing in this area. Ideally, however, as we learn how to forgive, we will be able to prevent bitterness from developing.

Jesus wants you healed from bitterness. He and the Holy Spirit are constantly interceding for you in this matter (Rom 8:26-27, 34; Heb 7:25; 9:24; 1 John 2:1). Forgiveness is part of the healing process. Psychology is actually beginning to see forgiveness as a therapeutic tool. Consider what Terry D. Hargrave, associate professor at Amarillo College, in Amarillo, Texas, who is also the author of a book *Families and Forgiveness*, published by Brunner/Mazel said, "For years, psychotherapy has been reluctant to label forgiveness as a therapeutic tool, instead focusing on anger, blame and carrying around one's negative emotions of family experiences." He also said, "In cases, for example of spousal infidelity or parental distancing and passivity, forgiveness can operate to restore trust and love in the damaged relationship." He continues, "But when a person has been irreparably damaged by the family, forgiveness becomes an important element to salvaging the self."[2]

The most important question is "Do you really want to be healed?" Jesus asked the same question to a man who was paralyzed for 38 years (John 5:6). I have known many people who have been paralyzed by bitterness for decades. They may not even realize that they are bitter. They need to be healed but think they never can be. The truth is that they can be healed by God, his word, Jesus and the Holy Spirit.

Source Notes

1. Everett L. Worthington, Jr., *Marriage Counseling: A Christian Approach to Counseling Couples*. (Downers Grove, IL: InterVarsity Press, 1989), p. 154.

2. Heather M. Little, "Patients, Therapist Praise the Healing Power of Forgiveness," *Lexington (Kentucky) Herald-Leader*, 10 December 1995.

1

Causes of Bitterness

Small things can make a person bitter. The song in 1 Samuel 18:7 sung by the women of Israel, "Saul has slain his thousands, and David his tens of thousands," made Saul very bitter. This song was known by people in Gath (1 Sam 21:11) and by other Philistines (1 Sam 29:5). Other people knew this song had to keep Saul continually bitter at David. Notice that after this song was first sung, it was not long until Saul tried to kill David.

The New World Dictionary of American English defines cause as "a reason, motive, or grounds for some action."

Every year across America a dubious record is being broken in many cities and small towns. It is the murder rate. In 1994, Indianapolis, Indiana broke the old record around Thanksgiving. This gave the city a little more than a month to "set" the new record. The faces of the victims appear on the national news and in local papers. They are the opening stories on the local news. They are some of the victims of bitterness.

Many health professionals don't recognize bitterness as a cause of many of the "evils" in our society. Psychology uses the *Diagnostic and Statistical Manual of Mental*

Disorders to diagnose mental and emotional problems. In its indexes bitterness does not even appear. In the Bible the word bitterness and associated words appear 84 times in the New International Version. The truth is our society has a problem with bitterness; many people are bitter even if psychology does not recognize it!

But who are these "bitter" people? They have a strong desire to seek revenge or get even. They are constantly dealing with physical illness. Their relationships have fallen, or are falling, apart. They are married or divorced, single, lonely, employed or unemployed, hurting because friends have betrayed them. They feel that trusting others only makes them vulnerable to deception and hurt. They are the victims of a sexual molestation and rape. They may be children from a broken home. They might have grown up in an abusive home where one parent was an alcoholic. They might be childless because of infertility, age or being single. Their dreams have been shattered. They may have stopped dreaming long ago. They could be any or all of us, and actually are many of us. They are like many people in our society. They are people of a bitter society.

Some bitter people are in a professional's office (doctor, counselor, minister) to deal with an issue that is destroying their life. If they come to a Christian counselor or minister, they want to be told sweet stories about Jesus, but do not want to be confronted with their true problem of bitterness. The truth will make them angry (Gal 4:16). If any person dare tell them the truth, they become very angry and defensive, only proving the diagnosis correct.

They are bitter, but do not want to accept it. They want to blame others for what they are feeling and not take responsibility for their own actions and emotions. Yes, they have been hurt and disappointed by circumstances and people. But, their bitterness is killing them and others.

How Bitterness Forms

I recently saw a picture of a mother standing over the fresh grave of her son, who was only 18 years old when he died. He, like her, was a victim of the civil war in Bosnia-Herzegovina. Death (loss) is a common occurrence with them. Years ago they faced the challenge of hosting the Olympics; now they face the challenge of surviving bitterness. Bitterness abounds in this region. This kind of loss is unwanted, unfair and unyielding. It will affect the survivors for a long time. When the war is over and the guns are silent, the civil war of bitterness will rage within the heart.

What can cause people to become bitter? They have been brought to the brink of bitterness by three very powerful events — loss, injustice and betrayal. They have become embittered by these events. These events have become an accustomed part of their existence. They are used to them, and they are used to being bitter. Bitterness is caused when people focus on and become stuck in painful events. Bitterness is unforgiveness. A person with an unforgiving heart is going through a punishment worse than death. Bitterness takes a bad, painful situation and makes it worse, a lot worse. It is important to realize that *any* betrayal, injustice, or loss can create bitterness. Bitterness can develop over trivial matters as easily as it can over earthshaking ones! Recently our newspaper ran a story about a woman who had put the ashes of her mother along with other items into a self-storage. She did not pay the monthly rent of $55.00 and the items were auctioned off. The lady was quoted as saying, "I can't believe they did this. I've lost everything. I've lost my mother." This loss, and any other, can create a good seed bed for bitterness to blossom and grow.

Bitterness is actually unforgiveness. Bitterness is a result of unforgiveness of betrayal, injustice and/or loss! Everett L. Worthington Jr. wrote, "Problems of forgiveness result from hurt and egocentrism of the party who was hurt. A relationship characterized by unforgiveness is built on mistrust of the spouse and either an air of martyred affliction or a desire to hurt the other person in return. Often, Christian couples can confess forgiveness, but still tend to act in ways that provoke their spouses. Over time, lack of forgiveness can lead to bitterness."[1] Over time, this lack of forgiveness will lead to bitterness! Unforgiveness will *always* result in bitterness.

When the snow starts to fall in central Indiana, it is easy to predict that winter is soon on the way. The cold winds begin to blow and the snow warnings become more frequent on the weather forecasts. Bitterness is as easy to predict as the seasons and the weather.

There appear to be some predisposing factors of bitterness that are found in the personality and environment. Some are: excessive pride, having been raised in a bitter environment, inappropriate self-esteem, insecurity, lack of self-control, and strong self-criticism. Proverbs 13:10 reads, "Pride only breeds quarrels...." Proverbs 22:24-25 teaches, "Do not make friends with a hot-tempered man, do not associate with one easily angered, or you may learn his ways and get yourself ensnared."

Scripture backs up the idea that bitterness is caused by loss, injustice and betrayal. Satan is the author and perfecter of loss, injustice and betrayal. He is hoping all three of these events happen to us. There is an old saying that things occur in threes. You will notice that I said there are three basic things causing bitterness. I believe there are three events that Satan will use to create bitterness because of what Ecclesiastes 4:12 states, "Though one may be overpowered, two can defend themselves. A cord of three strands is not quickly broken." Satan knows that the cord formed from loss, injustice and betrayal is not quickly broken. Consider the following diagram:

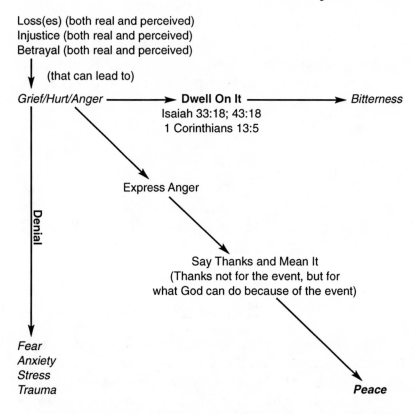

Loss(es) (both real and perceived)
Injustice (both real and perceived)
Betrayal (both real and perceived)

(that can lead to)

Grief/Hurt/Anger ⟶ **Dwell On It** ⟶ *Bitterness*
Isaiah 33:18; 43:18
1 Corinthians 13:5

Express Anger

Denial

Say Thanks and Mean It
(Thanks not for the event, but for
what God can do because of the event)

Fear
Anxiety
Stress
Trauma   ***Peace***

Bitterness is the universal language! It can be found in every culture since the beginning of time. It is an attitude, a bad attitude. The daily headlines in the papers across the nation confirm the bitterness epidemic — "Man kills estranged wife, then himself"; "Man intends to take bitter divorce to his grave"; "Fired worker returns to kill boss, then self"; "Fans bitter from coast to coast"; and "Welcome Back? Boos at Marlins, Dodgers reminder that baseball isn't totally forgiven." Even things like the loss of a World Series created by a professional baseball strike can create bitterness.

Bitterness has been around since the creation of the world. It was present when Cain killed Abel. It was there because Satan was there. Bitterness is one of Satan's favorite emotions. It is one of the stronghold emotions from which Satan operates. The other three are guilt, fear and inappropriate self-esteem.

What exactly is bitterness? An acrostic will help. Bitterness is:

B attering
I ntensifying
T erminal
T orment
E ndangering
R elationships
N eeding
E nergy
S atan
S timulated

Battering. Bitterness hammers away at all relationships. It attacks a person mentally, physically, spiritually and emotionally. Proverbs 18:14 states, "A man's spirit sustains him in sickness, but a crushed spirit who can bear?" Proverbs 15:13 teaches that heartache crushes the spirit. Proverbs 17:22 states that a crushed spirit dries up the bones. Bitterness batters the spirit of man crushing it. When the spirit is crushed, this effects the physical body. Bitterness makes the body more susceptible to illness and injury. Recent medical research has linked bitterness with cancer.

Intensifying. Bitterness grows in strength, becoming more destructive daily. The ideas on how to seek revenge grow daily until they consume the mind.

Terminal. Its end result is mental, physical, spiritual and emotional death and depression. Bitterness and depression are very similar in diagnosis. It is the leading cause of separation and alienation in relationships. It causes divorce and death, murder and misery.

Torment. It eats away at the mind; causes pain and a desire for revenge.

Endangering Relationships. Bitterness is the most deadly enemy of relationships. It will often destroy even healthy relationships. The truth is, when you are bitter at one person, you are probably bitter at all people. You may have a hard time believing this, but it is true. I believe that one reason people explode in minor situations is because they are angry at past situations. Frequently men who are angry at women in their past will take the anger out on their wives and vice versa.

Needing Energy. Energy is needed for bitterness to be maintained. Frequently fatigue and illness are common in people who are bitter. This energy is "stolen" from the body's immune system, leaving it vulnerable to disease and sickness.

Satan Stimulated. He is the author and prompter of bitterness. He understands it very well because it is what he is. Revelation 12:12 teaches that Satan is filled with fury. He is also full of bitterness and hatred.

More precisely what is bitterness? The Greek word for bitterness is *pikros* which means sharp, poisoning, piercing and violently bitter. It is the opposite of holiness (Heb 12:14-15). Bitterness attacks the Holy Spirit (Eph 4:30; Gal 5:17; 1 Thess 5:19). It is part of our human nature and is contrary to the Holy Spirit. In Galatians 5:17 the word "contrary" is the Greek word *antikeimai* which means "to lie opposite to." It is an emotion that hinders and entangles (Heb 12:1). The emotion of bitterness gets bound up in the heart (Prov 22:15). It causes a broken heart (Ps 69:20). Bitterness is like poison ivy — whatever it touches has some allergic reaction. It is like coffee. The more it brews the stronger it gets.

Bitterness is the result of a crushed spirit caused by

loss, injustice and betrayal (Ps 34:18; Prov 15:13; 17:22; 18:14). It may take months, years or even decades before it is fully developed. It begins when anger is held in past sunset. Jim Talley wrote, "As this anger (grows without resolution) intensifies and begins to alter the personality, it hardens into bitterness. In some instances this process can take a few months to solidify, but in others it may take a few years."[2] Think of bitterness as being like a slow cooker. It begins to cook the minute it is turned on, but it takes a while, a long while, before it is done. It is actually the emotion of repressed anger due to these three events that causes bitterness.

Emotions are something that all people have. There is a wide range of them. They are God given. But some of them are not to be kept inside the body. Anger is one that God intended to be unkept. It should be gotten rid of as soon as possible. Anger (held in) is like masking tape. The longer masking tape stays on an object the more difficult it is to remove. If masking tape is removed in a relatively short period of time, it is easier to remove. Anger is exactly the same way. The longer it stays in the body, not only does it do more damage to the body, but it is also harder to remove. Anger and past events can go unresolved forever.

Painful past events that are not resolved reside in the heart and will eventually be expressed in some way. This expression might take the form of an ulcer, cancer, high blood pressure or killing someone. The word "past" does not necessarily refer to events that took place 20 years ago, or two years ago but to events as recently as yesterday.

The past is also a teacher. One thing that is dangerous about the events in the past is they are often considered normal. This is one reason children who have at least one alcoholic parent often marry alcoholics; why children who have been abused often abuse. This is why spouses stay in abusive situations. It is not that they don't know better; it is because they don't know what normal is. Many people believe that being angry and bitter is a normal way of life. They may have seen it in their families for years. It becomes part of their family tree.

Bitterness and anger are closely related. William Backus, Ph.D. in his book *Telling the Truth to Troubled People* lists three basic reasons why people get angry: tension, expectations, and depression. He writes about expectations, "When you expect someone to provoke you, to be hostile, to be difficult, you are more likely to become angry in interaction with that person than when you have no particular prior expectations."[3] In the book *From Anger to Forgiveness*, Earnie Larsen writes, "Anger is always about injustice, perceived or real; it is the emotional response to injustice."[4] Anger can be the emotional response to loss and betrayal as well.

It is important to realize that God upholds us in times of loss, injustice and betrayal (Ps 37:17; 63:8; 145:14; 146:7). When you go through loss, injustice and betrayal, remember that Jesus' heart goes out to you (Luke 7:11-13). This will make the suffering easier to handle. He can understand and sympathize with what you are going through (Heb 4:15).

If injustice is one of the causes of bitterness, what is justice? One of the Old Testament words for justice is *mispat* which is from the root *sapat*, meaning to do what is right or just. Another word for justice is *sadaq*. This word is from a family of words conveying the idea that moral and ethical norms do exist. The New Testament word for justice is *dikaios* which has a similar meaning as *sadaq*.

What then is injustice? Isaiah gives some interesting descriptions of it. He writes that justice can be far from us, that it can be hard to find, that it can be driven back, and there are times when there is no justice (Isa 59:9, 11, 14, 15). These are great definitions of injustice. In Micah 3:9

we read that justice can be despised, and what is right can be distorted.

Two acrostic definitions of "past" are:

Painful	**Programming**
Activities	Advancing
Satan's	Satan's
Treat	Teaching

Ivern Ball said, "The past should be a springboard, not a hammock." In other words, people can rest and live in the past. We need to be aware that we are products of the past, but we don't have to be puppets. The past has no strings to control us. Because we are products, we can choose what will be the outcome of our past.

The past can be the foundation and fingerprints of the personality. It is where fears, shame, guilt, self-esteem and ideas about self and life are learned. You must choose to take control of your own life. Don't let the painful events in the past rule over your present and future.

The two D's of the past

One of the first things a person does with a painful past event is to *dwell* on it. Reaching back into the negative past and dwelling on it causes perpetual bitterness bondage and slavery. Ezekiel 35:5-9 lists some of the consequences of harboring (dwelling on) an ancient hostility. Two of the consequences are: God will give them over to bloodshed; and he will make their land desolate. The King James Version uses the phrase "perpetual hatred" in this passage. Ezekiel 25:15-17 is a supporting passage for this idea. The King James Version of this passage uses the phrase "old hatred."

If dwelling on the painful event is dangerous, should people just *deny* their past? No! Fear, anxiety, stress and trauma (physical) develop very quickly when a person

denies their betrayal, injustice and loss. Denial is the unac-
ceptance of the truth (Job 9:27-28). Denying loss, injustice
and betrayal leads to emotional and physical problems!
Denial makes the pain stay in the subconscious mind, where
it is not dealt with. The Center for Disease Control reports
that one of four people suffer from chronic stress headaches.
Their statistics report that 85% of all illnesses have stress
components. Could denial of bitterness be causing this?

Anger and bitterness are the most frequently denied
emotions on the planet. One way people deny being angry
is by the words they use to describe their anger. Words and
phrases I often hear to describe anger are: mad, upset, frustrated, disappointed, resentful, hacked off, teed off, ticked
off, bent out of shape, indignant, irate, aggravated, worked
up, hot under the collar, infuriated, sore, incensed, red-
faced, seething, boiling, bristled, flared, hit the ceiling,
stewed, steamed, steamed up, outraged, mad as a hornet,
and mad as a wet hen. The above words seem to be more
acceptable to use than the word "angry." By using a different word – this is a subtle form of denial.

Denial does not get rid of the pain, it only intensifies
it! Denial is the major reason for alcoholism and drug
abuse. People often use those substances as an escape from
the pain they have been through. They use them to numb
themselves from the pain in their past. Recent research
from an Associated Press (8/31/93) article stated that
nearly nine of ten alcoholic woman suffered physical or
sexual abuse as girls. This is from a study of 472 women
written in August 1993 in the Journal of Studies. Research-
ers say the study confirms existing evidence that abused
children are more likely to have alcohol problems later in
life. Denial causes anger to build. This anger will eventually
blow! Consider the follow statement:

> In many instances, there can be no healing and spiritual
> growth until we are released from the painful memories and

25

unhealthy patterns which now interfere with our present
attitudes and behavior. In denying our pain we give opportunity to the enemy. We may try to deny our feelings, but
we will live them out daily, and they will assume other
names."[5]

There are several forms of denial:

1. *Simple* denial: Believing the events never occurred.
2. *Minimizing*: Making less of what took place.
3. *Excuses*: Making excuses for what took place; defending
   the person who hurt you.
4. *Generalizing*: Saying that what happened to you happens to all people. Saying that yours was not all that bad.

Some people both dwell on and deny the past, thus
creating a pendulum of rapidly changing behaviors frequently labeled manic depression. People who have been
abused frequently have mood swings because of this pendulum (See diagram on p. 19). Suppressed emotions create
depression — 95 percent of depression is due to anger
repression.

I am frequently asked "How much of my past should I
remember?" I believe that all the painful past events do not
have to be remembered. Only the ones affecting the present are the ones that have to be dealt with. I do not
believe that people have to remember every painful event
to be healed. It is not important to remember the past
simply because you are curious.

Making peace with a person's past is a very difficult
task, but it is something that should be attempted and
accomplished. How do you make peace with a painful past
event? Peace comes from expressing the anger caused by
the event and then telling God "thank you" for the event.
(See diagram on p. 19) What exactly is peace? Peace is
something that God grants (Ps 147:14).

What does the Bible say about peace?

- ❖ Psalm 29:11 promises that the Lord blesses people with peace.
- ❖ Psalm 119:165 declares great peace is for people who love God's law.
- ❖ Proverbs 14:30 tells us that a heart at peace gives life to the body.
- ❖ Isaiah 26:3 says people can have perfect peace because they trust in God.
- ❖ Isaiah 48:18 promises if people would pay attention to God's commands, their peace would be like a river. One of God's commands is for people to say "thank you" to God for painful events (1 Thess 5:18; Col 3:15). Izaak Walton said, "God has two dwellings: one in heaven, and the other in a meek and thankful heart." When we thank God for a painful event we are turning our tears into rainbows. Telling God thanks for what he will do because of the event empowers him to act and gives us peace.
- ❖ Isaiah 54:10 promises God's covenant of peace will not be removed.
- ❖ Isaiah 57:19 links peace with God's healing.
- ❖ Isaiah 60:17 says peace can be our governor.
- ❖ Isaiah 66:12 God extends peace to his people.
- ❖ Philippians 4:7 God's peace transcends (rises above) all understanding. This is especially true with learning to say thanks. We have no understanding of how this brings peace, but it does. This type of peace is a great witness, and the world knows nothing about it.
- ❖ Hebrews 12:14 teaches that people should make every effort to live at peace and to be holy. In the next verse (15), the writer brings up the issue of bitterness. This passage suggests that the opposite of peace is bitterness.

There are some interesting Scripture passages dealing with the past. Isaiah 43:18-19 reads, "Forget the former things; do not dwell on the past. See, I am doing a new thing! I am making a way in the desert and streams in the wasteland." 1 Corinthians 13:5 states, "[Love] is not rude, it is not self-seeking, it is not easily angered, *it keeps no record of wrongs*" (emphasis added). Keeping a record of wrongs is how bitterness is formed.

Satan appears to have five purposes for bitterness: 1) *oppress* (Daniel 7:25), 2) *kill*, 3) *steal*, 4) *destroy* (John 10:10 — the word "and" means Satan wants all three and not just one of these three to occur), and 5) *ruin a Christian's faith* (Luke 22:31-32; Mal 3:14-15).

Bitterness is like the Chinese finger puzzle. The more people try to pull their fingers out, the stronger the grip of the puzzle is. Isaiah 58:6 visualizes what bitterness is. It asks, "Is not this the kind of fasting that I have chosen: to loose the chain of injustice and untie the cord of the yoke, to set the oppressed free and break every yoke?" It gives three illustrations of bitterness; 1) chains of injustice, 2) cords to a yoke, and 3) oppression.

Bitterness affects every area of life, including the personality of the bitter individual. Think of the personality as being like a hand. After going through loss, injustice and betrayal, the hand turns palm down, fist clinched (2 Cor 6:11-13). It is no longer open to be held, but is ready to fight and defend itself. Before loss, injustice and betrayal, the palm was up and open. It was affectionate and wanted to be loved.

A person's thoughts are also affected by bitterness. What does a person think about when going through these situations? These thoughts are subtle lies Satan tells to create bitterness:

During Loss a person thinks: *Love means leave. People always leave me. I knew it was going to happen. What's* *wrong with me?* Thoughts like these create low self-esteem. After loss, we tend to put a temporary restraining order on love that is hard to overcome and break! Many who go through loss make a promise to themselves that no one is going to get close to them. They make this promise so they won't get hurt anymore. Keeping this "promise made in bitterness" will result in loneliness and low self-esteem. Breaking this promise makes them angry and vulnerable. Either way they lose: this promise becomes a stronghold. No matter how they treat this promise, Satan has an area from which to operate.

During Injustice a person thinks: *No one cares about me. Life is unfair.* The word "unfair" is a verbal symptom of a bitter heart. This person might seek revenge to see that "justice" is served. Consider the following story:

> VINDICTIVE BOYFRIEND LEADS COPS TO ARREST (Joe Canan, *The Muncie Evening Press*, Wednesday, January 19, 1994, p. 1.)
>
> Deborah Olden got into an argument with her boyfriend Tuesday and called police to have him removed, but he got her back, according to county detectives.
> The boyfriend told police that Olden, a payroll clerk at Exide Corp., had participated in the theft and forgery of numerous payroll checks that had been cashed for more than $20,000, detective Robert Crabb said.

During Betrayal a person thinks: *From now on trust no one. Friendship is a joke, a lie. I always get hurt by those I love. I'm not protected by God. It always happens to me. All people are cruel.* After being hurt by betrayal people become negative toward anything the person who hurt them does, even positive things. They look for the flaws. Nothing can please them. They simply stop trusting! La Rochefoucauld is quoted as saying, "It is more disgraceful to distrust than to be deceived by our friends."

Healing for a Bitter Heart

The truth in these situations is:

Losses: *People are always moving in and out of your life. Love does not mean "leave," it means giving. You are a child of God. He will see you through this time in your life.*

Injustice: *People do care about you, but not all of them. Sometimes you don't get what you want out of life.*

Betrayal: *People break their promises at times. This is not a reason to totally distrust everyone. Friendship is a gift from God. You were protected, but the painful event was not prevented. Some people are cruel and you need to watch out for them.* God's protection is a very Biblical concept: Psalm 12:15; 91:14. Christians are told to watch out for people who will betray and lead them astray! (See Luke 21:8; Phil 3:2; 2 Tim 4:14-15.)

God will use these three situations for his glory. God has a purpose for pain (Ps 138:8). God will try to use these events to draw us closer to him (Jas 4:8). In crisis we either turn to God or completely away from him. God has many purposes in allowing these three events. One of God's purposes for these situations is to teach us to rely on him. Paul writes in 2 Corinthians 1:9, "Indeed, in our hearts we felt the sentence of death. But this happened that we might not rely on ourselves but on God, who raises the dead." Pain is frequently turned to God's glory (Isa 26:19; 54:11-12). What has been torn down by the storms in your life will be rebuilt by God beautifully. Consider the following story:

"A White Rose" By Pam Bennett

Once upon a time, there was a perfect white rose. It filled the world with beauty and sweetness, and it made the people who walked by feel more loving and gentle. They loved the white rose for all these good things.

Then one day some people who didn't care about gentle and beautiful and pure things walked by. They thought the

30

rose was something they could use for fun, and they thought being selfish and cruel was fun. They kicked dirt all over the rose, and they laughed. They didn't care that the rose was going to feel sick and dirty and sad. The rose hung its head and thought life would never feel clean and happy again. The rose was confused and thought it had become the dirt that it was smothering in. It didn't understand that it was still a rose.

Then one cold and gloomy day, a little girl who could easily see beautiful things was walking along the path where the white rose lived. She saw the sad rose hiding in the ugly weeds where it felt it belonged now. She knew it was something wonderful and she brushed off the dirt. She said, "See, little rose? The dirt was only on the outside. You are sweet and beautiful and pure, and people will love you for making the world a more sweet and pure place." The rose wasn't sure at first that this was true because it had been dirty so long, but it wanted this to be true so badly, it raised its head for all the world to see. Soon pure and sweet things it made the world feel. The rose soon saw that it was safe to be happy again, and it became the brightest rose in the garden.

C.S. Lewis, in a book titled *The Problem with Pain*, writes that God whispers to us in our joy and shouts to us in our pain.[6] God knows that these three events can be used to help us. William Penn wrote, "No pain, no palm; No thorns, no throne; No gall, no glory; No cross, no crown." Peter Marshall said, "God will not permit any troubles to come upon us, unless He has a specific plan by which great blessing can come out of the difficulty." Consider what Billy Graham wrote:

> Comfort and prosperity have never enriched the world as much as adversity has. Out of the pain and problems have come the sweetest songs, the most gripping stories.[7]

Another purpose is to create the ability to minister to hurting people. God trains us from past experiences so he

can use us in the present and future. If we had never experienced these situations, it would be impossible to witness
to others going through them. Paul writes in 2 Corinthians
1:3-4, "Praise be to the God and Father of our Lord Jesus
Christ, the Father of compassion and the God of all comfort, who comforts us in all our troubles, so that we can
comfort those in any trouble with the comfort we ourselves have received from God." Oswald Chambers said,
"The things we are going through are either making us
sweeter, better, nobler men and women; or they make us
more captious and fault-finding, more insistent upon our
own way." The world watches as Christians go through
these three events. This can be a dramatic witness for the
power of Christ. If the Christian does not become bitter,
the world will ask, "Why?" This is a great time to tell them
about Christ.

Another purpose God has for these events is so that
we can strengthen the brothers (Luke 22:31-32). These
events can show God's faithfulness. These events can
become a powerful witnessing tool (Mark 5:18-20). Let's
look in some depth at these three ingredients of bitterness.

Loss

Loss is often the main ingredient in the creation of bitterness (Ezek 21:6). Who or what the loss is, when the loss
occurred (I know of a person who had a son die on
Valentines Day and a daughter who died on Mother's Day
the same year.), why the loss occurred and how the person
found out about the loss can all contribute to the formation
of bitterness. Consider the following Associated Press story
by Jamie Friar dated August 18, 1992.

WEDDING GIFTS RIPPED OFF (Hookstown, Pennsylvania) AP

The bride and groom promised to stay together for richer,
for poorer. But they didn't expect to be poorer so soon.
Joseph and Theresa Novak had at least 600 dollars stolen

from a reception at the home of the groom's parents in Hookstown, Pennsylvania. Joseph Novak Sr. says the couple's presents, including envelopes containing cash, were left out in the open in his house. He says guests were relatives and close friends, which makes the theft so 'sad.'"

People in the Bible who had great losses and became bitter:

Naomi: She experienced multiple losses in a few years' time. As a result she became bitter. Her losses were:

Ruth 1:1 her relatives when she moved

Ruth 1:3 her husband

Ruth 1:5 her only two sons

Ruth 1:14 one daughter-in-law

Naomi asked to have her name changed from pleasant (Naomi) to bitter (Mara) Ruth 1:20-21.

Job:

Job's losses:

1:13-15 animals and farmhands

1:16 sheep and herdsmen

1:17 camels and servants

1:18-19 sons and daughters

Do you think Job was bitter at the three "friends" who came to give him advice? Let's take a quick look at their friendly advice:

- ❖ Eliphaz — "Who, being innocent, has ever perished? Where were the upright ever destroyed? (4:7)
- ❖ Bildad — "When a child sinned against him, he gave them over to the penalty of their sin." (8:1-7; v. 4 quoted)
- ❖ Zophar — "Oh, how I wish that God would speak, that he would open his lips against you..." (11:1-6; v. 5 quoted)

According to Job 2:13 Job's friends sat quietly with him for

33

seven days, the best kind of encouragement they could have given. They had originally come to give him comfort and encouragement because of his losses. They did an absolutely terrible job.

King Saul: "Samuel said to him, 'The Lord has torn the kingdom of God from you today and given it to one of your neighbors – to one better than you'" (1 Samuel 15:28). When Samuel used the word better, Saul became bitter!

Simon: Simon lost his reputation when the people compared him to the disciples (Acts 8:9-25). What was his request in Acts 8:18-19? Why did he make this request?

Peninnah: Her loss was due to the fact that her husband Elkanah loved his other wife, Hannah, more than he loved her even though she had given him children and Hannah was barren. She expressed her bitterness by constantly reminding Hannah of her barrenness. Hannah suffered from a broken heart because she was unable to have children, but, remarkably, showed little sign of bitterness. (1 Samuel 1:1-11)

Grief is a sign of bereavement or other loss. In the Bible, there are many accounts of grief over death. Some are:

- ❖ Abraham (Gen 23:2)
- ❖ Joseph (Gen 50:1)
- ❖ The Egyptians (Exod 12:30)
- ❖ Israel (Num 20:29; Deut 34:8; 1 Sam 25:1)
- ❖ Sisera's Mother (Judg 5:28)
- ❖ David (2 Sam 1:17; 2 Sam 12:15-23; 2 Sam 3:32)
- ❖ Mary and Martha (John 11:33)
- ❖ The disciples of Jesus (John 16:6)
- ❖ Dorcas' friends (Acts 9:39)

In summary, loss of any kind has the potential to create bitterness. Loss of a loved one, job, physical health, marriage, home, friendships, career, possessions, sexual purity, and innocence can create bitterness.

Injustice

Plato once said, "To do injustice is more disgraceful than to suffer it." Injustice is the second event that creates bitterness. Job 27:2 makes the connection between bitterness and denied justice (injustice). It declares, "As surely as God lives, who has denied me justice, the Almighty, who has made me taste bitterness of soul." A simple definition of injustice would be where the punishment does not fit the crime. Amos 5:7 refers to, "You who turn justice into bitterness and cast righteousness to the ground." If the punishment is seen as too severe, the perpetrator feels injustice, but if the punishment is not strong enough, the victim feels injustice. Frequently when this takes place you hear statements such as, "I'm going to take justice into my own hands." A sad verse on justice is Proverbs 28:5 which observes that the wicked don't understand justice.

A good example of someone taking justice into their own hands is found in Genesis 34. Simeon and Levi killed Hamor and Shechem, along with all the men in the town, because of the rape of their sister. Another story that has the theme of justice being taken into their own hands would be Absalom killing Amnon for raping his sister two years before (2 Sam 13).

Job understood justice. His losses were very unjust. He bemoans in Job 19:7, "Though I cry, 'I've been wronged!' I get no response; though I call for help, there is no justice." Job stated in 9:24, "When a land falls into the hands of the wicked, he blindfolds its judges."

Consider these five stories about sentences people received for their crimes. Bitterness could easily develop because of the discrepancy between the sentences and the crimes.

MAN KILLS UNFAITHFUL WIFE, SENTENCED TO 18 MONTHS (*Ball State Daily News* October 19, 1994, p. 1.)

Towson, Md. A man who shot his wife to death after catching her in bed with her lover drew 18 months in prison from a sympathetic judge in what women's activists say amounts to giving spouses a license to kill.

MAN GETS 5 MINUTES IN BEATING CASE (*The Star Press* Muncie, Indiana, Friday, August 9, 1996, p. 4C.)

Harrisburg, Pa. — A man who beat up a guy he caught in bed with his girlfriend was sentenced to 5 minutes' probation by a judge who suggested the victim had it coming. The person that got beat up required 32 stitches.

KISS HER GOOD-BYE (*The Muncie Evening Press*, Tuesday November 8, 1994, p. 1.)

Cleveland (AP)— It was the kiss of theft.
That's what a judge decided Monday, sentencing a woman to 50 years in prison for slipping men tranquilizer-laced champagne and robbing them as they slept.

VICTIM MUST PAY THIEF (*Evening Press*, Muncie, IN, Dec. 17, 1992, p. 5.)

Albion, IN, (AP) A homeowner who shot a burglar in his house has been ordered to pay the man $12,250.

MCDONALD'S CORP. WANTS NEW RULING OR A NEW TRIAL (*Evening Press,* Muncie, IN, August 31, 1994, p. 23.)

Albuquerque, N.M., (AP) McDonald's Corp. has asked a judge to rule in the company's favor or grant a new trial in a case of an Albuquerque woman who was awarded almost $2.9 million because she was scalded by hot coffee.

Justice is a major theme in one of the largest read magazines in America, *Reader's Digest*. Many of these issues deal with justice, crime and sentencing. For example: March 1993 had an article entitled, "When Criminals Go Free." The February 1994 issue contained an article on, "Revolving-Door Justice: Plague on America." November 1994 carried the article, "Must Our Prisons be Resorts?"

How common is injustice? The National Center for Policy Analysis in Dallas has estimated that:

A murderer could expect to spend 1.8 years in prison

For rape the expected punishment was 66 days

Robbery 23 days

Aggravated assault 7.6 days

Motor-vehicle theft 2.25 days

A U.S. Justice Department study of 79,000 felony probationers across the country discovered that 43% were re-arrested within three years. Princeton University Professor John J. DiLulio surveyed Wisconsin inmates in 1990 and found that over 40% admitted they had already been on probation two or more times.

The Bible speaks often of justice. The word "justice" occurs in the NIV 134 times. The word "injustice" occurs only 10 times. Below are some passages that deal both with injustice and justice. It is interesting to know if you break up the word "justice" between the "t" and the "i" the phrase formed is "*just ice.*" People often feel that the court's heart is made of ice after they have been through the judicial system. For bitterness to be gotten rid of, justice has to be done! Some verses dealing with injustice and justice are:

❖ *Deuteronomy 16:19-20; Deuteronomy 24:17; Proverbs 16:10; Proverbs 18:5* These four passages show how justice can be perverted, deprived, and betrayed. For more verses about justice being perverted look up Exodus 23:2; Leviticus 19:15; Job 8:3; Habakkuk 1:4.

Healing for a Bitter Heart

- ❖ _Proverbs 21:15_ Inverting this verse, it would read, "When injustice is done, there is no joy for the righteous and no terror for the evildoers." One reason this person has no joy is because of bitterness (Prov 14:10).

- ❖ _Habakkuk 1:4_ shows there are three negative P's that can happen to justice; it can be paralyzed, unprevailing, and perverted. Zechariah 7:9-10 uses two words to describe true justice: mercy and compassion (Jas 2:12-13, Eccl 8:11-12; Prov 17:23; 29:4, 7, 26; Isa 51:4).

- ❖ _Ecclesiastes 8:11_ states that justice can be slowly carried out. Consider John Wayne Gacy who was on death row for 14 years. He was sentenced to death back in 1980, but with appeals he was not executed until 1994. He actually outlived two of the jurists that sentenced him. He should have been executed 30 days after sentencing! Why was the sentence so slow in being carried out? Because our judicial system at times gives more rights to the criminals than the victims! The town where I live and pay taxes has just built a jail that is the Hilton of holding cells, the Howard Johnson of jails; at a cost of millions of dollars to taxpayers. What a message this sends to criminals. What a message this sends to law abiding citizens. Other countries of the world laugh at the United States' judicial and penal system.

- ❖ _Deuteronomy 25:1-3_ Is the spirit of this passage followed in the American court system today? Do the courts seem to be protecting the guilty more than the innocent? According to this verse there are different punishments for different crimes. Does the present justice system do this? Consider this article about justice. Who is being protected with this ruling?

38

VICTIM IN RAPE RULING FURIOUS OVER OUTCOME. (*Huntington Herald-Press*, Huntington, IN. Sunday, June 5, p. 6C.)

Allentown, PA (AP) The warning to women was clear: If a man attacks, don't fight, don't resist. Your life might depend on it.

Seven years ago, a college student took that advice. Today, she's fuming over a Pennsylvania Supreme Court ruling that she wasn't raped because her assailant didn't use force or threaten to use force.

"I did what we were supposed to do, what everyone taught us to do in college: If we were being raped, say 'no' and don't fight, because you could wind up dead," she told *The Morning Call* of Allentown in a story published Friday.

The Supreme Court overturned Robert Berkowitz's rape conviction last week, ruling the state definition of rape required force or threats.

During the trial, the woman acknowledged Berkowitz never restrained her or threatened her during the attack in his dormitory room at East Stroudsburg University in 1987. Both said the woman continually said "no."

Katie Leland from Wabash, Indiana wrote a research paper called, "Reclaiming Justice in America." In doing the research she talked to several foreign dignitaries and missionaries. She asked them about the punishment for rape in their countries. From these interviews she found the following information.

Country	Punishment
Haiti	Execution by hanging.
Iraq	Possible life imprisonment or hanging.
Israel	Imprisonment with extensive therapy — minimal chance for reduced sentence.
Laos	Imprisonment for 2-3 years. Repeated offenders are executed.

Malaysia	Imprisonment for several years without parole with possible caning.
Singapore	Caning: 10 strokes over one month.
United States	Average sentence: 7 years. Average time served: 66 days. Frequent reduced sentences.
Zimbabwe	Imprisonment 2-5 years and fine.

Betrayal

Betrayal — the third condition leading to bitterness. An acrostic definition of betrayal is:

Broken
Empathy,
Trust,
Respect,
Acceptance,
Yearnings,
And
Love

The Old Testament has two words it uses for betrayal. **Begad**, which means to deal treacherously (Ps 73:15; Isa 24:16; 33:1; Jer 12:6; Lam 1:2); and **Ramah**, which means beguile or deceive (2 Sam 19:26; 1 Chr 12:17). The New Testament word for betrayal is **paradidomi**. It means to hand over or deliver up. A simple definition of betrayal is getting from a friend what you expect from an enemy. Trust and loyalty become preconditions to betrayal.

It is broken empathy, trust, respect, acceptance, yearnings (goals) and love that causes overwhelming pain. It is the breaking of these traits of friendship that entrap a person in the bondage of bitterness. For betrayal to happen there has to be trust.

40

No one trusts very much anymore, not even corporate America. Consider the airline industry: several of them have bereavement rates so people can go to funerals in emergencies. But if you are going to use them, you might have to give the funeral home's name, the doctor's name, the name of the person that died, or even a death certificate to get the special fares. Why do you think the airlines require this information? It is because people have lied and taken advantage of the special rates for things other than funerals. I wonder how many people have gone on "funeral vacations."

Four kinds of betrayal are possible, and sadly common in our society.

❖ **Slander** – verbal betrayal

❖ **Gossip** – verbal betrayal (Proverbs 11:13; 20:19 "A gossip betrays a confidence....")

❖ **Adultery** – sexual betrayal. What about justice in divorce cases involving adultery? Who usually gets half the property? Why? Who usually loses half the property? Why? Can you understand why the victim of adultery is going to be bitter if a divorce occurs?

Sexual immorality (adultery) is a form of seeking revenge because of bitterness (Heb 12:16). One of my client's mother died. One month later his wife left him to go live with his natural father (they had fallen in love with each other). She took their two children with her. Way to stab your son in the back, dad! Satan loves the effects of double betrayal in single situations. This almost sounds like the Church in Corinth! (See 1 Cor 5). Who needs to watch "soap operas" when you have a life like this!

According to Frank Pittman, 50% of husbands and 25-35% of wives have been unfaithful. 53% of adulterous marriages end up in divorce. Many of those people who have affairs are largely motivated by anger. In a survey, he found that about 25% of people who had affairs were angry about some aspect of their spouse's behavior, or were retaliating for affairs their spouses had started.[8]

❖ **Sexual abuse** – sexual betrayal

Many people in the Bible can understand what it felt like to be betrayed.

David felt as if he was being betrayed and rejected by God! Look at all the passages found in the Psalms (6:3; 13:1; 35:17; 40:13; 43:2). David in Psalms frequently asked God "How long?" (4:2; 6:3; 13:1-2; 62:3; 94:3). He is waiting for God to do something other than to stand there and watch.

Job felt as if God were betraying and attacking him. He states in Job 30:20-23, "He throws me into the mud, and I am reduced to dust and ashes. I cry out to you, O God, but you do not answer; I stand up, but you merely look at me. You turn on me ruthlessly; with the might of your hand you attack me. You snatch me up and drive me before the wind; you toss me about in the storm. I know you will bring me down to death, to the place appointed for all the living." Job commented in 19:13, "He has alienated my brothers from me; my acquaintances are completely estranged from me."

Job also felt betrayal from family and friends. He lamented, "My kinsmen have gone away; my friends have forgotten me. My guests and my maidservants count me a stranger; they look upon me as an alien. I summon my servant, but he does not answer, though I beg him with my own mouth. My breath is offensive to my wife; I am loathsome to my own brothers. Even the little boys scorn me; when I appear, they ridicule me. All my intimate friends detest me; those I love have turned against me" (Job 19:14-19).

Joseph also understood betrayal. He could have been bitter at his brothers for what they did to him (Gen 37:12-36). He could have been bitter for being falsely accused by Potiphar's wife and being thrown in jail (Gen 39:6-23).

Paul is a man who experienced betrayal and desertion. Paul was deserted by John Mark in Pamphylia. This desertion caused a disagreement between Paul and Barnabas and they parted ways (Acts 15:36-38). Later in Paul's life he was reconciled to John Mark (2 Tim 4:11). Paul is forgiving, but it did not occur overnight; it was a process.

God understands being betrayed. Jeremiah 3:20-21 warns, "A cry is heard on the barren heights, the weeping and pleading of the people of Israel, because they have perverted their ways and have forgotten the Lord their God." (See also Jer 2:13, 27, 32; 5:11; 15:6; Hos 1:2; 4:1, 6, 10, 14; 9:1; Joel 2:12-13).

Jesus understood betrayal (Mark 9:31; Matt 20:17-19; 26:23-25, 31-35; 27:46). In Luke 21:16 Jesus said you *will* be betrayed. He did not say we might be betrayed. In Matthew 10:21 Jesus says this betrayal *will* occur!

These events can also change people's thoughts and lifestyles.

Losses: Losses can cause values to be placed in a correct or different order. It is through loss that we find out what is important (Ps 27:8; Matt 6:33). Loss often creates better relationships, because of the realization that life does not last forever.

Injustice: During times of injustice we can learn to trust God. We might learn that the Lord is a just God, but he does not promise justice on the earth that is visible and measurable by the victim (Ps 26:1; 2 Chr 19:7; Ps 20:7). God is not always invited into man's court. This is one reason why earthly justice is not always done. Recently

God has been taken out of the court system. Though the giving of the Ten Commandments is part of the frieze on the walls of the Supreme Court building, they have effectively been removed from the decisions of the court.

Betrayal: God teaches us in times of betrayal that he is the only one who will never let us down (Matt 28:20; Deut 31:6, 8; Rom 5:5; Isa 2:22).

Look at all of the reasons Jesus could have been bitter! Below is a list of some circumstances which could have caused Jesus to become bitter. Some of these situations were minor, but the accumulation of them could have worn Jesus down — if he were not God's Son. Even worse, Satan tried to get Jesus to be bitter to destroy his ministry.

His trials (Matt 27:11-26, 57-68); disciples not praying (Matt 25:36-46); Peter's lack of faith (Matt 14:22-35); Barabbas being freed (Matt 27:20-26); Judas' attitude (Matt 25:6-13); soldiers beating him (Matt 27:27-31); being crucified (Matt 27:32-44); the disciples' lack of faith during the storm (Matt 8:23-27); John's disciples questioning him on why he fasted (Matt 9:14); rejection by his own town's people (Matt 13:53-58); Peter's attitude about Jesus dying (Matt 16:21-28); disciples' lack of faith (Matt 17:14-23); what was done to his Father's house (John 2:12-16; Matt 21:12-13); man who told that Jesus healed him (Mark 1:40-45); Martha's attitude toward Mary (Luke 10:38-42); men on the road not recognizing him as Christ (Luke 24:13:35); his mother's request at the wedding (John 2:1-4); Nicodemus coming at night (John 3:1-2); Mary and Martha's attitudes about Lazarus' death (John 11:21-22, 32); the disciples deserting him (John 6:60-66); Peter's denial (Matt 26:69-75); people not receiving him or his word (John 1:11); Thomas' lack of faith (John 20:24-29); Judas' betrayal (John 18:3-14); being sold for thirty pieces of silver (Matt 26:14-16, 27:3-4); the Pharisees constantly trying to trick or trap him as when using the woman caught in adultery (John 8:3-6) and asking about paying taxes (Matt 22:15-22); the jealousy between the disciples (Matt 20:20-28; Mark 9:33-37); lack of family support (Mark 3:20-21); disciples falling asleep (Luke 22:45-46; Matt 26:40, 43); nine lepers not thankful for their healing (Luke 17:11-19); being arrested by people he knew and taught in the temple (Luke 22:52-53); chief priest and elders plotting to arrest and kill him (Matt 26:1-5); being betrayed with a kiss (Luke 22:47-48); being arrested (Luke 22:54); being accused of blasphemy (Matt 26:65); having his face spit into (Matt 26:67); being struck with fists (Matt 26:67); being slapped by religious leaders (John 18:22); Peter's threefold denial (Matt 26:69-75; Luke 22:54-62) being insulted by chief priest, elders and teachers (Mark 15:31-32, Luke 23:39); and being forsaken by his Father (Matt 27:45-46).

Jesus could have become bitter because of what the soldiers did to him:

- ❖ stripped him, put a robe on him (Matt 27:28)
- ❖ placed crown of thorns on his head (Matt 27:29)
- ❖ mocked him (Matt 27:29)
- ❖ spit on him (Matt 27:30)
- ❖ struck him on his head repeatedly (Matt 27:30)

As this chapter on the causes of bitterness ends, let's turn our attention next to how bitterness affects people. The next chapter will show the domination the emotion of bitterness has on people once it takes root in a person.

Source Notes

1. Everett Worthington, *Marriage Counseling,* p. 91.

2. Jim Talley, *Reconcilable Differences* (Nashville: Thomas Nelson Publishers, 1991), p. 56.

3. William Backus, Ph.D., *Telling the Truth to Troubled People* (Minneapolis: Bethany House Publishers, 1985), p. 161.

4. Earnie Larsen and Carol Larsen Hegarty, *From Anger to Forgiveness* (New York: Ballantine Books, A Hazelden Book, 1992), p. 17.

5. David Seamands in Jan Frank, *A Door of Hope* (San Bernardino, CA: Here's Life Publishers, 1987), p. 147.

6. C.S. Lewis, *The Problem with Pain* (London: Fontana Books, 1961).

7. Billy Graham, *Hope for the Troubled Heart* (Minneapolis: Grason Publishing Co., 1991), p. 104.

8. Frank Pittman, *Private Lies: Infidelity and the Betrayal of Intimacy* (New York: W.W. Norton and Co., Inc. 1989).

2

Crippling Effects of Bitterness

The New World Dictionary of American English defines effect as, "anything brought about by a cause or agent; result; the power or ability to bring about results."

My mom remembers Palm Sunday, April 11, 1965 when a group of ten tornadoes went ripping through 18 northern Indiana counties. 137 people died and 1724 were injured. The path of destruction was wide and costly. The results of that storm were still evident many years later as the landscape still bore the scars. Trees were uprooted and buildings destroyed. Rebuilding was long and expensive.

Bitterness is similar to the effects of this Sunday storm. Bitterness does much damage often without much warning. Death and injury is common. Anything in its path gets destroyed. It does not matter what it destroys, neither is it selective in the damage. As we begin this chapter on the effects of bitterness, several general concepts need to be addressed first about the brewing storm of bitterness.

❖ Bitterness is passed from generation to generation. It becomes part of the family tree and portrait. It usually affects

47

three to four generations (Ezek 16:44-47; Exod 20:4-5). Bitterness is considered normal and customary if you have grown up in it (Jer 13:23).

❖ Bitterness has the power to destroy the fruit of the Spirit, making Christians ineffective. Bitterness steals and drains the power of the Holy Spirit. The opposite of bitterness is any of the fruit of the Spirit (love, joy, peace, patience, kindness, goodness, faithfulness, gentleness and self-control — Gal 5:22-23). Ephesians 4:31 makes a contrast between love and bitterness. It proposes, "Get rid of all bitterness, rage and anger, brawling and slander, along with every form of malice. Be kind and compassionate to one another, forgiving each other, just as in Christ God forgave you." Bitterness overrides kindness, compassion and forgiveness transforming the personality into rage, anger, brawling and slander.

❖ Bitterness and revenge are part of our sinful nature (Exod 23:4; Jer 17:9; Gal 5:19-21; Eph 2:3). Lewis B. Smedes writes in *Forgive and Forget*, "The problem with revenge is that it never gets what it wants; it never evens the score. Fairness never comes. The chain reaction set off by every act of vengeance always takes its unhindered course. It ties both the injured and the injurer to an escalator of pain."[1]

Revenge is very common and often praised in our society. In two highly publicized hearings, the Bobbits and the Menendez brothers, the juries have seemed to legalize revenge. This is a very dangerous precedent. I recently met a woman who found out her husband was having an affair, so she washed his underwear with fiberglass drapes. This created a tremendous rash for her husband. He went to several doctors before his wife told him what she had done and why. This type of situation is seen regularly on daytime programming.

❖ Bitterness removes a Christian's breastplate of righteousness and makes a person unholy (Heb 12:14-15).

Without righteousness, there is no peace, quietness or confidence (Isa 32:17). Bitterness opens wide the heart to be attacked by Satan.

❖ Bitterness causes wretched days (Prov 15:15). Bitterness is the opposite of sweet (Prov 13:19) and pleasant (Ruth 1:20-21). There is no such thing as a bitter, happy person. There is little or no love, joy, peace patience, kindness, goodness, faithfulness, gentleness or self-control in a bitter person. Bitterness makes people wicked, without peace (Isa 48:22).

❖ Bitterness has no time limit. The feud can be forever! Consider what took place over ten years ago between Indianapolis and Baltimore. On March 29, 1984 the Baltimore Colts packed up in the night and left for Indianapolis. Ten years later some people still are bitter and hateful towards the owner, Robert Irsay. Mike Gathagan, who works in the front office of the Canadian Football League Colts, the new CFL team in Baltimore said, "So many people here hate Robert Irsay's guts. They'll do anything they can to make him look bad."[2] This is a pretty graphic illustration of bitterness.

❖ Bitterness is spiritual warfare! It is one of Satan's most powerful weapons in destroying families, churches, and countries. Resentment is a socially acceptable word for bitterness. Bitterness is not demonic possession; it is demonic, spiritual oppression (Ps 9:9; 10:18; 42:9; 43:2; 106:42; 129:1-2; Dan 7:25). One of the biggest problems with bitterness is that it takes away the whole armor of God. It leaves a person very vulnerable to Satan's attack.

❖ Bitterness is an evil cancer of character. It is not an incurable wound, but it won't be healed on its own (Jer 30:12, 15, 17). It can be healed only by the Master Physician Jesus. It, like evil spirits, won't leave of its own volition. It must be forced out and then replaced with something else (Matt 12:43-45).

❖ Bitterness is like a "bag of marbles" people carry around with them. The events of loss, injustice and betrayal add "marbles" to the bag. The bag becomes an anchor. This anchor stops growth. It also makes for some very dangerous personality characteristics.

What happens to a person as they become bitter? Consider the following stories:

POLICE: GIRL MURDERS STEPFATHER OVER TV *Muncie Evening Press*, Muncie, Indiana; 9/22/93, p. 1.

East St. Louis, Ill.,
  Police say a 13-year-old girl killed her stepfather because she was angry that he had turned off the television set.

The Muncie Evening Press, Muncie, Indiana; Friday, December 3, 1993, p. 1.

  Martinsville, Ind. (AP) A teenage girl pulled a loaded handgun on a fellow student and pulled the trigger, but the boy was saved when the weapon malfunctioned, police said.
  The two students who did not know each other said the near-homicide started with a bump in a high school hallway, investigators said.

What are some effects of bitterness?

Scripture gives some clear examples of how bitter people act or respond.

❖ In Psalm 73:21-22, David wrote, "When my heart was grieved and my spirit embittered, I was senseless and ignorant; I was a brute beast before you." Bitter people become *senseless*, *ignorant* and *brute beasts*. This verse confirms loss is one of the reasons for bitterness. Bitter people frequently do "senseless acts of violence" against others. This sounds like a hockey game.

❖ In Acts 8:23 Peter is quoted as saying to Simon, "For I

50

see that you are full of bitterness and captive to sin." Bitterness can become so consuming that it can be seen on the outside appearance of a person. *Bitterness is highly visible* to others. They can see it in the way you act and speak. *It fills the heart* (Esth 5:9). A bitter person's personality swings from Dr. Jekyll to Mr. Hyde. *It makes a person captive to sin.* Bitterness becomes a spiritual sinkhole that prevents any spiritual growth. Bitterness disables the spiritual aspect of man. It rots the mind like termites rot wood. It drains the body of power and life (Isa 37:27).

For a visual example of how bitterness fills the heart, take a bowl with water and put a corner of a paper towel in it. Watch what happens. Eventually the water is absorbed into all of the paper towel. With bitterness this "filling" process does not take place overnight. It may take weeks, months, years or even decades to become fully developed. In Acts 8:21 Peter declares that the heart is not always right before God; this is the condition of the heart after it is filled with bitterness. As bitterness fills the heart, it squeezes out love for God and man. The problem with this is found in Deuteronomy 6:5 which reads, "Love the Lord your God with all your heart and with all your soul and with all your strength." A bitter heart cannot fulfill this command. A bitter heart cannot love God when it hates man (1 John 4:20).

❖ Hebrews 12:15 reminds us, "See to it that no one misses the grace of God and that no bitter root grows up to cause trouble and defile many." The root of bitterness entangles itself around every aspect of a person's life. Bitterness causes people to *miss the grace of God. It grows* or becomes bigger. This is in direct contrast to the advice found in 2 Peter 3:18 telling believers to grow in grace. Bitterness and grace are direct opposites! Bitterness *causes trouble.* Bitterness is the basis for most fights in our society. Bitterness *defiles many* (even innocent people).

51

Usually when a person is bitter at one person, they are bitter at all people. It is important to realize that bitter people do not always express their bitterness to the person that has harmed them. Consider what happened to me one day. I was driving to my office when a driver in front of me got cut off by a semi-truck. She got out of her car, started yelling and making gestures to the driver, and then got back into her car and took off down the road. She did not realize that when she had gotten out of her car, her purse had fallen out onto the street. I inched my car up to her purse, opened my door, grabbed her purse, and took off after her, honking my horn and flashing my lights. When I finally got her attention, she gave me the same gesture she had given the truck driver. When I showed her the purse and asked if she wanted it, the gesture stopped. I gave the purse to her and she took off. If she had a dog, I bet she took all of this anger and bitterness out on it when she got home. If her husband is a truck driver, he better duck when he gets home!

Consider Michael Stone who apparently shot his 20-month-old son, Jeremy to death before killing himself. The writers of this story, Andrea Carter and Tammy Gay, wrote, "There were no apparent signs that Michael Stone's anger and frustration would be directed towards his own son, but eventually it was." Michael's wife reported that her estranged husband slapped her, pulled her hair, slammed her against walls and hit her with a portable phone. She also reported that he had hit and choked her son from a previous marriage.[3]

Consider the Federal Express pilot who landed his cargo plane safely in Memphis, Tenn. after he and his crew were attacked by a fellow employee. This employee had been awaiting a disciplinary hearing because he had allegedly falsified his credentials when he was hired. He probably was going to be fired. This employee attacked the three-man crew while in-flight from Memphis to San Jose. The attack occurred shortly after the plane had taken off from Memphis. The man had brought a hammer and spear gun onto the plane with him.[4]

❖ Proverbs 14:10 "Each heart knows its own bitterness, and no one can share its joy." A bitter person *knows she/he is bitter, bitterness resides in their heart,* and *has no joy.* Psalm 16:11, "You have made known to me the path of life; you will fill me with joy in your presence, with eternal pleasures at your right hand." One of the reasons why a bitter person has no joy is because bitterness squeezes out the feelings of the presence of God. In Lamentations 5:15 we read, "Joy is gone from our hearts; our dancing has turned to mourning." This is a great description of how bitterness robs people emotionally. It steals positive emotions and replaces them with negative ones.

❖ Job 21:25 "Another man dies in bitterness of soul, never having enjoyed anything good." A bitter person *dies in bitterness of soul* (Job 7:11; 10:1) and *sees nothing good in life.* Martin Luther on one occasion remarked, "When the heart is troubled and sorrowful, there follows also weakness of the body." Bitterness takes a tremendous amount of energy to keep it under control. This energy is stolen from the immune system leaving it vulnerable to illness and disease. Bitterness can and does kill a person physically.

❖ Deuteronomy 29:18 "Make sure there is no man or woman, clan or tribe among you today whose heart turns away from the LORD our God to go and worship the gods of those nations; make sure there is no root among you that produces such bitter poison." A bitter person *turns away from God, worships other gods* and *produces poison.*

❖ James 3:14 "But if you harbor bitter envy and selfish ambition in your hearts, do not boast about it or deny the

truth." Bitterness *is harbored in the heart* (Job 36:13; Ps
28:3; Ezek 25:15-17; 35:5-7), and it *causes people to deny
the truth.*

❖ In Romans 3:12-18 Paul addresses eleven consequences
of bitterness. (See Ps 5:8-9.) A bitter person *turns away
from God, becomes worthless, does no good, has a throat
that is an open grave, has a deceitful tongue* (Prov
12:20), *has lips full of poison and a mouth full of cursing,
has feet swift to shed blood* (they want revenge quickly),
has ruin and misery in his/her life, has no peace (Job
3:26), and *has no fear of God.*

Paul links bitterness to the mouth four times. Paul
then is indirectly linking bitterness to the condition of the
heart (Matt 12:34). This confirms Proverbs 14:10 where it
states that bitterness makes its home in the heart. Bitter
confrontations between people can involve words, vehi-
cles and deadly weapons. The tongue has the power of life
and death (Prov 18:21). The tongue becomes a sword in
the hands of a bitter soldier (Ps 55:21; 57:4; 59:7). The
tongue becomes a fire (Jas 3:6). The bitter tongue is full of
bitter poison (Jas 3:8).

Bitter statements often heard are: "It's too little, too
late," "She knows my phone number," "If he could do this
now, he should have done it before," "It's too bad it took
this crisis to cause this change," "After repeated rejection,
you quit asking," "The next money I spend on my wife will
be for her burial expenses," "It's never good enough to
please her," "I never forgot that," "She threw up to me
something I forgot," "Never get close to anyone, they may
not be here tomorrow." What a great communication pattern bitterness creates!

Many of the Proverbs describe the negative effects of
bitterness. Besides the few specific mentions of bitterness,
many actions and attitudes that are condemned could have
their roots in bitterness:

❖ Reckless words that pierce like a sword (12:18).
❖ Evil plots, and speech like scorching fire (16:27; see also Ps 64:6-8).
❖ Strife wherever they go (17:1).
❖ Fighting and quarrels (17:14).
❖ An unyielding attitude and strong fighting (18:19).

Many of Jesus' parables had bitter characters. It was often a common theme of Jesus' teaching. Some of these characters and parables are:

❖ *Older brother of The Prodigal Son*: (Luke 15:11-32)
The older brother was bitter at the preferential treatment the younger brother received when he got back home. The older brother was very angry because a banquet was served in honor of the rebellious runaway. He was very bitter at his father because his father had given him nothing that he could think of. This belief was not true. The father had given many things to the older son. He divided his property between these two sons (Luke 15:12). Bitterness impaired this son's judgment and thoughts. Bitter people don't celebrate. They become more bitter when the person who hurt them prospers.

❖ *The goats in The Sheep and the Goats*: (Matt 25:31-46)
Though the attitudes of those judged here is not recorded, the "goats" can well be imagined to be bitter because of the perceived unjust treatment they received from God. They did not realize they had not done kind things to God. On seeing the gifts the "sheep" received from God, they would have expected either the same or much better.

Unmet expectations (which can be perceived as injustice and betrayal, even when the expectations were unrealistic) are a common reason for bitterness. 2 Kings 5 tells about Naaman who wanted to be healed from leprosy. He expected Elisha to come out of his house and heal him. In verses 11-12 we are told, "But Naaman went away angry and said, 'I thought that he would surely come out to me and stand and call on the name of the LORD his God, wave his hand over the spot and cure me of my leprosy. Are not Abana and Pharpar, the rivers of Damascus, better than any of the waters of Israel? Couldn't I wash in them and be cleansed?' So he turned and went off in a rage." Why was Naaman in such a rage? It was because Elisha had sent a messenger out to tell Naaman how he could be healed (2 Kgs 5:10). Elisha did not even meet Naaman face to face.

King David had some unmet expectations that made him bitter. David had sent some of his men to the area where Nabal was shearing his sheep to ask for some food. David in a time past had protected Nabal's sheep from being killed or stolen. So what David expected from Nabal was only common courtesy. David expected Nabal to return a favor. David's men came back empty-handed. Nabal gave them no food. In fact Nabal actually criticized David. David became so bitter because of these two things that he was going to attack and kill Nabal, his men and all of his animals (1 Sam 25:1-22). Bitterness made David senseless in this situation.

❖ *The twelve-hour workers in the vineyard*: (Matt 20:1-16)

The workers who labored in the field for twelve hours show a bitter response to their wages. They received the same amount as the one-hour workers. This was definitely an unmet expectation and injustice according to the twelve-hour workers. The twelve-hour workers expected more when they saw what the one-hour workers got. This "lack of proper payment" clearly made them angry. It just was not fair for them to be treated this way. When I read Matthew 20:12, I see nothing but anger and bitterness: "'These men who were hired last worked only one hour,'" they said, "'and *you have made them equal to us* who have borne the burden of the work and the heat of the day'" (emphasis added). The twelve-hour workers were angry at the master. Any worker who worked more than one hour could have been bitter. This parable deals with God's grace. Bitter people have a really hard time understanding why grace should be given to anyone who has hurt them.

❖ *The son who said he would go work for his father but didn't*: (Matt 21:28-32)

There might have been a revenge motive here. This son might have wanted to get even with his father, because his father had hurt him in some way. This parable deals with a strong passive-aggressive trait often found in bitterness. A good proverb on passive-aggressive communication is Proverbs 26:18-19 which reads, "Like a madman shooting firebrands or deadly arrows is a man who deceives his neighbor and says, 'I was only joking'." Passive-aggression is expressing anger in such a way it cannot be confronted or detected as anger. James D. Mallory, Jr., M.D. writes:

> Anger that is not dealt with may also be expressed in a passively hostile way. The person who is chronically late, who drags his feet, who is an obstructionist at business meetings, bringing up all sorts of trivia, very likely has problems in dealing with anger directly.
>
> The husband who can't remember those things his wife asked him to pick up may well be clobbering her with his inability to remember things. Simply refusing to talk with someone or refusing to perform an act of kindness that would have been appreciated represents passive hostility.[5]

❖ *The Parable of the Soils*: (Matt 13:1-8)

This parable deals with the condition of a person's heart and how it accepts or rejects the word of God. The soil in this parable is the heart of man. In Matthew 13:19 the soil on the "path" is too hard to receive the word of God, and the evil one comes and snatches it away. This "path heart" has gone through loss, injustice and betrayal. This is what has made it so hard.

As this chapter has shown, Scripture gives many references to how bitterness effects people. Many of the parables that Jesus told have bitterness, not as the central theme, but as a secondary theme. Several verses in Proverbs make some reference to how bitterness causes problems. Let's turn now to look at people in the Bible who were bitter.

Source Notes

1. Lewis B. Smedes, *Forgive and Forget* (Harper and Row, 1984), p. 131.

2. *The Muncie (Indiana) Evening Press*, 29 March 1994, p. 11.

3. Story from *Lexington (Kentucky) Herald-Leader*, 31 March 1994.

4. Condensed from *The Evening Press*, Muncie, IN, 8 April 1994.

5. James D. Mallory, Jr., M.D., *The Kink and I* (Wheaton, IL: Victor Books, 1974), p. 174.

3

Profiles of Bitterness

The New World Dictionary of American English defines *profile* as, "a graph, diagram, piece of writing, etc. presenting or summarizing data relevant to a particular person or thing."

Søren Kierkegaard said, "When you read God's word, you must constantly be saying to yourself, it is talking to me, and about me." What would the personal profile of bitterness look like? How can you tell when a person is bitter? Scripture gives many clear profiles of bitterness.

"Aren't She Beautiful, Mommy?"

My boy Joshua had been the only child for 3 years. When his little sister, Caity, was born, Joshua first saw her in the arms of my wife. I will never forget the words that he said to my wife Janelle. He said to her, "Aren't she beautiful, Mommy?" She was a very beautiful child. Bitter people on the other hand are very ugly and mean. They may appear very beautiful on the outside, but on the inside they are totally ugly. If you are around these people enough, their inside ugliness overshadows their external appearance.

How would you describe a bitter person? They could

be described in many words. Mean, critical, lonely, unforgiving, dishonest, self-centered, rebellious, revengeful, hateful, apathetic, harsh, a killjoy, rejecting, condemning, unloving, unpredictable, plotting, untrusting, intolerant, demanding, spiteful, hostile, and absent when needed by others. Most of the time a bitter person is unaware of how they are portraying bitterness.

As I wrote in the last chapter, bitter people become senseless. They do things without considering the possible consequences. Consider the following stories and think about how bitterness played a part in them.

SERBIAN PLAYER IMPROVING *Evening Press*, Muncie, IN, April 30, 1993, p. 17.

A Serbian basketball player was reported improving today after spinal surgery to repair a neck injury suffered when he slammed his head into a concrete block in anger at a referee's decision.

Doctors at the Athens KAT hospital in Greece said Slobodan Jankovic, a 30-year-old center, may recover use of his arms and legs as a result of the operation late Thursday.

Jankovic rammed his head against a cement support of the basket after being called for the fifth foul that put him out of a semi-final game in the Greek championship play offs.

A's STAR AGREES TO SEEK COUNSELING *Pharos-Tribune*, Logansport, IN, April 3, 1992, p. A 10.

Miami (AP) — Baseball star Jose Canseco, arrested on charges for ramming his Porsche into his wife's BMW, has agreed to seek counseling. If he completes 26 sessions with his therapist, authorities will drop a charge of aggravated assault, Assistant State Attorney Margaret Rosenbaum said Thursday. (*One sad note, I recently read this couple has gone through a divorce. Bitterness could be the contributing factor!*)

SHOOTING ALLEGEDLY OVER YARDWORK FEUD *The Star Press*, Muncie, IN, Monday, August 5, 1996, p. 4C.

New Orleans — A man who had a running feud with his neighbors over yardwork put down his Bible and picked up his gun, fatally shooting a woman as she swept her sidewalk and injuring her husband as he mowed, police said.

Bitterness frequently has some "hidden" costs associated with it. In one of the above cases it was car repair and the cost of a divorce. In many cases, though, it is family repair. Many children are hurt because of and by a parent's bitterness. In a bitter divorce it is not uncommon for children to be used as pawns and go-betweens. The children are placed in the crossfire of both parents.

Bitter people frequently do things they regret later. Proverbs 14:15 states, "...a prudent man gives thought to his steps." Proverbs 14:16 states, "...but a fool is hotheaded and reckless." (I did not write these verses; I just call them as I see them.) Do you think that Jose later regretted what he did to his cars? Do you think that Slobodan Jankovic later regretted what he did?

Bitterness is obviously in society, but let's look at how bitterness has invaded the church and how a person's actions were reckless! Consider the following example:

OFF KEY SINGING LEADS TO DRAIN-CLEANER ATTACK *The Post and Courier*, Charleston, SC, Nov. 26, 1991, p. 5-A.

Lexington, Ky. (AP) — A choir member threw liquid drain cleaner into the face of a fellow singer during a church service, causing serious burns, for singing off key at rehearsal, police said.

Five other church members were splashed by the chemical but were not seriously injured.

The attack took place Sunday just as a service was beginning at the East Second Street Christian Church.

Police said the fight stemmed from a continuing argument about who was singing off key. The pastor, the Rev. Raymond

Brown, said it was more elaborate than that, but he refused
to provide more details.

You won't find the above four stories mentioned in
the Bible, but the Bible is a biography of bitterness. Consider the following as examples of people whose experiences either did or could have made them bitter (it is not
always clear how they did react):

- ❖ Lamech (Gen 4:23)
- ❖ Noah (Gen 9:20-27)
- ❖ Sarai (Gen 16:1-6; 21:10)
- ❖ Esau (Gen 27:41-42)
- ❖ Simeon, Levi (Gen 34:25-28)
- ❖ Joseph's brothers (Gen 37:23-28)
- ❖ Potiphar's wife (Gen 39:13-15)
- ❖ Pharaoh (Exod 10:20, 27; 11:10)
- ❖ Moses (Num 11:10-15; Exod 14:10-12)
- ❖ Naomi (Ruth 1:20-21)
- ❖ King Saul (1 Sam)
- ❖ Brother of David (1 Sam 17:28)
- ❖ David (1 Sam 25:1-38; 2 Sam 11:14-17)
- ❖ Absalom (2 Sam 13:1-29)
- ❖ Joab (2 Sam 3:22-27/18:14)
- ❖ Prostitute who stole the baby (1 Kgs 3:16-28)
- ❖ Jezebel (1 Kgs 21:1-16)
- ❖ The Shunammite Woman (2 Kgs 4:8-36)
- ❖ Naaman (2 Kgs 5:11-12)
- ❖ Athaliah (2 Kgs 11:1-3)
- ❖ Michal (1 Chr 15:29; 2 Sam 6:16-23)
- ❖ King of Aram (2 Chr 18:28-34)
- ❖ Sanballat, Tobiah and Geshem (Neh 2:19; 4:1-3; 6:1-7; 7:8-11)
- ❖ Haman (Est 5:9)
- ❖ Job (Job 7:11; 10:1)
- ❖ Adulteress (Prov 5:3-4)
- ❖ Jonah (Jonah 4:1-3)

- ❖ Herodias (Mark 6:19; Matt 14:1-12)
- ❖ Paul (Acts 15:36-41)
- ❖ Satan (Rev 12:7-12)
- ❖ Hezekiah (Isa 38:1-5)
- ❖ Peninnah (1 Sam 1:1-11)
- ❖ Samson (Judg 14:19-20)

This is not a short list. When I first started compiling it, I was shocked to find as many as I did. If I looked harder, I could find even more, because there are more.

This part of the manual will look at the life of **King Saul** and how bitterness destroyed his life and kingship. Realize that Saul is just like us, and what bitterness did to him, it can do to us. Some biblical signs and symptoms of bitterness in Saul's life are:

- ❖ 1 Samuel 18:9, 15, 30 (Jas 3:14)

Jealousy. In James 3:14 the phrase "bitter envy" is used. In Galatians 5:21 the Greek word *phthonos* is used for envy. It means to have a feeling of displeasure produced by witnessing the prosperity of others. This is what Saul felt when he looked at David. He was jealous of David's new found popularity after he killed Goliath.

- ❖ 18:10

Depression. When bitterness takes hold of a person, this is one of the most common side effects. This depression or oppression is because it takes energy to hold the anger inside the human body, thus creating depression.

- ❖ 18:11, 25; 19:11, 15 (Ps 37:12; Jer 9:8)

Planning and seeking revenge. This is another very common sign of bitterness. Revenge is never satisfied, because you could have done something more or different. People don't want to get even, they want to get slightly above even. Revenge says you want to hurt the person who hurt you more than what they did to you. This becomes a cycle. Another one of the problems with seeking revenge is that God will do to you what you have done to others. Ezekiel 35:11 states, "therefore as surely as I live, declares the Sovereign Lord, I will treat you in accordance with the anger and jealousy...."

❖ 18:15, 29

Fear is another common outcome of bitterness. People who are bitter fear that others will advance beyond them. They fear that they will lose what they have.

❖ 18:20-21; 19:11; 24:8-9; 26:18-19

Recruiting others for their schemes. Bitterness always has a prompter and person behind it, just like fire always needs wood (Prov 26:20-21). There are three good illustrations in the Bible that show bitter people often prompt others to seek revenge. These three recruits of bitterness are:

❖ *Nebuchadnezzar:* Daniel 3:8-12 records that several astrologers told Nebuchadnezzar that Shadrach, Meshach and Abednego were not paying attention to his decree. The astrologers told Nebuchadnezzar this because they hated the Jews and wanted to give them a bad name (Dan 3:8). They were jealous at the advancement of the Jewish boys in the king's service due to their superior wisdom (1:20; 2:49). The astrologers knew the consequences for breaking the king's decree, and even reminded the king (3:11) because they wanted the Jews to die. These astrologers used Nebuchadnezzar as a way of expressing their bitterness. He probably did not realize that he was being used!

❖ *Daughter of Herodias:* Matthew 14:8 says, "Prompted by her mother, she said, 'Give me here on a platter the head of John the Baptist.'" Herodias, the girl's mother, had a problem with John because he was opposed to Herod's marriage to her and publicly condemned them. She wanted him dead (Matt 14:3-4; Mark 6:17-29).

Mark 6:21 states, "Finally the opportune time came...." Herodias had been waiting for this time for a while. Her daughter's dance and Herod's attitude gave her the perfect opportunity.

❖ *King Xerxes:* The book of Esther is a story of Haman's plot to kill all the Jews. He tries to use King Xerxes to do it (Esth 3:12-14). This cost Haman his life. This is a prime example of how bitterness-based revenge blows up in a person's face.

Consider this following example of recruitment. I have a client who was recently put in her grandmother's will. She actually replaced her mother in this will. I believe this woman treats her granddaughter well to get at her daughter. This is an intentional behavior of revenge by using other people.

❖ 1 Samuel 18:25 (Jer 9:8)

Hypocrisy. Bitter people say one thing but mean another. They speak out of both sides of their mouths. Saul promised David he would not attempt to kill him anymore. This promise was short lived. 1 Samuel 19:6; 26:21 shows that bitter people tell lies about what they are going to do and not do.

❖ 18:29; 19:17

Seeing others as enemies. Bitter people see many people as enemies. You become an enemy the minute you support someone they hate. King Saul saw both of his children as his enemies. He was mad at Jonathan because he was David's best friend (1 Sam 18:1, 4; 19:1, 4). If Satan can "convince" us to see others as enemies, he can work without being detected or disturbed.

❖ 18:29; 23:14

Insatiable desire to "get even." Saul's goal in life with David was to kill him. This became his life's purpose. He even used his daughter Michal to be part of his plan.

❖ 23:14 **Day after day searching**. A bitter person becomes consumed with the idea of seeking revenge.

❖ 19:16-17; 20:30; 22:13

Feeling betrayed by people who support the "enemy." This occurs frequently in divorce situations where the children support the "wrong" parent.

❖ 19:17

Tension with other people. Psychology recognizes that emotions can be transferred from one person to another. This is called transference. For those of you who have been through a painful divorce, it is important you forgive the ex-spouse for any pain they have caused before getting involved with someone else. If this is not done, the painful emotions you have towards your ex-spouse will be transferred onto the new relationship. This transfer of emotions can take place in any relationship. Take this as a warning! Consider this example of transference of bitterness:

I have been counseling professionally for over 10 years. As a counselor I work with a lot of bitter people. One case in particular sticks in my mind. This man had been married for quite a long time, had a good job and a fine family and home. All of this was shattered within a very short period of time. In a couple of months there was a severe change in his whole personality when he became involved with a younger woman.

On his wife's birthday he told her he was in love with another woman. On Christmas day he left his home and went to live with his mistress. On Valentine's day he filed for divorce. Three of the most important days of the year were ruined by this man's timing of events. In dealing with this man I have repeatedly asked him what his wife did to deserve this. He never gave a satisfactory answer. He was definitely bitter at someone, but it was not necessarily his wife! Bitterness is the leading cause of divorce. Bitterness is simply the hardening of the heart (Matt 19:8). Bitterness will funnel and tunnel into every relationship.

This man was abandoned by his mother when he was very young. She was the object of his bitterness, but this bitterness was transferred to his wife. It was this man's past experiences that made him treat his wife the way he did. He never got a chance to express his anger towards his mother. It was hidden inside his heart until it came out towards his wife.

If you are bitter or angry at one person, the bitterness, if it is not resolved, resides in your heart. It will spread to people who are not responsible for your pain. Bitterness is one cause of child abuse. The parent, or whoever abuses, is frustrated and angry at events that are happening in their life. Instead of getting rid of the frustration they keep the anger inside; and eventually they take it out on a child.

❖ 1 Samuel 20:30 (Rom 3:14; Eph 4:31)

Anger, cursing. Bitter people often express anger in very extreme forms. They may hit things with their fists or with their words.

❖ 22:18-19

Innocent people being hurt.. Bitterness hurts everyone it comes in contact with. Children of bitter parents will be hurt. In this example in Saul's life, Saul had a whole town wiped out because he was bitter with David. He felt that the town of Nob had conspired against him and supported David. Doeg the Edomite was the one who killed eighty-five priests. He also killed all the men, women, children and infants. Doeg also killed all of Nob's cattle, donkeys and sheep.

❖ 26:21

Acting like a fool. Bitter people do many foolish things. They say many foolish things. Saul even admitted to David that he had acted like a fool.

❖ 28:8

Losing faith in God. Bitter people often believe that
when they go through their loss, injustice and betrayal,
that God is cold and distant. In Saul's life, he was so bitter
with David and also God that he consulted with a witch at
Endor.

❖ 31:4

Suicide is at times an attempt to hurt the person that
you are bitter at or it can also be a way of relieving the pain
bitterness has created. At times, bitter people believe that
the only way the pain will go away is through death.

What loss, injustice or betrayal is found in Saul's life?
He lost his kingdom. This would really hack a person off.
Consider David as an innocent victim of bitterness. Psalm
35 is David's story. What did David do that made Saul
bitter? He killed Goliath and this made Saul look bad. Saul
had to blame David for all his losses. Saul believed that he
had a right to be bitter with David. He convinced himself
he was totally justified in his response even though Samuel
had twice told him he was going to lose his kingdom
because he had disobeyed God's orders on two different
occasions (1 Sam 13:14; 15:26-28).

Why would an army of Saul's be after David? David
caused the soldiers to look bad when he killed Goliath!
When David killed Goliath he did something the "trained"
fighting men did not even attempt to do. When they went
back to their hometowns and villages, they faced a lot of
jeers and remarks from the citizens about what David did.
They also had to answer questions like, "Why didn't you go
out and face Goliath?" David made these soldiers "lose
face." David was very confident, and even his own brother
hated him when he was at the battlefield (1 Sam 17:28). It
is these same soldiers Saul told to pursue David. Eliab, his
brother, was possibly in the army pursuing David.

Psalm 35 has language similar to what David said to Saul in 1 Samuel 24. David possibly wrote this Psalm while fleeing from Saul. In Psalm 35:4 David writes that people are seeking his life. First Samuel 24:2 states Saul took 3000 chosen men with him to look for David.

In Psalm 35:11, 15 David tells about ruthless men that question him about things he knows nothing about. He was being slandered without ceasing. In 1 Samuel 24:9 David asks Saul why he listens to men who make false accusations about him and his behavior.

Psalm 35:20-21 describes 1 Samuel 24:9 in which David asks Saul why he listens to men who are telling Saul lies. In Psalm 35 he asks God to contend against those who contend against him. More than just one man was attacking David.

In Psalm 35:23-24 and 1 Samuel 24:15 David asks for God to vindicate him and fight for him.

General questions on bitterness in Saul's life:

If you were "ex-king" Saul, with whom would you be bitter? Why?

What did Samuel do in 1 Samuel 15:26-28 that caused Saul to be bitter?

What word did Samuel use in 1 Samuel 15:28 that caused Saul's bitterness?

Why did Saul ask Samuel to come and worship God with him? (1 Sam 15:30) Was this request made so Saul might save "face" in front of his people?

Why were the soldiers who watched David kill Goliath bitter at him?

How do you think they felt when David killed Goliath?

What pain did David create for the soldiers as they went home?

What kinds of questions and criticisms do you think the soldiers might have faced at home?

What kinds of "losses" did the soldiers face at home?

Let's look at **Jonah** and his expressions of bitterness. All the references are in the book of Jonah. (It is interesting to note that Jonah was a prophet and not just an ordinary man [2 Kings 14:25]. If he can become bitter, so can you!)

❖ 1:1-3 **Running from God's commands**. Rebellious people are often bitter — they know what God would like them to do, but they refuse to do it. They have their own agenda. Jonah's agenda was that he wanted Nineveh completely destroyed.

❖ 4:1 **Anger with God** because he is forgiving and kind to the people Jonah hated. Realize again Jonah wanted the people of Nineveh not to be saved but to be destroyed.

❖ 4:2 **Lack of compassion for hurting people**. Bitter people are very apathetic and un-compassionate to their enemies. They do not want to love them. They want to see them suffer.

❖ 4:3 **Wanting to die**. When Jonah's favorite vine was eaten by a worm, this made him very angry. He was so angry at God for forgiving these people, his only solution was to die.

❖ 4:5 **Wanting the destruction of people you hate**. Plutarch once said, "A man should not allow himself to hate even his enemies, because if you indulge this passion, on some occasion, it will rise of itself in others: if you hate your enemies, you will contract such a vicious habit of mind, as by degrees will break out upon those who are your friends, or those who are indifferent to you."

❖ 4:6-8 **Self-centeredness**. Concern for a vine which was giving him relief, but not for people whom he considered his enemies. Jonah wanted the vine to live and the people to die. God wanted the people to live and the vine to die.

A possible reason for Jonah's bitterness was because he felt betrayed by God when God told him to go to Nineveh. Jonah knew the prophecies in Isaiah about Assyria rising up against Israel. Jonah probably did not want to go to Nineveh because it was the capital of Assyria. He knew if Nineveh was destroyed, Assyria would not pose as great a threat to Israel.

Now that we have seen several traits of bitterness in Saul's life, as well as Jonah, let's look at five newspaper headlines and story summaries to see how bitterness might be a cause of behavior.

BRILLIANT STUDENT GUNS DOWN FOUR, THEN HIMSELF *The Evening Press*, Muncie, IN, Nov. 2, 1991

Iowa City, Iowa (AP) — Gang Lu, a student at the University of Iowa, went on a shooting rampage after being passed over for an academic honor. He killed the rival student who was nominated for the honor. He also killed three professors, critically wounded a university administrator and another staffer before killing himself.

MAN KILLS WIFE, HURTS FOUR OTHERS AT DIVORCE COURT *Press-Enterprise*, Bloomsburg, PA, May 6, 1992, p. 17

In Clayton, Mo., a woman waiting for a divorce court session to open was shot to death Tuesday by her estranged husband, who also wounded four other people in the courthouse before police shot him.

In Grand Forks, N.D., a judge hearing a case over child support was critically wounded. A court reporter said a man who had been called to testify at the hearing pulled out a gun while approaching the witness stand and fired twice. Another court employee said the man had been subpoenaed because of allegations he had not paid his ex-wife child support for their teen-age son.

71

GUNMAN MOTIVE: 'REVENGE' *Reading Eagle*, Reading, PA, May 3, 1992, p. A 1-2

Olivehurst, Calif. (AP) — Eric Houston's revenge for flunking history three years ago is four dead, 11 wounded and about 80 terrorized hostages at his former high school.

THREATS WERE DISMISSED AS FANTASIES *The Evening Press*, Muncie, IN, May 4, 1992, p. 24

Olivehurst, Calif. (AP) — Hundreds of students received counseling at a rural high school where a dropout angry over a failing grade killed his former teacher and three students, wounded nine others and held scores hostage.

ANGRY HUSBAND TORCHES HOME *South Bend Tribune*, South Bend, IN, Nov. 7, 1992, p. A1

North Liberty, IN (AP) — A man angry about an impending divorce set his car on fire and burned down the family home about 12:30 p.m. Friday...

Angered by divorce papers, he apparently filled up his car with gasoline and doused the inside of the vehicle with fuel before leaving a local convenience store. He then drove several miles and burned down his tri-level home.

The three R's of bitterness: Resentment, Retaliation, Revenge. Let's look further into what the Bible teaches about these three.

Resentment is defined in The American College Dictionary as "the feeling of displeasure or indignation at something regarded as an injury or insult, or against the author or source of it."

Previously I stated, bitterness is frequently expressed toward innocent victims. Consider the following quote, "A wife's feeling of resentment toward her divorced spouse may be reflected on her relationship with her son."[1] The resentment for the husband went to the son.

The Bible teaches that:

- ❖ Job 5:2 "Resentment kills a fool, and envy slays the simple."
- ❖ Job 36:13 "The godless in heart harbor resentment."

H. Norman Wright writes in *Making Peace with Your Past*, "Resentment means you have given that other person control of your emotional state."[2] Actually it is Satan who has control of your emotional state when you resent! In 2 Corinthians 2:5-11, Paul links forgiveness (verse 7) and the Devil (verse 11). It is one of Satan's schemes that people not forgive. It is through unforgiveness that he gains his greatest stronghold. One of Satan's schemes or plans is to create bitterness.

Earnie Larsen and Carol Larsen Hegarty write, "The key to forgiveness is the realization that the price we are paying for the resentment is simply too high. The goal is to refuse to pay this price any longer. That is why we forgive. It's for ourselves; it is not about them. It is about our own quality of life."[3]

Retaliation:

Exodus 23:4-5 "If you come across your enemy's ox or donkey wandering off, be sure to take it back to him. If you see the donkey of someone who hates you fallen down under its load, do not leave it there; be sure you help him with it." When a person is thinking about retaliation, they plot and scheme about what to do and when to do it.

Revenge:

Bitter people frequently have one thing on their mind: they want to get even with the people who hurt them. They believe this will be sweet. It only leads to emptiness and wanting to seek more revenge. Human beings' desire to seek revenge or get even will not go away until they feel justified by their actions. An acrostic definition will help you understand what revenge is:

Rehearsing
Every
Vengeance
Enhancing
Need to
Get
Even

William H. Walton said, "To carry a grudge is like being stung to death by one bee."

Seeking revenge is just like the cartoon coyote trying to get the roadrunner. No matter how complicated and correct his schemes appear to be, they always seem to fall back on him! The desire for revenge often blows up in the person's face! Numbers 32:23 warns, "But if you fail to do this, you will be sinning against the LORD; and you may be sure that your sin will find you out." Proverbs 26:27 promises, "If a man digs a pit, he will fall into it; if a man rolls a stone, it will roll back on him." Ecclesiastes 10:8 declares, "Whoever digs a pit may fall into it; whoever breaks through a wall may be bitten by a snake." Proverbs 17:13 gives one of the best reasons for not seeking revenge. "If a man pays back evil for good, evil will never leave his house." This also applies if a person repays evil for evil (Prov 22:8; Gal 6:7).

❖ Leviticus 19:18 instructs "Do not seek revenge or bear a grudge against one of your people, but love your neighbor as yourself. I am the Lord."

❖ Deuteronomy 32:35 explains "It is mine to avenge; I will repay. In due time their foot will slip; their day of disaster is near and their doom rushes upon them."

❖ Hebrews 10:31 states, "It is a dreadful thing to fall into the hands of the living God."

❖ Proverbs 25:21-22 (quoted in Romans 12:20) teaches "If your enemy is hungry, give him food to eat; if he is thirsty, give him water to drink. In doing this, you will heap burning coals on his head, and the LORD will reward you."

❖ Proverbs 20:22 and Proverbs 24:29 warn "Do not say, 'I'll pay you back for this wrong!' Wait for the LORD, and he will deliver you." "Do not say, 'I'll do to him as he has done to me; I'll pay that man back for what he did.'" God says, "Don't even say it," because saying something is one step away from doing it! You plan it, say it, and then do it.

❖ In Matthew 5:38-39 Jesus teaches, "You have heard that it was said, 'Eye for eye, and tooth for tooth [Exod 21:24; Lev 24:20; Deut 19:21]. But I tell you, Do not resist an evil person. If someone strikes you on the right cheek, turn to him the other also." God gave the "eye for eye" ruling to make sure that there was not a greater punishment than what the behavior called for. Gandhi is quoted as saying, "If we all live by 'an eye for an eye' the whole world would be blind. The only way out is forgiveness."

❖ In Romans 12:17 Paul says the same thing: "Do not repay anyone evil for evil. Be careful to do what is right in the eyes of everybody."

❖ Romans 12:19 continues "Do not take revenge, my friends, but leave room for God's wrath, for it is written: 'It is mine to avenge; I will repay,' says the Lord."

❖ Romans 12:21 then concludes "Do not be overcome by evil, but overcome evil with good."

Consider this story about resentment, retaliation and revenge.

DAUGHTER ACCUSED OF SETTING FIRE *The Evening Press*, Friday, November 25, 1994, p. 22.

Avella, Pa. (AP) — A college student home for Thanksgiving set her house on fire, killing her father, because her

75

mother had been arguing with her about going to a nearby bar, police said.

Melanie Vicheck, 19, was charged with murder and arson. She sprayed WD-40 lubricant throughout the basement and living room and ignited the fire early Wednesday, according to a state police affidavit.

Edmund Vicheck rescued his wife, Patricia, by dropping her from a second-story window, and later died of smoke inhalation, County Coroner Tim Warco said.

Police said Miss Vicheck had planned the crime for about a week because of a running dispute with her mother. Hours before the fire, Miss Vicheck had been arguing with her mother about going to the bar.

She was arrested after returning home about 9 a.m.

Mrs. Vicheck was in serious condition Thursday night with burns, a broken wrist and back and knee injuries.

How important is forgiveness in getting rid of bitterness and resentment? Bitterness affects our physical bodies in many ways. I was recently told by a nurse that bitterness builds up acetic acid in the body, which eats away the joints and can cause arthritis. I believe that bitterness will actually shorten a person's life span. Louis Proto writes,

The connection between the development of cancer and the holding on to resentments has long been established. Dr. Carl Simonton and his wife Stephanie found in a survey that the typical cancer patient evinces a strong tendency to hold on to resentment and a reluctance to forgive. Earlier, a New York psychologist Lawrence LeShan, in a survey of 250 cancer patients, came up with a 'cancer profile'. He found that they all suffered from feelings of self-hatred and an inability to come to their own defense if attacked. They also suffered tension in their relationships with their parents."[4]

O. Carl Simonton, MD, Stephanie Mathews-Simonton and James L. Creighton wrote in *Getting Well Again*, "Processes that help people release resentment, express negative feelings, and forgive past wrongs (whether real or imagined) may well be a major part of the preventative medicine of the future. And because cancer patients often have unresolved resentments, and other emotional ties to the past (as we have seen, perceived abandonment or rejection by one or both parents may be an antecedent to the development of cancer), helping our patients learn to release the past is often essential in helping them get well."[5] Everett L. Worthington writes, "Bitterness is due to long-lasting lack of forgiveness. It shows up as cynicism by either party and by an unwillingness to take risks to make the marriage better. Bitterness is a disease of the soul that has consequences for the body."[6]

Bitterness is a gradual transforming of the heart so that it subtly becomes hardened to God's commands. Hardening of the heart causes man to seek revenge and to stay bitter. It is a growing epidemic within our society. Look at what Zechariah 7:11-12 states about the hardening of the heart and God's response. Nowhere in Scripture does God ever want these three R's to occur, no matter what has happened. If you do any of these R's, you have lost your witness and have become a detriment to the kingdom of God.

Look at the life of King Saul and his attack on David. Saul is filled with the three R's. He resents David for becoming more popular than he is. He resents the song the people sang about David, "Saul has slain his thousands, and David his tens of thousands" (1 Sam 18:7-8). This song was very popular and was actually sung in foreign countries (1 Sam 21:11). The soldiers in Saul's army would sing this song repeatedly to keep Saul pursuing David. They wanted him dead. The soldiers knew the only way to kill David was to make sure Saul was continually embittered!

Bitter people bear grudges against the person who hurt them. The word "grudge" appears four times in the NIV. In all of those verses, it deals with revenge and bitterness (Gen 27:41; Gen 50:15; Lev 19:18; Mark 6:19). The book of Esther is a great book showing how bitterness, grudges and revenge backfire.

In the book of Esther there is a very bitter man named Haman. Haman is bitter at one Jew in particular, Mordecai, who refuses to rise when Haman walks by or to show fear (3:5; 5:9). Mordecai just happens to be the Queen's foster father. This is one of the things that leads to Haman's downfall.

Haman's bitterness at Mordecai spreads to all Jews. Haman convinces the king to decree that all the Jews in the country shall be killed. Wanting to kill someone is a dead giveaway that there is bitterness. (Pun not intended). Esther 5:9-14 records that Haman is very happy when the decree to kill the Jews goes into effect. This same passage states that even though Haman was the second most powerful man in the kingdom, he still had no satisfaction or joy (Prov 14:10). The reason no one can share his joy is that there is none! How are Haman and Esau alike (Gen 27:41-42)? What brought Esau consolation?

In chapter 6 of Esther, Haman is asked by the king, "What should be done for the man the king delights to honor?" Haman was thinking the man the king was talking about was himself. Wrong! Haman told the king that this man should have a royal robe the king has worn. He should have a horse the king has ridden. He should be paraded through the streets of the city with people shouting, "This is what is done for the man the king delights to honor!"

The king was delighted with Haman's suggestions. He tells Haman to make it so. Haman finds out this royal treatment is for Mordecai. The reason for this fancy treatment was that Mordecai had once uncovered a plot to kill the king. Mordecai had saved the king's life. This was King Xerxes' way of saying thank you! When Haman found out who the king was going to honor, Haman had a change of heart and wanted to tell the king that a simple handshake would do just fine. This is a good example of how bitterness backfires.

Esther eventually tells the King, her husband, she is a Jew and there is a plot out to destroy her people. The king asks who is the one behind this plot. Esther told him that it was the vile Haman (7:6). Haman had gallows made 75 feet high. They were built for the purpose of killing Mordecai, but it was Haman who died on it (5:14; 7:9-10). Bitterness was the sin that found Haman out, and it cost him his life (Num 32:23).

Source Notes

1. Martin Hoffman, "The Role of the Father in Moral Internalization," *The Role of the Father in Child Development*, ed. Michael E. Lamb (New York: John Wiley and Sons, 1981), p. 371.

2. H. Norman Wright, *Making Peace with Your Past* (Old Tappan, NJ: Fleming H. Revell Company, 1985), p. 68.

3. Earnie Larsen and Carol Larsen Hegarty, *From Anger to Forgiveness* (New York: A Hazelden Book, 1992), pp. 122-123.

4. Louis Proto, *Be Your Own Best Friend* (New York: Berkley Books, 1994), p. 61.

5. O. Carl Simonton, MD, Stephanie Mathews-Simonton and James L. Creighton, *Getting Well Again*, (New York: J.P. Tarcher, 1978), p. 149.

6. Everett L. Worthington, *Marriage Counseling*, p. 154.)

4

How Bitterness
Affects Christians

The strongest effect bitterness has on people is that it spreads into all
relationships and will eventually destroy them. Christians are not
immune from this effect! In fact, bitterness is the fastest growing negative emotion found in churches today.

Bitterness is something that can affect all people. It
can be expressed in a wide variety of ways. Our society has
experienced a rash of killings because of bitterness. Consider the following two newspaper articles:

RESENTMENT AGAINST GROUPS, INSTITUTIONS FUELS MURDER
SPREES by Fred Bayles AP national writer. *The Evening
Press*, Thursday, December 9th, 1993, p. 11

A man with a grudge against lawyers stalks a high-rise,
killing eight people. A gunman resentful over denied jobless
benefits shoots government workers. A man who hates
whites and Asians is accused of shooting passengers on a
commuter train.

"There's a tremendous amount of resentment out there and
increasingly it's being translated into murder," said James
Alan Fox, dean of criminology at Northeastern University.
"It's not all that random and not at all spontaneous."

OUR VIOLENT NATION SHOWING ITS WORST SIDE By Robert
Dvorchak, AP National Writer, *The Muncie Star*, Muncie, IN
Sunday December 19, 1993, p. 1A. (Excerpts taken from
this story)

The repetitiveness of multiple killings seems like a stac-
cato burst from some fiendish gun aimed at America's sense
of security.

Six commuters killed on a New York train. Four pizza-
parlor workers slain in a Denver suburb by a man police say
is a former employee. Two shoppers gunned down in
Oklahoma; the gunman commits suicide. A police officer
and three unemployment workers killed in California;
police shoot the gunman.

Can you see where bitterness played a large role in the
crimes committed in the above two stories? Can you see
the large number of innocent victims that were killed
because of their race or color? The sad thing is that in
America these kinds of stories are not that uncommon!

Bitterness has several unique ways it affects just
Christians. Satan loves these effects. He wants Christians to
have them all. Satan personally knows about these effects,
because they happened to him. What happens to
Christians when they choose not to forgive people that
have hurt them?

1. **It interferes with our relationship with God**
(1 John 2:9-11; 3:15; 4:8, 20). It causes a person to not
know God. It causes a person to not love God. Bitterness
contaminates the heart, but when a Christian forgives, he
has a sincere heart towards God and can approach him
with full assurance of faith (Heb 10:22). Realize the love
you have for your greatest enemy is equal to the love you
have for God! A bitter person is in darkness, is lost, and is
believing lies.

The reason bitterness ruins our relationship with God

is that bitterness goes completely against his nature. Anything that goes against his nature is sin! When a person is bitter because of loss, injustice or betrayal, it is normal for them to be bitter at God. (Look at Naomi in Ruth 1:20-21). In order for people to become bitter at God, they have to blame God for the painful event. Blaming God for painful events will put distance between you and God. People do a wide variety of things when they are bitter at God: rebel against his teachings, stop praying and going to church, turn to other "gods," and stop giving money to church, to name only a few.

When King Saul went to the witch at Endor (1 Sam 28), he went to a necromancer, one who inquires of the dead. Necromancy was one of several occult practices forbidden in the Old Testament (Deut 18:10-11). When Saul did this he was showing total disregard for God's commands. This is one of the major symptoms of bitterness. This showed how Saul's relationship with the Lord had deteriorated.

2. **Bitterness makes it impossible for God to forgive** (Matt 6:14-15; 18:21-35). For Christians, forgiving others equals forgiveness from God. If God does not forgive, then Hell is one of the consequences (both an eternal hell as well as a living hell on earth!). As I wrote previously, bitterness is a result of unforgiveness. Shortly after Jesus was resurrected he said, "Whose soever sins ye remit, they are remitted unto them; and whose soever sins ye retain, they are retained" (John 20:23, KJV). It would appear from this verse that when a person does not forgive, the unforgiving person retains the sin. This is why God cannot forgive the unforgiving person.

3. **Bitterness hinders prayers** (1 Pet 3:7). This is one of the many devastating effects of bitterness. Bitter people often feel that their prayers are going no higher

than the ceiling. They are right! Bitterness is sin! Sin causes God not to be able to hear prayers. Isaiah 59:2 accuses, "But your iniquities have separated you from your God; your sins have hidden his face from you, so that he will not hear." Isaiah 58:4 states, "Your fasting ends in quarreling and strife, and in striking each other with wicked fists. You cannot fast as you do today and expect your voice to be heard on high." In Mark 11:25 we read, "And when you stand praying, if you hold anything against anyone, forgive him, so that your Father in heaven may forgive your sins." Therefore, *bitterness causes God not to hear prayers*. The problem lies with the heart. Prayer comes out of the heart, and this is where bitterness resides. Proverbs 14:10 reads, "Each heart knows its own bitterness."

4. **It ruins *all* relationships** – it is only a matter of time (Heb 12:15). Bitterness funnels and tunnels into all relationships and will destroy them. Bitterness at one person means bitterness at them *all* until you give up your revenge and forgive.

5. **It is a spiritually blinding prison** in which a person dies (Acts 8:23; 1 John 2:9-11). Bitterness causes spiritual suicide. When you are bitter, you murder yourself daily. You lose your eternal life with God when you are bitter (1 John 3:15).

6. **It causes people to overreact** (Ps 73:21-22; Dan 3:19). Dr. Harry Emerson Fosdick is quoted as saying, "Hating people is like burning down your own house to get rid of a rat." Consider the father who was upset with his son's baseball coach because his son was not playing an infield position. This father threatened the coach with a bat and gun during the practice of the 7 and 8 year old boys team. Bitterness also changes personalities and attitudes. This change occurs after painful event(s). After such an

event they make a promise to themselves that no one is ever going to get close to them again, so they won't be hurt. A sudden change in attitude usually denotes a "promised" bitter heart! The person who has changed is now more defensive and protective. Such persons are now hurting themselves. Consider this story.

"MAJOR SPAT" RISON'S GIRLFRIEND ARRESTED AFTER FIRE DESTROYS MANSION. *The Muncie Evening Press*, Muncie, Indiana Friday, June 10, 1994, p. 11.

Alpharetta, GA. (AP) Hip-Hop star Lisa "Left Eye" Lopes surrendered to police today to face charges that she set a fire that destroyed the home of her boyfriend, Atlanta Falcons receiver Andre Rison.

Police said Lopes, 22, a singer with the group TLC is accused of setting fire to cardboard in a whirlpool tub at the two-story mansion early Thursday, shortly after Rison and a group of friends returned after being out all night.

Police said Lopes slapped and cursed at Rison before setting the fire and also smashed a white Mercedes-Benz sedan, a red Mercedes-Benz roadster and a Toyota 4-Runner parked at the home.

Bitterness Interferes with Worship of God

Charles Swindoll in *Stress Fractures* writes, "We have become a generation of people who worship our work, who work at play, and who play at our worship."[1] Bitterness could be one of the reasons why people "play" at worship. Ezekiel 33:31-32 states, "My people come to you, as they usually do, and sit before you to listen to your words, but they do not put them into practice. With their mouths they express devotion, but their hearts are greedy for unjust gain. Indeed, to them you are nothing more than one who sings love songs with a beautiful voice and plays an instrument well, for they hear your words but do not put them into practice." This passage is similar to James 1:22-

24. Isaiah 29:13 reads, "The Lord says: 'These people come near to me with their mouth and honor me with their lips, but their hearts are far from me. Their worship of me is made up only of rules taught by men.'" The Septuagint on this passage says, "They worship me in vain, their teachings are but rules taught by men." How does bitterness affect worship? How does bitterness interfere with worshiping God? There are at least three ways. These effects should scare Christians and make them very forgiving.

1. **It makes offerings unacceptable to God** (Matt 5:23-24). Cain must have already been bitter with Abel. This is why God rejected his offering (Gen 4:1-8). Cain's heart was not fully devoted to the offering. It was second best. Bitterness makes any ministry or offering to God second best. Second best is never acceptable to God!

2. **It causes Christians to take communion in an unworthy manner** (1 Cor 11:27-30). If a person takes communion with a bitter heart, he is guilty of sinning against the body and the blood of the Lord. In verse 30 Paul links bitterness and communion with weakness and sickness of the body. There is modern evidence that bitterness steals energy from the body's immune system, leaving the body vulnerable to illness and disease. Bitterness makes taking communion a "condemning" activity instead of a freeing one. Communion should never be taken if a person realizes they are bitter. This needs to be stressed from the pulpit.

3. **It changes a person's commitment and attitude toward God** (1 Kgs 8:61; Prov 28:14). A good example of this change is found in King Saul's life.

Picture bitterness being a chain connected between your heart and the person with whom you are bitter. On Calvary Jesus took one of the nails that was pounded into his flesh and broke this chain. At Calvary Jesus freed you from the effects of bitterness. Satan will repeatedly try to reattach you to this chain!

Source Notes

1. Charles Swindoll, *Stress Fractures* (Grand Rapids: Zondervan, 1994).

5

God's Healing Steps to Get Rid of Bitterness

"No one ever moved from bitter to better until the 'I' moved out."
—Unknown

"My conviction is that it is legitimate to pray for healing and deliverance and that God may give it.... If there is a medical or psychological process that will help bring healing, that process is from God."[1]

As we begin the healing process to rid ourselves of bitterness, it is important to understand that bitterness is a choice! (Deut 30:19) Satan cannot make people bitter. He can cause events that will tempt people to be bitter. This is exactly what he did with Job. Satan was hoping Job would become bitter at God and turn away from him. Satan attempts to do the same thing to Christians today. How exactly does one get rid of bitterness and the effects it has in our lives?

Stages of the healing process:

1. Painful event(s).
2. Blaming of self.
3. Punishing of self because of the blame.

4. Stoppage of painful event(s).
5. Gradual realization that you were the victim.
6. Shifting blame for the event to the real source.
7. Private confession of the event.
8. Possible public confession of the event.
9. Forgiveness for the event and perpetrator.
10. Healing from the painful event(s).

Later in this chapter I will give twenty-four biblical healing principles to purge ourselves of bitterness, and to create abundant living. These steps are not in any particular order. You may not have to do them all since we are all at different steps in this healing process (Ps 107:20; 119:71).

For there to be healing, there has to be sickness. One Old Testament word used for healing is *rapha*. The basic meaning for this word is "to heal," or "to make healthy." Bitterness is spiritual sickness. Isaiah 1:5 teaches that "your whole heart is afflicted." This is a good illustration of bitterness and how it affects the whole heart.

Only God can heal the bitter heart. Isaiah 53:5 is my favorite verse on healing. It reads, "...and by his wounds we are healed." Exodus 15:26 reads, "...I am the LORD who heals you." Hosea 6:1 states, "Come, let us return to the Lord. He has torn us to pieces but he will heal us; he has injured us but he will bind up our wounds." 2 Chronicles 7:14 promises, "If my people, who are called by my name, will humble themselves and pray and seek my face and turn from their wicked ways, then will I hear from heaven and will forgive their sin and heal their land." Further references on healing are found in Isaiah 57:18-19 and Jeremiah 33:6.

In step number 13 of this chapter I will stress the importance of expressing anger to help in healing. One important factor to recognize is that anger is frequently linked with "needed gifts" (i.e., love, trust, tenderness, touch, gentle words, and protection). It may seem paradoxical that victims of hurt would feel a lot of fear and anger when receiving these needed gifts. This unwanted linking of emotions usually occurs as a result of what the perpetrator said to the victim while hurting them. Many times the perpetrator tells the victim they love them and then abuses them. This creates some negative "definitions" for positive terms. Love becomes leave; trust becomes betrayal; hope becomes disappointment. If the abuse and linking occurred during childhood, it will be very difficult to break these false definitions.

People who become angry over positive gifts usually will go round and round with relationships and get nowhere. They will frequently feel obligated and expect pain shortly after receiving a positive gift. In their thinking, if they don't receive gifts they won't be hurt.

These victims have learned from their pasts. A lot of what they have learned makes them bitter. This "learning" has to be unlearned, then learned correctly! People who are caught in the cycle will look for flaws in relationships, so that they can get out before they get hurt. These flaws may be very small. If they cannot find them, they create them. They are so afraid of getting hurt, that they hurt others before it is done to them.

These victims will often "push away" from healthy relationships and go to unhealthy ones. This is what they are used to. This is one reason children of alcoholics frequently marry alcoholics. Any painful experience a child has been through repeatedly becomes normal and accepted. These victims will frequently expect hurt from relationships. When they don't get it they might feel they are not loved. They believe they are loved when abused. This is the only "love" they know!

God's Steps to Healing from Bitterness

At the Christian Campus House at Ball State University there is a picture of a butterfly being released from its cocoon. The location of this picture is very significant: it is above a baptistry! The words next to this picture say, "Released from bondage." This is what Jesus did when he died at Calvary, he released mankind from the bondages of sin. He also released people from the bondage of bitterness by being our model of forgiveness. His death brought us many victories.

It is important to claim victory through Christ over the bitterness in your heart (Matt 12:20; 2 Cor 2:14). Isaiah 14:3 describes bondage as being cruel. I regularly ask clients to figure out the number of days they have been in bondage to the person that hurt them. To get this figure they multiply the number of years since the event they have not forgiven took place by 365.25. This might be a staggering number.

Justice is one of the best ways to heal bitterness or even prevent it in the first place. There has to be a penalty for the offending party to pay so that the victim can feel vindicated. Restitution is a necessary part of justice (Exod 22:3-6, 11, 12, 14; Lev 5:16; 6:5; 22:14; 24:18, 21; Num 5:7, 8). There has to be vindication (being set free from the burden and shame) for healing to take place! David frequently asks for vindication from God. Vindication is having a burden removed so you are free to move again. The American College Dictionary defines "vindicate" as, "to clear, as from charge, imputation, suspicion, or the like." Consider the following verses on vindication: Psalm 17:2, 24:5, 26:1, 35:24, 27; 54:1, 135:14, Jeremiah 51:10. Vindication occurs only after the person realizes he was a victim of an event.

An Old Testament concept dealing with justice is the "Avenger of Blood." He was the executioner who was the executor of justice and punishment (Num 35:19, 21, 24-25, 27, 29-32; Deut 19:6, 12; Josh 20:3, 5, 9; 2 Sam 14:11). Another concept of justice, mentioned in Numbers 35, Deuteronomy 19, and Joshua 20, is the "city of refuge." Joshua 20:9 describes these cities and their purpose. "Any of the Israelites or any alien living among them who killed someone accidentally could flee to these designated cities and not be killed by the avenger of blood prior to standing trial before the assembly" (Num 35:6, 11-14; Josh 20:2; 1 Chr 6:57, 67).

A simple acrostic definition of justice is:

J esus'
U nderstanding
S entence
T o
I ncrease
C hild's
E dification

Jesus' Understanding because he is the only Judge with true justice (Ps 50:6). He knows what it is like to be a victim of abuse (Heb 4:15).

Sentence the payment required for a crime (Rom 6:23).

To Increase to make grow.

Child's the Christian victim of abuse (John 1:12).

Edification building up and healing from bitterness.

There are three kinds of justice: 1. legal justice, 2. God's physical justice, and 3. God's spiritual justice. The first one is very visible and measurable. The second might be visible and measurable. The third is neither visible nor measurable.

Jesus was just in the way he treated people. Some of the things Jesus did to bring about Godly justice were:

1. He allowed people to talk about what they had been through. The woman at the well is a good example of this (John 4:1-25). Jesus knew all about this woman's past, but he gave her the opportunity to talk about it. Jesus understood the healing power of confession.

2. He was compassionate (Matt 9:36; Lam 3:22, 32).

3. He never blamed the victims of the painful event (John 9:1-3).

4. He was sympathetic and suffered with them (Heb 4:15).

Jesus' type of "justice" is different from the legal aspect. Legal justice is also very important in ridding ourselves of bitterness. When a victim does not see man's justice he feels cheated. If he never sees God's physical justice, he may become bitter. Some of the legal-justice punishments mentioned in the Bible are:

banishment	Ezra 7:26; Revelation 1:9
imprisonment	Genesis 39:20-23
confiscation	Ezra 7:26
beatings	Daniel 25:1-3; 2 Corinthians 11:24
scourging	Matthew 27:26
enforced labor	Judges 16:21
burning	Leviticus 20:14; Daniel 3:6
hanging	Genesis 40:22; Esther 7:10
stoning	Leviticus 24:14; Acts 7:59
beheading	2 Kings 6:30-33; 2 Timothy 4:6
maiming	Deuteronomy 25:11-12
crucifixion	Matthew 27:31

According to 2 Thessalonians 1:6-9 retribution is part of God's divine justice. Psalm 9:16 teaches that God is known for his justice! He loves justice (Ps 99:4; Isa 61:8).

One major theme in the Old Testament deals with criminal justice. The Bible's judicial system includes penalties for:

Assault Exodus 21:18-27; Deuteronomy 25:11-12
Theft Exodus 22:1-4; Leviticus 19:35-36
Fraud Leviticus 6:1-7; Deuteronomy 25:13-16
Property Damage Exodus 22:5-15

What kind of justice do you find in the following story? Who might become bitter because of the sentence this man received?

JURY PUTS MURDERER ON PROBATION *The Evening Press*, Muncie, IN, March 24, 1993, p. 22.

Fort Worth, Texas (AP) — An all-white jury convicted a skinhead of murder in the drive-by shooting of a black man, then let him off with probation.

"Black folks' lives still ain't worth a damn in Texas," fumed Dallas County Commissioner John Wiley Price, who is black. "I'm mad as hell. Until black folks start taking to the streets nothing is going to happen."

Christopher William Brosky, an 18-year-old white supremacist, received 10 years probation Tuesday for the 1991 slaying of 32-year-old Donald Thomas. He could have received life in prison.

"We just felt like this might be a man who might be able to turn his life around," juror Richard Higgs said. "If we had sent him to Huntsville [prison], he might have come back in worse shape."

According to testimony, Brosky helped plan the shooting and was in the car.

Believing in God's spiritual justice is by faith only. Ecclesiastes 12:14 reminds us, "For God will bring every deed into judgment, including every hidden thing, whether it is good or evil." Job 34:21-22 says, "His eyes are on the way of men; he sees their every step. There is no dark place, no deep shadow, where evildoers can hide."

95

God's physical justice or consequences is the punishment a perpetrator receives from God for the sin he has committed, sometimes immediately, but not always. It might be ulcers, stress, depression, guilt, unhappiness, substance abuse, or a failed marriage. There will be times it will take faith in God's physical judgment to help heal bitterness. You may never see the person who hurt you suffer, but be assured they will. In Jeremiah 30:11 and Jeremiah 46:28 we read, "'I am with you and will save you,' declares the LORD. 'Though I completely destroy all the nations among which I scatter you, I will not completely destroy you. I will discipline you but only with justice; I will not let you go entirely unpunished.'" Nahum 1:2-3 states, "The LORD is a jealous and avenging God; the LORD takes vengeance and is filled with wrath. The LORD takes vengeance on his foes and maintains his wrath against his enemies. The LORD is slow to anger and great in power; the LORD will not leave the guilty unpunished" (See also Exod 34:7; Num 14:8; Job 10:14; Ezek 30:11; 46:28). You may have thought that the person who harmed you gets by with no punishment at all. This is not true. God does punish the people that have caused us pain! There are many passages in the Bible that deal with the idea of the Lord repaying people for the wrong they have caused others (Deut 7:10; Judg 9:56; 2 Sam 3:39; 16:8; 1 Kgs 2:32; 2 Chr 6:23; Job 34:11; Ps 28:4; 94:23; Prov 14:14; Isa 66:6; Col 3:25). To overcome bitterness, it is important you believe in the second and third judgments of God! Believing that God will not let the guilty go unpunished should help remove bitterness.

It is important to recognize that forgiveness by God does not stop all the physical consequences that God gives because of sin. Jesus forgave the thief on the cross, but he still died for the crimes he committed (Luke 23:39-43). For more proof that forgiveness does not stop the physical consequences of sin, consider what happened to Adam and

Eve; Abel; the people of Israel; and David and Bathsheba after God forgave them. Adam and Eve were kicked out of the garden (Gen 3:23-24). Cain had to wear a mark and was put out of the presence of the Lord (Gen 4:10-16). God forgave the people of Israel for their disbelief, but he did not allow them to enter the promised land (Num 14:20-23). The child born to David and Bathsheba through adultery died (2 Sam 12:13-23). In three of these cases, God later blessed them with children (Gen 4:1-2, 5:3; Gen 4:17; 2 Sam 12:24-25).

Forgiveness erases the spiritual consequences of sin. Jews, in Jesus' day, understood the physical consequence of sin (John 9:1-3 and John 5:14). King Saul was afflicted by an evil spirit after he had sinned against God; this was part of God's physical judgment (1 Sam 16:14-15, 18:10, 19:9). David wrote that men will be cursed by God for what they have done to him (1 Sam 26:19; Deut 27:15-26). Zechariah 2:8 says God will plunder those who hurt his people.

In Psalm 31:10 David tells of his affliction. This word is also translated "guilt." Guilt is often one of the physical judgments of God. John 16:8 tells us the Holy Spirit "will convict the world of guilt in regard to sin and righteousness and judgment." David wrote many verses in Psalm 38 dealing with the physical consequences of guilt and sin. I am assuming David had already asked God to forgive him, but he still had to go through the physical punishment for his sin. God's forgiveness does not end the judgment of man nor God's physical consequences of sin.

Consider what the verses below say about the consequences for sin. Even though this is for David's sin, I assume these consequences can happen to all people.

Psalm 38:2   arrows have pierced him, God's hand was upon him.

   38:3   no health in the body, no soundness in his bones.

97

38:4	guilt has overwhelmed him. It is a burden too heavy to bear. This burden of guilt has to hinder and entangle around a person (Heb 12:1).
38:5	wounds fester and are loathsome.
38:6	bowed down, constant mourning.
38:7	back filled with searing pain.
38:8	crushed, feeble and anguished.
38:9	sighing.
38:10	heart pounds, strength fails.
38:11	friends and companions stay away.
38:12	paranoia, irrational fear of people seeking his life.
38:17	pain is constant.

When the person who hurt you suffers, don't gloat! Proverbs 17:5 teaches us that, "He who mocks the poor shows contempt for their Maker; whoever gloats over disaster will not go unpunished." Proverbs 24:17-18 reads, "Do not gloat when your enemy falls; when he stumbles, do not let your heart rejoice, or the LORD will see and disapprove and turn his wrath away from him." This is great advice to follow.

Steps to Healing

1. **Do I want to be healed?** See John 5:6. This is the first question you must ask yourself if you are serious about being healed from bitterness. It is important that you consider what your definition of healing is going to be. Admitting to yourself you are tired of the effects of bitterness in your life is a crucial start to ending the cycle of bitterness. Another question Jesus will ask is, "What do you want me to do for you?" (Luke 18:40-41). It is important to answer this question when Jesus asks it. Tell him you want to be healed from bitterness, the cancer of the heart! The

word "heal" or an associated word occurs often in Scripture. "Heal" occurs 44 times; "healed" occurs 73 times; "healing" occurs 28 times; and "heals" occurs 6 times in the New International Version. What is Jeremiah's plea (found in Jer 17:14)?

Once you have made the decision that you want to be healed from bitterness, what's next? It is important that you begin praying daily for yourself and the situations that have embittered you. If you do not know what the situations are, pray that the Holy Spirit will reveal to you the situations that have caused your heart to be the way that it is. Prayer should not be a call to 911. Not our last defense, but our first attack to defeat bitterness. Prayer should bring quietness and confidence (Isa 32:17), which can defeat bitterness. Dr. Sadler, a psychiatrist from Chicago, writes in his book, *The Practice of Psychiatry*: "When we set ourselves to the work of collecting or re-collecting the scattered pieces of ourselves, we begin a task which if carried to its natural conclusion ultimately becomes prayer."[2] When you are praying it is important that you remember who you are praying to. Consider these verses:

2 Chronicles 24:8 which promises that God has power to help.

Job 26:14 which tells us God's power is limitless.

Psalm 62:11 which states power belongs to God.

Usually this power is linked with prayer. Isaiah 40:31 teaches that, "They that wait upon the LORD shall renew their strength." When you pray it is important you believe that what you are praying for will happen.

It is important that you pray and ask God for healing. Prayer is bending your knee at Calvary. It is also important that you believe your prayers will be answered. James 1:6-8 reads, "But when he asks, he must believe and not doubt, because he who doubts is like a wave of the sea, blown and tossed by the wind. That man should not think he will receive anything from the Lord; he is a double-minded man, unstable in all he does." Praying without believing is wasted breath.

One of my favorite stories about prayer being answered is found in Acts 9:32-43. Peter comes across a paralytic who had been bedridden for eight years. Peter said to him, "Jesus Christ heals you. Get up and take care of your mat." The man, Aeneas, got up immediately. It is important that you realize that the only way you are going to be healed from paralyzing bitterness is through Jesus Christ.

2. **Have faith that you will be healed**. Have faith that God has the power to heal you (Luke 4:40). Jeremiah 32:27 declares, "I am the LORD, the God of all mankind. Is anything too hard for me?" In Acts 14:9-10 we read that the faith to be healed can be seen.

The New Testament uses the Greek word ***dunamis*** for power, which is the root of the English words "dynamic" and "dynamite." Psalm 147:3 assures us, "He heals the brokenhearted and binds up their wounds." Psalm 103:3 reminds us that God is the God, "who forgives all your sins and heals all your diseases." God can heal you from the sin of bitterness. You must believe this to be healed.

In Hebrews 11:6 we read that faith pleases God. Many times in Scripture, faith is linked with healing. Several verses in Mark link faith with healing (2:5; 5:34; 7:32-35; 8:22-26; 9:23-27; 10:4-52). As faith increases, bitterness decreases. The opposite of this is also true. To conquer bitterness, you must believe God can deliver you. You must believe that you through God's help can defeat the bitterness harbored in your heart. If you believe it cannot be overcome, it never will. Look at how the faith of Shadrach, Meshach, Abednego and Daniel kept them alive and free from bitterness (Daniel chapters 3 and 6). Look especially at 3:16-18.

One of the greatest stories of healing, found in Ezekiel 37, is the story of the valley of dry bones. In 37:5-6 we read, "This is what the Sovereign LORD says to these bones: I will make breath enter you, and you will come to life. I will attach tendons to you and make flesh come upon you and cover you with skin; I will put breath in you, and you will come to life. Then you will know that I am the LORD." Ezekiel did as the Lord commanded and the bones came back to life and formed a vast army (7-10). To be healed from bitterness and have your heart put back in order, you must have the faith of Ezekiel!

Paul Tillich wrote this about faith: "The strong usually have a strong conviction. Everybody needs a place to stand upon. Without a foundation no strength is possible." He also wrote, "Don't give up the faith that alone can make you ultimately strong because it gives you the ultimate ground on which to stand."[3]

Consider the following quote about faith:

Human pain works its way out of our consciousness over time. There is a season of sadness. A season of anger. A season of tranquility. A season of hope. But seasons do not follow one another in a lockstep manner. At least not for those in crisis.

The winters and springs of one's life are all jumbled together in a puzzling array. One day we feel as though the dark clouds have lifted, but the next day they have returned. One moment we can smile, but a few hours later the tears emerge. It is true that as we take two steps forward in our journey, we may take one or more steps backwards. But when one has faith that the spring thaw will arrive, the winter winds seem to lose some of their punch.[4]

3. Be careful of the people you allow to be around you (Prov 4:14; 12:26; 1 Cor 15:33). It is very difficult to be healed when you are around sick people. Being around bitter people is like drinking milk past its expiration date. Both put a bad taste in your mouth. Bitterness rubs off on people like smoke from a camp fire rubs off into clothes. Augustine once said, "Bad company is like a nail driven into a post, which, after the first or second blow, may be drawn out with little difficulty; but being once driven up to the head, the pincers cannot take hold to draw it out, [except] by the destruction of the wood."

Let's do an assignment about your friendships. Make a list of friends that you have who would help you heal from bitterness. Make a list of your friends who would encourage you to be bitter. Beware of this second group; they are being used by the Devil. When you are around them, you can become just like them. If I could rewrite Proverbs 22:24-25, I would take out the word "may"; and put in the word "will." So the passage would read, "Do not make friends with a hot tempered man or associate with one easily angered, or you will learn his ways and get yourself ensnared."

If you are around bitter people, it will be easy to "learn" and will be difficult to overcome (Deut 18:9; Josh 23:6-8). If you have been raised by bitter parents, you have a greater chance of becoming bitter. Ezekiel 16:44 states basically "like mother, like daughter."

If you are to overcome bitterness, it is vitally important that you have a strong Christian fellowship around you. Ecclesiastes 4:8-12 says "There was a man all alone; he had neither son nor brother. There was no end to his toil, yet his eyes were not content with his wealth. 'For whom am I toiling,' he asked, 'and why am I depriving myself of enjoyment?' This too is meaningless — a miserable business! Two are better than one, because they have a good return for their work: If one falls down, his friend can help him up. But pity the man who falls and has no one to help him up! Also, if two lie down together, they will keep warm. But how can one keep warm alone? Though one may be overpowered, two can defend themselves. A cord of three strands is not quickly broken."

Christians are like Moses; even he needed two people to support him during his battles, Aaron and Hur (Exod 17:10-13). To conquer bitterness, you need to have some strong friends in whom to confide. Proverbs 27:17 states, "As iron sharpens iron, so one man sharpens another." Hebrews 3:13 commands, "But encourage one another daily, as long as it is called Today, so that none of you may be hardened by sin's deceitfulness." In Hebrews 10:25 we read, "Let us not give up meeting together, as some are in the habit of doing, but let us encourage one another — and all the more as you see the Day approaching." One of the best reasons for constant fellowship is found in Matthew 18:20, "For where two or three come together in my name, there am I with them."

4. **Be careful about what you watch, listen to, and read**. A study by *TV Guide* reported that in a single day TV showed 1,846 acts of violence, 389 assaults, 362 uses of guns and 273 punches (NBC NIGHTLY NEWS, 5/21/93). How would this create bitterness and violence? (See Prov 4:23; 23:7; Matt 6:22). Albert Bandura did research on young children and television back in the 1960s. In one study, young children watched an actor on television being aggressive in some very unusual ways against a large inflated toy clown. After watching, the kids were placed in a room with many different toys, including the toy clown. In general, the results of the study revealed a strong imitation behavior. In some cases the children actually appeared to be carbon copies of the models they observed hitting this clown.

Time Magazine (June 12, 1989) reported that by the age of 16, the average American child has seen more than 200,000 acts of television violence, including 33,000 murders. The Center for Media and Public Affairs commissioned *TV Guide*'s Neil Hickey to study violence on television. He studied one day—Thursday, April 2, 1992. The study covered ten stations and 180 hours of programming. His study tallied:

> 1846 individual acts of violence
> 175 scenes resulting in one or more fatalities
> 389 scenes depicting serious assaults
> 362 scenes involving gun play
> 673 depictions of punching, pushing, shoving, dragging and other physically hostile acts
> 226 scenes of menacing threats with weapons

Hickey said his day included all types of programming. Cartoons led the way with 471 violent acts. TV promos came next with 265. Movies had 221, toy commercials 188, music videos 123, commercials of theater movies 121, TV dramas 69, TV news 62, reality shows (such as *Top Cops* and *Hard Copy*) 58, sitcoms 52, and soap operas 34. (Neil Hickey, "How Much Violence on TV?" Ethics: Easier Said Than Done, Issue 21, 1993, p. 53.)

The Chicago Tribune did an article about the link between watching TV violence and violence entitled "22-Year study links TV, violent behavior" (*Chicago Tribune*, 4/19/92)

> Youngsters who watch excessive amounts of television violence tend to engage in more violent behaviors and criminal activity as adults, a University of Illinois at Chicago study found.
>
> A 22-year study of 875 8-year-olds from a semi-rural New York county showed that by age 30 those who had watched more television violence at 8 were convicted of more serious crimes, said psychologist Leonard Eron.
>
> They were also more aggressive under the influence of alcohol and punished their children more harshly, said

Eron, who heads the American Psychological Association's commission on Violence and Youth.

The findings support earlier results, which showed that boys who were low in aggressive behavior at 8 but who watched more television violence became more aggressive at 19 than boys who originally were highly aggressive but watched less television violence. A more recent three-year study of suburban Chicago youth showed the same effect of TV violence, he said.

"Television violence affects youngsters of all ages, of both genders, at all socioeconomic levels and all levels of intelligence, and the effect is not limited to children who are already disposed to being aggressive and is not restricted to this country," Eron said.

There is a lot of bitter material in the world today. Many times the nightly news is just bitterness updates. Being exposed to this material repeatedly causes desensitization. If a person watches enough talk shows or reads the newspaper column from noted advisors, bitterness is seen all the time. It is important to guard what you allow your eyes to watch and ears to hear. A children's song comes to mind, "Oh, be careful, little eyes, what you see." This would be a good song for adult Christians to consider. I would encourage you to stay away from daytime programming on TV that exploits abuse. Watching these type of shows could cause shame, guilt and flashbacks and might promote bitterness. Flashbacks cause you to feel the same way you did when you were going through the painful event! Flashbacks turn the tape player in your mind on that plays the old stuff again. Flashbacks are when Satan reminds you of a painful event and it causes you to experience the same emotions all over again.

5. **Change your thought pattern from the negative**. A prayer to help you change your thoughts might be, "I want more of your thoughts in my mind, Lord, and less of mine. Father, what is hurting my thought pattern? Help me to identify it and get rid of it."

One of the best ways to change your thought pattern is by daily Bible reading. This allows the Spirit of God to teach you how to think. David asks God to create in him a pure heart (51:10) He also asks God to get rid of any thoughts he has that displease God (Ps 139:1, 23-24). Philippians 2:5 gives the Christian thinking pattern. One can attain mental purity by living according to God's word (Ps 119:9). The Bible teaches that we should read it day and night (Josh 1:8). The Bible is an excellent source for teaching, reproof, correction and training in righteousness so that we can be fully equipped for every good work (2 Tim 3:16-17).

What have people in the past said about the Bible? Sir M. Hale said, "The Bible is the only source of all Christian truth; the only rule for the Christian; the only book that unfolds to us the realities of eternity." Flavel stated, "The Scriptures teach us the best way of living, the noblest way of suffering, and the most comfortable way of dying." Mark Twain wrote, "It ain't those parts of the Bible that I can't understand that bother me, it is the parts that I do understand." D.L. Moody said, "The Bible will keep you from sin, or sin will keep you from the Bible." And James Jennings said, "If a man's Bible is coming apart, it is an indication that he himself is fairly well put together." It is by reading the Bible that our thoughts become transformed into God's thoughts (1 Cor 2:16).

Bitterness feeds on negative thinking. Ephesians 4:23 tells believers, "to be made new in the attitude of your minds." Paul writes in Philippians 4:8, "Finally, brothers, whatever is true, whatever is noble, whatever is right, whatever is pure, whatever is lovely, whatever is admirable — if anything is excellent or praiseworthy — think about such things." 1 Peter 1:13 encourages, "Therefore, prepare your minds for action; be self-controlled; set your hope fully on the grace to be given you when Jesus Christ is revealed." This new attitude is one that is righteous not bitter. Paul's positive thinking pattern is a great defense against bitterness!

One benefit of a positive thinking pattern is that it keeps bitterness away from the heart. Consider what Hans Selye, a stress researcher, said about thoughts, "Nothing erases unpleasant thoughts more effectively than concentration on pleasant ones." Consider the following quotes about thoughts: "The whole course of human history may depend on a change of heart in one solitary and even humble individual—for it is in the solitary mind and soul of the individual that the battle between good and evil is waged and ultimately won or lost."[5] Dan Polson wrote, "The Devil can have no more power over you than the thought he can inject into your mind."[6]

1 Corinthians 14:20 gives the pattern of thinking God wants. It also gives Satan's desired thought pattern. "Brothers, stop thinking like children. In regard to evil be infants, but in your thinking be adults." God wants Christians to be infants when it comes to evil and adults in normal thinking. Satan wants just the opposite of this. How does Romans 16:19 relate to this idea?

It is important to understand the power thoughts have. Every behavior has a thought motivating it. Self-talk, the talk that takes place inside the head that no one hears, has a great deal of control over behavior. In the King James Version of the Bible Proverbs 23:7 reads, "For as he [a man] thinketh in his heart, so is he." Below are verses that speak about thoughts.

1 Corinthians 13:11 — Thoughts should change as we mature.
Colossians 2:8 — We can be taken captive by thoughts. Thoughts can be hollow, deceptive and based on human tradition.
Romans 12:2 — Minds can and should be renewed.

> 2 Corinthians 10:5 — We should take captive every
> thought and make them obedient to Christ.
> Deuteronomy 6:5; Matthew 22:37 — "Love the Lord,
> your God, with all your heart...."

According to the Bible many things should come out
of the heart. Some of them are:

> 2 Samuel 17:10 — courage, bravery, boldness
> Psalm 19:14 — meditations that can please God
> Psalm 28:7 — trust in God
> Proverbs 11:16 — kindness
> Proverbs 12:20; 15:30; Psalm 28:7 — joy
> Proverbs 13:12 — hope
> Proverbs 14:13 — laughter
> Proverbs 14:30; Colossians 3:15 — peace
> Proverbs 15:13 — happiness
> Proverbs 17:22 — cheerfulness
> Matthew 11:28-30 — gentleness, humbleness
> Matthew 18:35 — forgiveness
> Acts 2:26 — rejoicing, gladness, hope
> Romans 5:5 — love
> 2 Corinthians 4:5 — the light of Jesus
> Colossians 2:2 — encouragement
> Colossians 3:16 — gratitude to God
> 1 Peter 1:22; Philemon 7 — love.

These qualities are the opposite of bitterness! They
oppose bitterness, making it difficult for Satan to get into
the heart. According to Matthew 18:35 forgiveness comes
from the heart. Neil T. Anderson in *The Bondage Breakers*
writes, "How do you forgive from the heart? First you
acknowledge the hurt and the hate. If your forgiveness
doesn't visit the emotional core of your past, it will be
incomplete. This is the great evangelical cover-up. Christians
feel the pain of interpersonal offenses, but we won't
acknowledge it. Let God bring the pain to the surface so he

can deal with it. This is where healing takes place. Ask God
to bring to your mind those you need to forgive...."[7]

Negative qualities also come out of the heart, produc-
ing and maintaining bitterness (Matt 15:19). Below is a list
of some negatives the heart can produce:
Genesis 42:28 — fear, depression
Leviticus 19:17 — hate
Deuteronomy 15:7 — hardness
Deuteronomy 15:10 — grudges
Deuteronomy 20:3 — fainting, weakness, fear, terror,
    panic
1 Samuel 1:8 — depression
1 Samuel 28:5 — terror
Psalm 13:2 — grief, sorrow, wrestling, struggles
Psalm 25:17 — troubles
Psalm 38:8 — anguish
Psalm 55:21 — war
Proverbs 6:25 — lust
Proverbs 11:20 — perversion
Proverbs 12:20; 26:24 — deceit
Proverbs 12:23 — blurts out folly
Proverbs 12:25 — anxiety
Proverbs 13:12 — sickness
Proverbs 14:10 — bitterness
Proverbs 16:5 — pride, proud
Proverbs 22:15 — folly
Proverbs 23:17 — envy
Proverbs 25:20 — heaviness
Ecclesiastes 2:20 — despair
Isaiah 35:4 — fear
Isaiah 59:13 — lies
Jeremiah 17:9; Proverbs 26:24 — deceitfulness
Ezekiel 33:31 — greed
Mark 3:5; Romans 2:5 — stubbornness

Healing for a Bitter Heart

> Luke 21:34 – dissipation, drunkenness, anxieties of life
> John 14:27 – trouble, fear
> Acts 8:22 – wickedness
> Romans 2:5 – unrepentance
> Hebrews 3:12 – sin, unbelief
> 1 John 3:20 – condemnation.

What is the purpose of the heart?

> Deuteronomy 8:5 – knowledge, discipline
> Deuteronomy 30:2; Psalm 119:34 – obedience
> 1 Samuel 12:24; Jeremiah 32:40 – praise, thanks, worship of God
> 1 Samuel 24:5 – violation, conscience, guilt
> 1 Kings 3:12 – wisdom and justice
> 1 Kings 3:9 – discerns good and evil
> Psalm 9:1 – to praise God
> Psalm 62:8; 1 Samuel 1:13 – prayer
> Psalm 112:8 – security
> Psalm 119:11 – place to hide God's word
> Proverbs 6:21 – place where God's word should be
> Proverbs 16:9 – planning the course of life
> Proverbs 16:23 – guides the mouth
> Proverbs 22:17 – to be applied to knowledge
> Proverbs 23:19 – to keep us on the right path
> Ecclesiastes 2:15-17; Psalm 16:7 – decisions, thought
> 2 Corinthians 9:7 – decisions, thought
> Isaiah 6:10 – understanding, healing
> Joel 2:12 – conversion
> Matthew 9:2 – forgiveness
> Romans 2:5 – repentance
> Romans 12:2 – renewing and changing
> 2 Corinthians 1:20-22 – place where God's Spirit lives, deposit
> Hebrews 10:22 – place where the cleansing from guilt occurs

These purposes of the heart keep it free from bitterness!

What verses can be used in prayer to change a bitter heart?

Deuteronomy 30:6 — Circumcise my heart so that I love you.

1 Samuel 13:14 — Give me a heart after your own heart.

1 Samuel 16:7 — Lord, look at my heart.

Ezra 1:5 — Move my heart.

Ezra 7:27 — Put things in my heart that praise and honor you.

Psalm 17:3 — Probe my heart; examine me.

Psalm 19:14 — Let the meditation of my heart be acceptable.

Psalm 51:10 — Create in me a pure heart.

Psalm 51:17 — Break my heart if it needs it.

Psalm 57:7 — Make my heart steadfast.

Psalm 111:1 — Teach me to praise you with my whole heart.

Psalm 112:8 — Make my heart secure.

Psalm 125:4 — Make my heart upright.

Psalm 138:3 — Make me bold and stouthearted.

Psalm 139:23-24 — Search my heart, get rid of what you hate.

Proverbs 15:11; Acts 16:14 Lord — open my heart.

Proverbs 21:1 — Put my heart in your hands. Direct my heart.

Proverbs 23:26 — Father, I give you my heart.

Isaiah 57:15 — Revive my heart.

Malachi 2:1 — Set my heart so that it honors you.

Luke 24:32 — Make my heart burn when I read the Bible and pray.

Acts 2:37 — Cut me to the heart.

Romans 2:15 — Write your laws on my heart.

Romans 12:2 — Renew my mind.

1 Corinthians 2:16 — Make my mind like yours; give instruction.

Ephesians 1:18 — Enlighten my heart.

Ephesians 3:17 — Dwell in my heart, Lord Jesus.

Hebrews 10:16 — Put your laws in my heart. Write them on my mind.

God would actually like us to have his mind and thought pattern (1 Cor 2:16). Consider this quote:

> The Lord's thoughts are all working towards 'an expected end.' God is working with a motive. All things are working together for one object: the good of those who love God. We see only the beginning. God sees the end from the beginning. He knows every letter of the Book of Providence; He sees not only what he is doing, but what will come of what he is doing.
>
> As to our present pain and grief, God sees not these things exclusively, but he sees the future joy and usefulness which will come from them. He regards not only the tearing up of the soil with the plow, but the clothing of that soil with the golden harvest. He sees the consequences of affliction, and he accounts those painful incidents to be blessed which lead up to so much happiness.
>
> Let us comfort ourselves with this.[8]

How does one go about transforming the bitter mind? It must begin with daily personal Bible study and meditation. In Psalm 1:2 we read, "But his delight is in the law of the LORD, and on his law he meditates day and night." Joshua 1:8 says, "Do not let this Book of the Law depart from your mouth; meditate on it day and night, so that you you may be careful to do everything written in it. Then you will be prosperous and successful." In Hebrews 4:12 we read, "The word of God is living and active. Sharper than any double-edged sword, it penetrates even to dividing soul and spirit, joints and marrow; it judges the thoughts and attitudes of the heart." Reading the Bible on a regular basis is going to have an effect on your thoughts. Psalm 119:11 reads, "I have hidden your word in my heart that I might not sin against you." Second Timothy 3:16 teaches that, "All Scripture is God-breathed and is useful for teaching, rebuking, correcting and training in righteousness...."

6. **Be sure not to cross responsibility**. Don't blame yourself for the actions of others (Deut 24:16; Ezek 18:1-4; Jer 31:29-30). Doing this makes it impossible to forgive. Two side effects of crossed responsibility are depression and fatigue. When you blame yourself for others actions, you are in bondage. Bondage is:

B laming
O urselves
N eedlessly
D estroying
A ny
G od given
E steem

Colossians 2:8 tells us to, "see to it that no one takes you captive through hollow and deceptive philosophy, which depends on human tradition and the basic principles of this world rather than on Christ." Blaming yourself for the actions of others is one of those hollow and deceptive philosophies! Later in this book we will address God's steps to forgiveness. Step one is holding the person who hurt you accountable and 100% responsible for their sins against you.

To help you get rid of crossed responsibility, make a list of the events that other people have done to you that you blame yourself for. Write out the proof of why you blame yourself. Who taught you to blame yourself? More than likely it was the person who hurt you that taught you this. It could also be that Satan is the one who taught you to blame yourself (2 Tim 4:1). It is a Biblical fact that Satan is a teacher!

Healing for a Bitter Heart

The State of Oregon passed a law that was to be enacted September 9, 1995 that makes the parents legally responsible for misdemeanor infractions of their children under the age of 15. This law creates crossed responsibility! In Ezekiel 18:2 there is the following proverb, "The fathers eat sour grapes, and the children's teeth are set on edge." In Jeremiah 31:30 we read, "Instead, everyone will die for his own sin; whoever eats sour grapes — his own teeth will be set on edge." This Oregon law and the Bible disagree. The Bible makes the person who does the behavior, responsible for the behavior. This Oregon law does not do this.

7. **Build your self-esteem on Christ**, not on the way people treat you. Knowing three things will help prevent bitterness:

1. **Who God is.**
2. **Who you are in God's sight.**
3. **Whose you are.**

In the book of Daniel there are two stories about four people who could have been bitter. Shadrach, Meshach and Abednego were thrown into a fiery furnace because they refused to bow down and worship an idol. Daniel was thrown into a den of lions because he prayed to God and not to the king (Dan chapters 3 and 6). These four people were not bitter because they knew who God was; who they were in God's sight; and whose they were. This is what saved them from death. God would not have saved them if they had been bitter. They would have burned or been eaten by lions!

Blaise Pascal once said, "Apart from Christ we know neither what our life or death is; we do not know what God is nor what we ourselves are." Consider these verses on what the Bible says Christians are:

Deuteronomy 7:6 — We are his people, his treasured possession.

114

Psalm 23; Isaiah 40 — Sheep
Psalm 139:13-14 — We were knit together, fearfully made.
Isaiah 43:4 — Precious, Honored, Loved
Isaiah 43:21 — Formed to proclaim his praise.
Isaiah 49:15-16 — We are engraved on the palm of God's hand.
Isaiah 65:24 — A people God listens to.
Zechariah 2:8; Deuteronomy 32:10; Psalm 17:8 — Apple of his eye.
Matthew 26:52-53 — The only reason Jesus died.
Matthew 27:11; John 1:12 — Prince, Princess
John 10:18 — The reason Jesus choose to die.
2 Corinthians 5:20 — Ambassadors
Philippians 2:15 — Blameless, pure, children of God, stars. Blameless is an interesting word to describe forgiveness. It is found 13 times in the NIV New Testament (1 Cor 1:8; Eph 1:4; 1 Thess 3:13).

8. **Build the "C's"** in order to avoid bitterness. It is the Bible and the Holy Spirit that teach these characteristics to Christians. God would like Christians to be:

Competent — adequate, capable, qualified, sufficient, suitable (2 Cor 3:4-5).

Confident — a belief of adequacy and reliance on God's ability (Heb 10:35-36; Ps 27:3; Prov 3:26).

Complete — whole, full, entire, total (Ps 23:1; 2 Tim 3:16-17).

Courageous — a quality of mind that enables one to be steadfast in the face of opposition, hardship, danger and fear (Josh 1:9; Matt 14:27; Deut 31:6,8; Prov 28:1).

Committed — willing to follow through and execute fully (2 Chr 16:9; Jer 2:2).

Correct — striving to gain mastery of the word of God (2 Tim 2:5).

9. **Sing praises to God**. Singing praises to God is one of the best ways to break the bonds of bitterness. A praising heart has sawed through the chains of bitterness (Acts 16:25-26). Christians must learn to praise God during trials. (Ps 47:7; 52:9; 59:17; 61:8; 63:4, 5, 7; 64:10; 66:10; 101:1) The word "praise" appears 340 times in the NIV. "Praises" occurs 19 times; "praising" occurs 16 times. 2 Chronicles 20:1-30 tells of a battle plan where a choir preceded an army of the Lord into battle, giving thanks in song to God. This is a good illustration of praise in action. What happened to the armies of the Moabites, Ammonites and some of the Meunites right after the choir sang? God destroyed them.

In Acts 16:25-26 Paul and Silas are in prison. At midnight they are singing praises to God and praying. Shortly after this there is an earthquake and the prison doors open. The chains binding the men fall off. What kind of chains would fall and doors would open if Christians would sing praises and pray? The chains of bitterness would be one of the first to fall! In Isaiah 58:6 we read, "Is not this the kind of fasting that I have chosen, to loosen the chain of injustice, to untie the cord of the yoke, to set the oppressed free, to break every yoke." Bitterness is a chain binding people to their past. David in Psalm 100 addressed the issue of singing praise to God. He writes:

100:2 Worship the LORD with gladness;
    come before him with joyful songs.
100:4 Enter his gates with thanksgiving.
    and his courts with praise;
    give thanks to him and praise his name.

10. **Tell God "thank you"** for what he will do through what has happened (1 Thess 5:18; Ps 50:23). Saying thanks releases you from bitterness, causing freedom. Habakkuk 3:17-19 reads, "Though the fig tree does not bud and there are no grapes on the vines, though the olive crop fails and

116

the fields produce no food, though there are no sheep in
the pen and no cattle in the stalls, yet I will rejoice in the
LORD, I will be joyful in God my Savior. The Sovereign LORD
is my strength; he makes my feet like the feet of a deer, he
enables me to go on the heights." Nothing in this passage
mentions feeling thankful. I believe that you do not have to
feel thankful before saying it. After *saying* thanks you will
gradually start feeling it. Saying thanks to God is like turning
on a light switch and allowing the power to flow. Saying
thanks allows God to act in the painful situation! Saying
thanks acknowledges God's power to transform the situation into good (Rom 8:28). God will use what you have
been through to comfort others (2 Cor 1:3-4). Before saying
thanks a couple of biblical principles must be understood:

1) Genesis 50:19-20 — God works through harmful
events and uses them for good.
2) Lamentations 3:33 — God does not willingly bring
affliction or grief to the children of men.
3) Romans 5:3-4 — Suffering produces perseverance;
perseverance, character; and character, hope.
4) Romans 8:28 — In all things God works for the good
of those who love him, who have been called
according to his purpose.
5) James 1:2-4 — Consider trials of many kinds pure
joy, because the testing of faith develops perseverance. Perseverance, when it is done working,
makes Christians mature and complete.
6) Psalms 119:67, 71 — Affliction can teach God's
word.

Why should Christians give thanks to God for loss,
injustice and betrayal? It is being obedient to God and his
word. 1 Thessalonians 5:18 declares that Christians should
give thanks *in all* situations. It is God's will that thanksgiving occur for all events! How does this relate to what Paul
wrote in Ephesians 5:20, which tells us to be "always

117

giving thanks to God the Father for everything, in the name of our Lord Jesus Christ"? How does this relate to Psalm 34:1, 2?

Three Forms of Thanks

1) Saying thanks before an event turns out well — is called **faith**.
2) Saying thanks as an event is turning out well — is called **worship**.
3) Saying thanks after an event turns out well — is called **praise**.

God wants us to offer all three forms of thanksgiving when we go through trials. When there is no thanksgiving for loss, injustice and betrayal, depression sets in. How does saying "thank you" take our personal Valley of Achor and make it a door of hope? (Josh 7:24-25; Hos 2:15) Because eleven things happen when Christians say thanks for loss, injustice and betrayal:

1) *They are being obedient to God and his word*. He blesses obedience (1 Thess 5:18; Deut 28:1-14). John 14:15, 21, 23 link obeying God's commands with love. Christians are loving God when they say thanks!

2) *They are allowing God to fight*. Psalm 35:1-3 shows God is a warrior. He will fight for Christians. When people say thank you for painful events they are handing the battle over to the Lord. A good example of this is found in 2 Chronicles 20:15 — Jehoshaphat is told the battle he is about to go into is not his, but the Lord's (Deut 20:4).

3) *They are allowing God to protect them* from bitterness that so easily destroys relationships. Psalm 91:4 says God will cover you with his feathers and under his wings you will find refuge. When you say thank you, you are stepping into the loving protection of God (Ps 25:20-22).

118

4) *They are claiming victory* over the situation. As stated in #2, God fights when people say thanks. When God fights he never loses (Ps 44:4, 7; 60:12; Prov 21:31; 1 Cor 15:57; 1 John 5:4; Deut 20:4; 1 Sam 17:47).

5) *They are increasing faith in their God* and putting more hope in him. Psalm 20:7 says some trust in horses and chariots, but Christians should trust in the name of the Lord.

6) *They are taking away a stronghold* Satan tries to set up in their lives. Ephesians 4:26-27 says people should not hold anger inside them past sunset. Such pouting gives the devil a stronghold. Paul writes in 2 Corinthians 10:4 that the weapons Christians fight with have divine power to demolish strongholds. Stronghold is from the Greek word **ochuroma** which means fortress; it means to make strong or firm. It is a place that Satan tries to establish in a person's life to control him or her. George Otis, Jr. said, "A studied observation of the territorial variety (of strongholds) reveals two universal characteristics—they repel light and they export darkness." Ed Silvoso said about strongholds, "A stronghold is a mindset impregnated with hopelessness that causes us to accept as unchangeable something that we know is contrary to the will of God."

7) *They are becoming a child of God*. This is what he wants for all Christians (Matt 18:3; 19:13-15). If this change is not made, then the person will not enter heaven.

8) *They are worshiping God*. Psalm 22:3 says God lives in the praises of his people. It is important to understand that saying thanks for painful activities is actually a form of worship and offering to God (2 Chr 29:31; 33:16; Ps 50:14, 23; 56:12; Jer 17:26; 33:11). This kind of offering is actually a pleasing aroma to God (Num 15:3, 7, 10, 13, 14, 24; 18:17; 28:2, 6, 8, 13, 24, 27). This process of saying thanks goes against your human nature, but so do a lot of things God asks of us.

9) *They are acknowledging his transforming power.* God is being allowed to change their minds and make them like his (Rom 12:2; 1 Cor 3:18; Eph 4:22-24).

10) *They are dumping the garbage of the past,* allowing new things to come and replace it. They are starting the rebuilding process in their life (Neh 2:20).

11) *They are allowing God to heal the past* (Isa 57:19; Jer 17:14; Mal 4:2).

Why is it hard to say thanks?

When saying thank you to God for loss, injustice, and betrayal, people might hear themselves saying:

1) I want more of what has already happened to me.
2) I enjoyed what happened to me.
3) I deserved what I got.
4) I appreciated what happened to me.

Saying thanks is like putting hydrogen peroxide on a sore. When you say "thank you" for the loss, injustice and betrayal, you are allowing the infection of bitterness to be removed and healing to begin. Saying thanks is like going through surgery — you don't thank the doctor for the cutting and discomfort, but for the healing that occurs afterwards. Saying thanks allows God to perform surgery on the painful experiences of the past. It allows the painful events to be removed and God's forgiveness and healing power to be put in its place.

Look at the diagram on page 19. After saying thanks to God, peace develops. Peace is what every human being is looking for in a tiring and stressful world. In one of the best verses on peace in the whole Bible, Isaiah 57:2, we read, "Those who walk uprightly enter into peace; they find rest as they lie in death." One of the cries of all people today is to find peace with the events in their past. The peace they are searching for is only found in Jesus Christ. It is a gift God gives us (Isa 9:2; Isa 32:17-18; Eph 2:14-17). "By the same measure it may be said with equal force that if peace is absent from a person's life it is apparent that Christ really has not come in. It is a delusion to believe or think one is a Christian whose life is marked by constant battling, bitterness or belligerence."[9]

Christians, searching for peace, need to be receptive to the teaching about giving thanks. This is a hard teaching because it goes against human nature. One of the reasons Jesus gave the Sermon on the Mount was to show people that without God in their lives, they cannot live in ways that please him. Philippians 4:4-9, 12-13 is a passage about thanksgiving that Paul most likely wrote in jail (Phil 1:12-14). These are things that brought Paul peace:

4:4 Rejoice in the Lord always.

4:5 Let our gentleness be evident to all. The Lord is near.

4:6 Be anxious about nothing. Pray about everything. Prayer should include thanksgiving.

4:7 God's peace transcends our minds. The peace of God guards our hearts and minds in Christ Jesus.

4:8 There is a Christian thinking (thanking) process that is to be dwelled on.

4:9 Practice what has been seen and heard from Paul. The God of peace is with us.

4:12 Paul has been in a variety of situations, through which he learned the secret of being content in any and every situation. The secret Paul learned (rejoice always) is in 4:4. This secret still works today!

11. **Confess to others what has happened to you.** Talk to trusted people about how you feel about the loss, injustice and betrayal (Jas 5:16). Why is it so difficult to be open with people about your past? You might expect them to not believe you, to betray your confidence, to treat you differently after you tell them what has happened to you, to

laugh at you, to blame you, or even scold you. They might be unemotional when you tell them and they might ask you "why didn't you tell me this sooner?"

Confession has often been referred to as a "talking cure." One major benefit of confessing what has happened in the past is that it takes bitterness away from the heart. Your feelings, the hurt, the bitterness, the secret is now being shared by someone else. Confession of this kind frequently gives a different perspective on what took place and who is to blame! Be cautious who you share with! You need to confess to someone who is trustworthy, someone who is not going to gossip or use it against you later.

Jesus in his time of need had friends with whom he shared his feelings. Peter, James and John were with him at the most critical time in his life. Jesus says to them, "My soul is overwhelmed with sorrow to the point of death. Stay here and keep watch with me" (Matt 26:38). It was also during this same time that he confesses to his father exactly how he feels about what is going to take place. "My Father, if it is possible, may this cup be taken from me. Yet not as I will, but as you will" (Matt 26:39). Jesus also encouraged his disciples to pray for him (Matt 26:41). If you are struggling with bitterness, I would encourage you to be very transparent to three Christian friends. Ask them to pray for you.

One of the reasons people don't openly talk about what has happened to them is that they feel guilty and want to keep it secret. An acrostic definition will help define what secret is and its power:

Shame
Encouraging
Constant
Repression,
Enduring
Timelessly

People frequently blame themselves for the abuse that has happened to them. This creates shame. Shame is feeling that you did something wrong and that you are guilty. Shame will cause you to hide from people because of a fear of exposure (John 3:20). An acrostic definition for shame is:

S in's
H umiliation
A nd
M onumental
E mbarrassment

Galatians 6:2 tells us to, "Carry each other's burdens, and in this way you will fulfill the law of Christ." With this type of confession (confession of your past abuse), you are allowing people to carry your burdens. The purpose of Christ is found in Luke 4:18-19: "The Spirit of the Lord is on me, because he has anointed me to preach good news to the poor. He has sent me to proclaim freedom for the prisoners and recovery of sight for the blind, to release the oppressed, to proclaim the year of the Lord's favor." I believe this is what happens when we are open to people about the painful events in our lives! We become free from bitterness.

12. **Forgive the perpetrator** (Matt 6:14-15). Be careful not to have a judgmental attitude (Matt 7:1-5). Be bigger than both the person who harmed you and the offense (Ps 119:165; 1 Cor 6:7). The last chapter of this book will deal with forgiveness in detail.

13. **Learn to express anger in a timely and appropriate manner**. I recently had problems with my clothes dryer due to overheating. The problem was diagnosed as poor venting. It is the same way with the heart. When anger is not vented properly, it overheats. Harriet Goldhor Lerner wrote, "When we vent our anger ineffectively, we can easily get locked into a self-perpetuating, downward

cycle of behavior. We do have something to be angry about, but our complaints are not clearly voiced and we may elicit other people's disapproval instead of their sympathy. This only increases our sense of bitterness and injustice; yet, all the while, the actual issues go unidentified."[10]

I found some very interesting quotes about anger:

> I can't think of a single person I've met who would willingly expose a child or spouse to the fury of a full-grown lion, but I know many husbands and wives who are letting another deadly killer walk right through their front door without a fight—unhealthy, unresolved anger.
>
> Self anger is the negative emotion we feel when a person or situation has failed to meet our needs, blocked our goals, or fallen short of our expectations.
>
> (*Love Is a Decision*, by Smalley and Trent, Word Publishing Co., 1989, p. 75, 77.)

"When a pot boils over, it cools itself." — German proverb

"Anger punishes itself." — Chinese proverb

"Do not remove a fly from your neighbor's face
with a hatchet." — Chinese proverb

Two major reasons for expressing anger are:

1. It takes away a stronghold that Satan tries to set up (Eph 4:26-27).

2. It gets rid of bitterness stored in the heart (Eph 4:31). I like the way the King James Version states Ephesians 4:26-27, "Be ye angry, and sin not: let not the sun go down upon your wrath: Neither give place to the devil." Thomas Secker said, "He that would be angry and sin not, must not be angry with anything but sin." If anger is kept inside past sunset, this is a dangerous state. Remember, those that anger you, are controlling you. Anger is only one letter away from

danger. The "D" is added to anger when it becomes dusk. Consider the following quote about what anger can do:

Anger not only leads to deadly violence when unchecked, it also kills in more subtle ways. There are millions of drug addicts who are shooting up, snorting up, or washing down some chemical that will soothe the anger-ridden mind of the user.

Blood pressures can peak because of unresolved anger. Some scientists say that cancers grow best in a metabolism prepared by the chemical reactions produced by anger. The lives are wasted away in depression as the temper is left unexpressed and turned inward. Anger is a thief that steals life from individuals and potential from relationships. And in its most destructive form, for both individuals and relationships, anger fuels a fire that burns up the will to survive.[11]

Seneca is quoted as saying, "If anger is not restrained, it is frequently more hurtful to us, than the injury that provokes it."

How does anger affect the body?

Anger:

    causes an increase of adrenaline and nonadrenaline
    causes an increase of various pituitary and adrenal hormones
        testosterone (or estrogen)
        thyroxine
        insulin
    causes an increase of cholesterol and fat blood levels
    causes an increase in the time the body needs to rid itself of cholesterol (3 to 4 times longer)
    causes a pre-diabetic state
    causes an increase in the time for the clotting elements of the blood to precipitate out
    causes a narrowing of the small capillaries nourishing the coronary blood vessels[12]

Hebrew has four words for anger. The definition for each of these words follows the word.

ap: flaring nostrils
hemah, haron: burning and heat
gesep: violation of relationship that causes heated anger
ebrah: fury

Greek has two words for anger. The definition of each of the words follows the word.

thymos: outburst of anger
orge: brooding, deliberate anger

The emotion of anger takes many forms and this is what makes it so hard to diagnose. Some of these forms may be depression and hatred. There are many angry people in our society who do not even recognize that holding anger in creates bitterness.

The four quadrants of anger:

As you saw in the diagram on page 19, bitterness can result from anger being held in and dwelled on. Anger is usually expressed in more secure relationships. Anger expressed to a person does not necessarily mean anger at a person. The following diagram gives the four ways anger is expressed in relationships:

1. timely/inappropriate;   2. timely/appropriate;
3. untimely/inappropriate;   4. untimely/appropriate.

	Inappropriate	Appropriate
Timely		*God wants this one*
Untimely	*Satan likes this one*	

126

The two brothers of Dinah in Genesis 34 would fall into the quadrant that Satan likes. They were angry at Shechem for raping their sister Dinah. How long did they hold their anger in? For at least three days, Genesis 34:25 indicates. How is three-day-old anger expressed? In this case Simeon and Levi killed every male in the city where Shechem lived. This was definitely untimely–inappropriate anger expression. Their anger intensified during those three days and became bitterness.

Which quadrant would Absalom fall into? (2 Sam 13) Absalom killed Amnon for raping his sister Tamar. According to 2 Samuel 13:23, it took Absalom two years to express his anger. That means he held his anger inside for two years!

Verses that deal with anger being timely:

> Ephesians 4:26: Don't let the sun go down while you are angry.
> James 1:19: Be slow in getting angry; don't be a flare or a hothead.
> Psalm 7:11: Express anger on a daily basis.
> Psalm 30:5: God's anger lasts only a moment, and so should ours.

Verses that deal with anger being expressed appropriately:

> Ephesians 4:26: Don't sin in your expression of anger.
> Proverbs 21:14: Being nice to people soothes anger.
> Proverbs 29:11: Keep your anger under control.
> Proverbs 16:32: Be patient, control your temper.
> Proverbs 19:11: It is good to overlook some offenses.
> Proverbs 15:1: Answer gently when you are in an angry situation.
> Ephesians 4:31: Get rid of all anger and bitterness.
> Psalm 103:9: God does not harbor his anger forever.
> Psalm 145:8: God is slow to anger (thoughtful in how to express it).

Verses that deal with anger being untimely:

> Ephesians 4:26: Anger prolonged past sunset.
> Ecclesiastes 7:9: Being quickly provoked.
> Proverbs 27:14: Don't express yourself too early in the morning.
> Proverbs 18:13: He who answers before listening.

Verses that deal with anger being expressed inappropriately:

> Ephesians 4:26: Expressing anger in any sinful way.
> Proverbs 26:17: Getting involved in quarrels that are not yours.
> Proverbs 29:11: Giving full vent to your anger.
> Ecclesiastes 7:9: Letting anger reside within.
> Proverbs 20:2: Expressing anger by harming someone.
> Proverbs 16:14: Expressing anger by killing or hurting someone.
> Proverbs 27:4: Being cruel in your anger.
> Proverbs 27:14: Anger expressed loudly.

What did Nehemiah do with his anger? (Neh 5:1-8) He made accusations. He confronted the people with the problem and called together a meeting to deal with what made him angry (Neh 5:7-13). What does the word "pondered" mean? (Neh 5:7)

When Jesus was angry in the temple, he made a whip (John 2:15). This gave him time to consider the problem, how he felt, and what he wanted to do about it. I encourage a lot of my clients who are angry to make a "whip." This "whip" is doing something physical before expressing their anger. This gives them a chance to cool down and not say things they will regret later. A good example of a "whip" would be going for a walk.

I would encourage those of you who are angry to move to Alaska! (Eph 4:26) Alaska in the summertime has

128

some of the longest daylight hours in the world. There are several other reasons why I would encourage you to move to Alaska. It is far away. It is desolate. There are not a lot of people living there. This would be a great state to be angry in! But one of the problems with living in Alaska is the wintertime. It has some of the shortest daylight hours in the world! You might want to try to live there six months out of the year, and move to the south pole during the winter months. I frequently tell angry people they had better start walking west, driving west, or flying west. This gives them more daylight to deal with their anger.

Three equations will help in understanding the expression of anger: R is the response to a situation. S is the situation.

R = S appropriate

R < S denial, inappropriate

R > S Painful past conflicts have brought up a lot of pain, leading to too much expression of anger. The man who expresses his anger with an inappropriately strong response will usually be seen as a "raving lunatic."

I believe in an angry Jesus! A steamed Savior. In what situations did Jesus express anger? Mark 3:1-6 gives us a clear example of Jesus' anger. He is in the temple on the Sabbath. A man with a shriveled hand is there. Mark 3:5 says, "He looked around at them in anger and, deeply distressed at their stubborn hearts, said to the man, 'Stretch out your hand.' He stretched it out, and his hand was completely restored." Jesus used his anger here to heal! Another story about Jesus getting angry is found in John 2:12-16. This is when Jesus cleared the temple. His reasoning for doing this was because the temple had become a marketplace, not a house of worship. In John 2:16 Jesus says, "Get these out of here! How dare you turn my Father's house into a market"! This is when Jesus made a whip from cords and drove the people out of the temple. Jesus used his anger in this situation to show love for his Father!

Scripture also teaches that God can be provoked to anger. Psalm 106 gives many examples of how God is angered by wicked deeds. (Also see Deut 4:25; 9:7, 18; Judg 2:12; 1 Kgs 14:9, 15, 22; 15:30; 16:13, 26; 21:22, 53; 2 Kgs 17:11, 17; 21:6, 15; 22:17; 23:19; 2 Chr 28:25.) In my searching through the Bible I have found three godly reasons for anger. The reasons are:

1) When God's laws are being broken (John 2:12-16; Zech 1:2-6, 7:11-12).
2) When God's creation is being hurt (Mark 3:1-5).
3) When people interfere with a person's relationship with Jesus and God (Mark 10:13-16). Matthew chapter 23 is a great record of Jesus' anger at people who get in the way of a person's relationship with God (vv. 13-15).

Proverbs 31:8-9 comes to mind. It tells us that Christians should do several basic things: 1) speak up for those who cannot defend themselves; 2) speak up and judge fairly; 3) defend the rights of the poor and needy.

What is man's anger? How is man's anger different from God's? Man's anger is anger for unbiblical reasons. God's anger is always for biblical reasons. Mankind gets angry:

when he did not get his way. This is pouting anger.
when things are not fair. This is manipulating anger.
when he does not win. This is childish anger.

These three reasons are in direct contrast to the three reasons stated above as to why God gets angry. This is why James writes in James 1:19-21, "My dear brothers, take note of this: Everyone should be quick to listen, slow to speak and slow to become angry, for a man's anger does not bring about the righteous life that God desires. Therefore, get rid of all moral filth and the evil that is so prevalent and humbly accept the word planted in you, which can save you."

Why is anger so difficult to express and deal with appropriately? One reason getting rid of anger is so difficult is due to the lies Satan tells about anger. He has at least fourteen lies about anger. Later in this book I will discuss the power lies have and why Satan tells them. People often believe that anger will only make things worse. They don't understand that there is value in expressing anger. It relieves that pressure in the heart. It takes away one of the grips of Satan!

Some of Satan's lies about anger:

1. Christians should never be angry.
2. Anger is a sign of immaturity.
3. Anger is close to becoming mentally ill. (Expressing anger is next to nuts.)
4. If I express my anger, nothing will change.
5. If I express anger, there will be retaliation.
6. Anger is wrong and unhealthy.
7. Expression of anger is a sin.
8. Expressing anger will only hurt relationships.
9. Expressing anger is a maneuver to get pity and sympathy.
10. Expressing anger is a weakness.
11. Expressing anger hurts other people's feelings.
12. Expressing anger shows disrespect.
13. Anger shows an inability to accept circumstances.
14. Anger shows an inability to control your emotions.

Can you imagine telling Jesus he is immature, mentally ill, or any of these other lies, because he was angry? Then why do you say them to yourself? The fact is, our God is an angry God (Exod 4:14; Num 11:10; 12:9; 25:3-4; 32:14; Deut 6:15; 7:4; 29:20; Josh 7:1; 23:16; Judg 2:14, 20; 3:8;

10:7; 2 Sam 6:7; 24:1; 2 Kgs 13:3; 24:20; 1 Chr 13:10; 2 Chr 25:15; Isa 5:25; Jer 3:12; 4:8, 26; 7:18, 20; 10:10; 11:17; 12:13; 15:15; 23:20; 25:37; 30:24; 51:45; 52:3). God causes or creates a path for his anger to be expressed (Ps 78:50).

All or some of these fourteen statements might sound true, but they are lies! Most of these lies about anger are learned in childhood. Holding childhood beliefs about anger in adulthood will keep you bitter! Paul, in 1 Corinthians 13:11, wrote, "When I was a child, I talked like a child, I thought like a child, I reasoned like a child. When I became a man, I put childish ways behind me." Probably one of the most difficult tasks of growing up is putting childish ways (thoughts) behind and thinking like an adult. Why are these lies taught during childhood? Satan wants them taught in childhood so that bitterness will be the outcome. This way, children develop a pattern of not expressing their anger, and this gives Satan a stronghold (Eph 4:26-27). Consider the following quote about things learned in childhood.

> The stereotype of a deluded mental patient is one who walks around in a daze and complains about hearing voices. The truth is that we all are subjected to voices, especially those from our childhood. These voices and the content of their messages play over and over in our heads. They may not be audible, but their effect can be devastating, especially for driven people. Like a broken record that drums and throbs the same bar of music, the same messages follow these people throughout the years. No matter how hard the people try, they can't get away from the sound.[13]

People frequently hear the echoes of past teaching on anger. This causes anger to be stifled instead of expressed. The truth about anger is that it is a very healthy, normal emotion. It is not something of which to be afraid. Jesus, in Mark 3:1-5, was angry and he healed a man. It is too bad we don't see anger as healing. In John 2:12-16 Jesus was angry as he drove the merchants from the temple of God because of his love for God. There are things in our society that God expects will make us angry (Ezek 9:3-6). What is the consequence of not being angry or grieved by what is taking place, according to this verse? God had these people killed!

Anger is an emotion that is not merely a sign of frustration, but can also show love. Most people do not understand that anger can show love. Do you become angry at your son when he runs across the street without looking? How do you feel when a loved one is hurt? Do you feel angry? This is normal. This is love!

Below is a simple five-step approach to dealing with anger.

1. *Admit you are angry.* Realize that you are allowed to be angry. Jesus was angry, so it cannot be a sin! God is described in Scripture as an angry God, (Num 11:33; 12:9; 14:18; 25:3-4; 32:10, 13) so anger is an acceptable emotion. Paul in Ephesians 5:1 tells Christians to imitate God, so it is fine to be angry. In Job 20:23 Zophar states that God vents his anger. 1 Chronicles 13:10 says God's anger burned. We need to be careful about what angers us. We need to be sure it is something which would anger God!

2. *Admit why you are angry.* Be specific about the reasons for your anger.

3. *If possible and profitable, confront the person who hurt you* (confrontation without condemnation). Forgiveness requires some type of confrontation. "Possible" means a physical confrontation can actually occur. It is not possible to confront a dead person face to face, but they can be confronted in other ways. Profitable means you believe confronting the person who hurt you will have some benefit or reward. If you believe the person will not listen, will blame you more for the event, or will call you a liar, I would encourage you to go to this person in your mind.

You might want to do this by writing the person a letter and not mailing it. Consider this example:

Dear Dad,

I am very mad and sad that you got divorced! And it's just not even that I have to live through this and you didn't. And you know what else, I didn't even know you got the divorce. Dad I love you, but, I don't understand why you did it and what makes me really mad is that you always say things are better this way, but they're not! Also you say you don't like the drive! Well I've got some advice for you: first of all things are not better for me. Second, if you want not to drive so far, then you shouldn't of gotten divorced.

WE DO NOT EVEN GET TO SEE EACH OTHER ANY MORE,

Always loving you,

P. S. I'll love you no matter what you do.

A good way to start writing an unmailed letter is to complete the sentence "You had no right to....." as many different ways as you can think of. The "You" is referring to the person who hurt you. This is a good way to uncover the true emotions that have been buried inside. The more specific and detailed you can be in completing these statements, the greater and more accurate your expression of anger will be.

4. *Tell them how their actions affected you.* Do not minimize what they did. Do not use the words "only" or "just" when telling them about the event. When talking to the person who hurt you it is important that you speak the truth. In Proverbs 24:26 we are told, "An honest answer is like a kiss on the lips." It is important to be honest with the person you are confronting! In Proverbs 27:5 we read, "Better is open rebuke than hidden love." Remember that a gentle answer turns away wrath (Prov 15:1). Do not use words as weapons, or the bitterness you have will only be compounded. Using words to seek revenge will not satisfy

the desire to get even. Any attempt to hurt the person who hurt you will only make you more bitter and angry. You will need to speak the truth in love (Eph 4:15). Tryon Edwards said, "Accuracy of statement is one of the first elements of truth; inaccuracy is a near kin to falsehood." Speak with grace (John 1:14), and with mercy and compassion (Jas 5:11). Henry Wadsworth Longfellow is quoted as saying, "Being all fashioned of the self-same dust, let us be merciful as well as just." Lloyd D. Mattson said, "He who has mastered the grace of forgiveness is far more triumphant than he who has managed to see that no wrong to him is gone unavenged."

5. *Do not expect them to change or to admit they were wrong.* Haliburton said, "When a man is wrong and won't admit it, he always gets angry." Thomas à Kempis once said, "Be not angry that you cannot make others as you wish them to be, since you cannot make yourself as you wish to be."

If your "hidden agenda" is to get them to admit they were wrong, you will be more angry after talking to them. You are expressing anger not for them to apologize, but to release it. This will make you feel better. Do not expect them to say these eight words, "I'm sorry, I was wrong, please forgive me." (See chapter # 9: God's Steps to Forgiveness.)

In situations where you have done what the Bible says and there is no change, accept it! This is their choice! At this point, it is important to develop a sense of humor. More information about laughter and the healing process will be given in step # 15 below.

A good example of the above five steps for removing anger took place in Milwaukee, Wisconsin, during the Jeffrey Dahmer hearing. Dahmer was convicted of brutally killing 15 boys. The judge, Laurence C. Gram Jr., allowed one family member of each of the victims to tell Dahmer how they felt. Consider the following excerpts from a story by Lisa Holewa, an Associated Press writer, dated February 18, 1992.

SENTENCING OF DAHMER CLEARS WAY FOR HEALING FOR VICTIMS' FAMILIES

Milwaukee — Some relatives of Jeffrey Dahmer's victims say they can "let the healing start" now that the serial killer has been sent to prison with no chance for parole.

"I feel sorry for him," said Shirley Hughes, mother of victim Tony Hughes. "He has feelings, too. I don't hate him."

Dahmer told the Judge before being sentenced Monday to 15 consecutive life prison terms that he expected neither forgiveness nor freedom.

"I feel so bad for what I did to those poor families, and I understand their right to hate," Dahmer said in a low monotone. "I have seen their tears and if I could give my life right now to bring their loved ones back, I would do it."...

...Nine relatives of victims told the judge of their suffering before Dahmer was sentenced. By sentencing him to consecutive — rather than concurrent — terms, Milwaukee County Circuit Judge Laurence C. Gram Jr. made parole out of the question.

"It's not going to bring David back," said Inez Thomas, mother of victim David Thomas. "But I hope my family and I can get on with our lives and let the healing start."

What Judge Gram did is the best thing he could have done for the family members of the victims. Inez Thomas said, "But I hope my family and I can get on with our lives and let the healing start." There are two reasons this healing process started. First, in the eyes of the victims' families, justice was served. Secondly, the judge allowed the family members to express to Dahmer how they felt. These events were vital for the healing process to take place.

I called and talked to Judge Gram. He told me that he allowed the family members of the victims to speak because this gave them some part in the judicial process. He told me that in the case of murder the person pressing the charges is not the family members, but the State. At the sentencing hearing, allowing them to speak gives the family members a part in the justice system. What Judge Gram was also doing was giving the victim's families a chance to be released from bitterness.

I wish that this process of allowing people, who have been hurt by the actions of others, to speak out would take place more often in courts. I have been told by a Christian deputy prosecutor in Indiana that there are laws in Indiana that give this right to the victims of crime. This expression of hurt from the victim should take place in rape cases, adultery and molestation cases. Many of the molested children I work with are in dire need of confronting the person who hurt them. This confrontation would greatly aid their healing process by giving the victim a chance to vent anger. This will prevent bitterness from developing. Confrontation is one of the tasks of the Holy Spirit. Acts 13:9-11 is one of my favorite confrontations found in the Bible. Paul confronts a man named Elymas. "Then Saul, who was also called Paul, filled with the Holy Spirit, looked straight at Elymas and said, 'You are a child of the devil and an enemy of everything that is right! You are full of all kinds of deceit and trickery. Will you never stop perverting the right ways of the Lord? Now the hand of the Lord is against you. You are going to be blind, and for a time you will be unable to see the light of the sun.'"

Questions that might help in confronting the person who hurt you:

1. What questions would you like to ask that person?
2. What statements would you like to make to that person?

137

3. What emotions would you feel if you did the first two steps face to face with the one who hurt you?
4. What things would you like to hear from them?
5. If you did 1 & 2 face to face, how do you think they would respond?
6. How would you feel if you just wrote 1 & 2 and did not verbalize it to them; or if you mailed it?

14. Do good things for yourself without feeling guilty (Matt 14:22-23). Guilt caused by doing good things for yourself comes because you believe it is selfish. If you don't do good things for yourself you will never be healed from bitterness. Treat yourself like your best friend (Matt 22:39). If you were your best friend, how would you treat yourself? What type of things would you be doing for yourself? I would encourage you to start doing some of them today. It is not selfish to be good to yourself, as long as you are not mistreating others when you do it.

15. Learn to laugh. Laughter is the emotion that gives the heart a short vacation from bitterness. When God created it, he gave us a prescription for health and long life. It is sad, but during times of loss, injustice and betrayal, laughter is frequently absent. Laughter should be part of a person's daily diet. *Readers' Digest* has regular features to make people laugh ("Laughter, the Best Medicine"; "Life in These United States"; "All in a Day's Work"; "Campus Comedy"; and "Humor in Uniform"). This is one of the reasons I like reading this magazine. B.C. Forbes said, "Cheerfulness is among the most laudable virtues. It gains you the good will and friendship of others. It blesses those who practice it and those upon who it is bestowed." Consider what the following article tells us about happiness:

"If You're Happy and You Know It..."

You may be nuts, contends Richard P. Bentall writing in the

Journal of Medical Ethics (June 1992). The psychologist argues that happiness should be classified as a psychiatric disorder.

Happiness "is statistically abnormal and consists of a discrete cluster of symptoms," writes Bentall. "There is at least some evidence that it reflects abnormal functioning of the central nervous system; and it is associated with various cognitive abnormalities—in particular, a lack of contact with reality." In fact, "happiness should be included in future taxonomies of mental illness, probably as a form of affective disorder."

He suggests that the word happiness "be replaced by the more formal description 'major affective disorder: pleasant type', in the interest of scientific precision and in the hope of reducing any possible diagnostic ambiguities."[14]

The idea that laughter is a medicine is not a new idea. The book of Proverbs has some absolutely wonderful verses about laughter and joy that disagree with Bentall's point of view. One of my favorite Proverbs is 17:22 which says laughter is good medicine. I also like 15:13, 15 which say a happy heart makes the face cheerful, and a cheerful heart has a continual feast. Psalm 30:5 says joy comes in the morning. Nehemiah 8:10 says the joy of the Lord is my strength. When a situation cannot be changed and you have done all you can to correct the situation, laugh!

It is God's patience (Exod 34:6) and sense of humor that prevented him from destroying the world. In Psalm 37:13 we read, "but the Lord laughs at the wicked, for he knows their day is coming." Consider the following quote about laughter and humor:

> In laughter, we transcend our predicaments. We are lifted above our feelings of fear, discouragement, and despair. People who can laugh at their setbacks no longer feel sorry for themselves. They feel uplifted, encouraged and empowered.
>
> Comedians, cartoonists, and comedy writers know the power of humor for conquering painful circumstances.

Healing for a Bitter Heart

Several studies have revealed that many nationally known comedians experienced intense isolation, depression, suffering, or loss in their childhood. They found that kidding around about their losses and difficulties was a way of gaining power over them.

During the Civil War Lincoln used laughter to get him through the hard times. During one meeting, he was reading a book of humor. After he finished he told those people attending the meeting: "Gentlemen, why don't you laugh? If I did not laugh I should die, and you need this medicine as much as I do."[15]

Consider these quotes about laughter:

"A keen sense of humor helps us to overlook the unbecoming, understand the unconventional, tolerate the unpleasant, overcome the unexpected, and outlast the unbearable." *Billy Graham*

"Like a welcome summer rain, humor may suddenly cleanse and cool the earth, the air, and you." *Langston Hughes*

"Good humor is the health of the soul, sadness its poison." *I.V. Stanislaus*

"Humor is just another defense against the universe." *Mel Brooks*

"Laughter is a tranquilizer with no side effects." *Arnold Glasgow*

"You can turn painful situations around through laughter. If you can find humor in anything — even poverty — you can survive." *Bill Cosby*

"Laughter is a safe and civilized alternative to violence." *Dr. Martin Grotjahn*

"When people are laughing, they're generally not killing one another." *Alan Alda*

Below is a list of a few of the psychological benefits of laughter:

extinguishes body tension

**gives a psychological boost
reduces stress**

Cardiovascular benefits:

**decreases blood pressure
lowers heart rate
enhances circulation**

Muscular benefits:

**strengthens heart muscles
relaxes muscles throughout the entire body
helps to move nutrients and oxygen to muscles**

(From Bernard Siegel, M. D.; author of two best selling books *Love, Medicine and Miracles* and *Peace, Love and Healing*)

16. **Maintain a biblical perspective of God**. It is through the eyes of the heart that a person sees God. When a heart is full of bitterness, the image of God it sees is distorted greatly. It is like looking at God through beveled glass. This is one of the reasons why Satan likes bitterness. Isaiah 32:6 states "For the fool speaks folly, his mind is busy with evil: He practices ungodliness and spreads error concerning the Lord…." W. L. Carrington wrote, "Some people seem to have grown up with a very distorted idea of God, which endows him with an almost sadistic revengeful spirit, which would be unbecoming even to an average human being."[16]

In Job 36:26 we read, "How great is God — beyond our understanding! The number of his years is past finding out." Job continues in 36:29, "Who can understand how he spreads out the clouds, how he thunders from his pavilion." In Job 37:5 we find, "God's voice thunders in marvelous ways; he does great things beyond our understanding." In Ecclesiastes 11:5 we read, "As you do not know the path of the wind, or how the body is formed in a mother's womb, so you cannot understand the work of God, the Maker of all things."

It is not with the human mind that the comprehension of God is maintained. It is only with the spiritual mind. Paul wrote to the church at Corinth, "For the message of the cross is foolishness to those who are perishing, but to us who are being saved it is the power of God" (1 Cor 1:18). A simple prayer is to ask God to reveal himself to you.

Erich Fromm, in his book *Art of Loving*, says a mature concept of God can be constructive. He also writes, "Quite obviously the majority of people have in their personal development not overcome this infantile stage, and hence the belief in God to most people is the belief of a helping father — a childish illusion."[17] A person's belief in God should mature as the person matures. How does Jeremiah 20:11 describe God? This passage is even more colorful in the King James Version. It states, "But the LORD is with me as a mighty terrible one: therefore my persecutors shall stumble, and they shall not prevail: they shall be greatly ashamed; for they shall not prosper: their everlasting confusion shall never be forgotten." Exodus 15:3 also relates the idea that God is a warrior. It reads, "The LORD is a warrior; the LORD is his name." Ask yourself this question: do you view God as being a wimp or warrior; as an Ernest P. Worrell or an Arnold Schwarzenegger?

One reason people maintain bitterness is their faulty view of God during trials. When going through trials people often see God as being disappointed, discouraged, disinterested, dissatisfied, or disgusted with them. If this is the way you see God, bitterness has a very fertile ground for growth. Who is indifferent to your pain, apathetic to your needs, tolerant of evil and consoled by your grief? It is Satan. In Nahum 1:7 we are told, "The Lord is good, a refuge in times of trouble."

In loss, injustice and betrayal many people have learned God "backwards." That is, they see God the way Satan is. This is not surprising because of what Paul wrote in 2 Corinthians 11:14, that Satan masquerades as an angel of light. The way we should see God during trials is found in Zephaniah 3:17 and James 5:16. It is important to see God as being a FLAG when going through struggles.

Faithful – Lamentations 3:23; Psalm 146:6
Loving – Jeremiah 31:3-4
Angry – Mark 3:5 (at the people that have hurt you)
Grieved – Jeremiah 42:10

Traits of Jesus and God as Father:

- Compassionate – Matthew 9:36
- Forgiving – John 8:1-11
- Gentle – Luke 7:11-15
- Willing – Luke 5:12-13
- Stern – Luke 4:35; 13:15-17
- Loving – John 3:16
- Caring – 1 Peter 5:7
- Complimenting – Matthew 8:5-13; 15:21-28
- Merciful – Matthew 9:27-31
- Confrontive – Matthew 23; Mark 4:40; Luke 17:11-19
- Sensitive – John 11:35; Luke 13:34-35
- Allowing for mistakes – Matthew 14:25-31
- Demanding – Luke 14:25-26; Mark 8:34-38
- Active in involvement – Luke 8:49-56
- Timely – Matthew 14:31
- Dedicated to task – Luke 22:42
- Concerned – Exodus 3:7
- Consistent – Hebrews 13:8
- Accepting – Luke 7:36-50
- Present and future oriented – John 5:14
- Teaching – Matthew 7:28-29
- Angry for the right reasons – Mark 3:1-5; 10:13-16
- Blunt – Matthew 15:16; Mark 9:19
- Restoring – John 21:15-19

Several verses give us a clear picture of the emotions

and personality of God. David had a fantastic relationship with God. He also had a great perspective on how he viewed him. Look at God in the Psalms from David's point of view:

Psalm 5:4 – God takes no pleasure in evil.

    7:11 – God is a righteous judge who expresses his wrath daily.

    9:9 – The Lord is a refuge for the oppressed.

    10:16 – The Lord is King.

    11:7 – The Lord is righteous and loves justice.

    12:7 – The Lord is a protector of his people.

    22:28 – The Lord rules over the nations.

    24:1-2 – The Lord owns the earth; he is the creator.

    25:8-10 – The Lord is good and upright; he guides and teaches.

    28:8 – The Lord is the strength of his people.

    33:13-15 – The Lord sees all mankind; he watches over all who live on the earth; He formed the heart of all; he considers everything man does.

    34:15-16 – His eyes and ears are attentive to the righteous.

    57:10 – God's love is great.

    62:11-12 – The Lord is strong, loving and rewarding.

    68:20 – The Lord saves.

In times of sorrow, loss, injustice and betrayal this picture of God fades and gets fuzzy. This is exactly what Satan is hoping for. Consider Job's fuzzy picture:

Job 19:8-12 says, "He has blocked my way so I cannot pass; he has shrouded my path in darkness. He has stripped me of my honor and removed the crown from my head. He tears me down on every side till I am gone; he uproots my hope like a tree. His anger burns against me; he counts me among his enemies. His troops advance in force; they build a siege ramp against me and encamp around my tent."

What would it be like to believe in Job's God in the above passage? What would it be like to believe in a God who could *not* relate to human suffering? Satan tries to teach this idea! It is actually a bold-faced lie. God and Jesus both fully understand our weaknesses and suffering. Hebrews 4:15 explains, "For we do not have a high priest who is unable to sympathize with our weaknesses, but we have one who has been tempted in every way, just as we are — yet was without sin."

Remember the following ten characteristics of God and Jesus when going through your trials. They will bring hope and strength. Realize that Jesus and the God of the Bible are Jesus and God today (Mal 3:6; Heb 13:4). Initials from these ten characteristics form the acrostic "SCARS." SCARS were his penalty. SCARS are his personality! A wise person once said, "Faith in God is not blind. It is based on his character and his promises." The emotions you give to the Lord when you are hurt are very important to your healing. At the time you were being hurt, God was angry! Understanding this will greatly enhance your relationship with the Lord.

Jesus and God:
  See our trials

  ❖ **Genesis 29:31** — God sees when people are not loved.
  ❖ **Exodus 3:7; Acts 7:34** — God sees misery.
  ❖ **Exodus 3:16** — God watches over his people.
  ❖ **Job 28:24** — God sees everything under the earth.
  ❖ **Job 34:21** — God sees man's every step.
  ❖ **Isaiah 38:5** — God sees tears. Tears are emotional stitches. Tears are part of prayers and healing! (2 Kgs 20:5; Job 16:20; 31:38; Ps 6:6; 42:3; 56:8; 119:136; Eccl 4:1; Isa 25:8; 38:5; Jer 9:1, 18; Luke 7:38; Acts 20:19; 2 Cor 2:4; Ph 3:18; Heb 5:7.)
  ❖ **Matthew 6:4, 6** — God sees what is done in secret.
  ❖ **Jeremiah 24:6** — God watches over people for their good.

Have Care, Compassion, Concern

- ❖ **1 Peter 5:7** – God cares about people.
- ❖ **Psalm 103:8** – God is compassionate.
- ❖ **Matthew 9:36** – God has compassion on the harassed and helpless.
- ❖ **Matthew 20:34** – Jesus had compassion on two blind men.
- ❖ **Psalm 145:8-9** – God is compassionate on all he has made.
- ❖ **Deuteronomy 32:36** – God has compassion for his servants.
- ❖ **Isaiah 49:13** – God has compassion on his afflicted ones.
- ❖ **Isaiah 49:10** – God has compassion and will guide Christians.
- ❖ **Isaiah 60:10** – God will show compassion with favor.
- ❖ **Exodus 3:7** – God is concerned about people's suffering.

Act, Answer

- ❖ **Isaiah 45:2** – God goes before us with mighty acts.
- ❖ **Psalm 106:2** – God has mighty acts that should be proclaimed.
- ❖ **Psalm 145:4** – Generations should pass down God's mighty acts.
- ❖ **Psalm 145:6** – God's acts of power are awesome.
- ❖ **Psalm 99:6** – God answers prayers.
- ❖ **1 Kings 18:24, 38** – God answers Elijah's prayer with fire.

Remember, Respond

- ❖ **Genesis 8:1** – God remembers Noah and the animals in the ark.
- ❖ **Genesis 19:29** – God remembers Abraham's situation.

- **Genesis 30:22** – God remembers Rachel's suffering and listens to her.
- **Exodus 2:24** – God remembers his promises.
- **Exodus 6:5; Leviticus 26:42, 45** – God remembers his covenant with his people.
- **1 Samuel 1:19** – God remembers Hannah's suffering.
- **Psalm 98:3** – God remembers his love.
- **Psalm 103:14** – God remembers what we are made of and how fragile we are.
- **Psalm 105:8** – God remembers his covenant forever.
- **Psalm 136:23** – God remembers our low estate.
- **Jeremiah 2:2** – God remembers our dedication to him.
- **Hebrews 8:12; 10:17** – God remembers our sins no more.
- **Psalm 102:17** – God responds to the prayers of the destitute.

Sensitive, Sympathetic

- **Hebrews 4:14-16** – God can sympathize with our weaknesses.
- **John 11:35, 38** – Jesus weeps over the death of Lazarus at least twice.
- **Isaiah 53:3** – Jesus can sympathize because of his suffering and sorrow.

Patrick M. Morley writes, "The turning point of our lives is when we stop seeking the God we want and start seeking the God who is."[18] The book of Isaiah has many pictures of the Christ who is. One I would encourage you to dwell on during loss, injustice and betrayal is: Jesus as a righteous Judge who executes justice (Isa 11:3-4).

I would encourage you to see God as carrying the painful burdens that you have been through (Ps 68:19). God is merciful during your pain (Ps 51:1; 56:1). I would also encourage you to believe that when you were being hurt, you were actually in the shadow of God's wings (Ps 36:7; 57:1; 63:7; 91:4). God can also become your stronghold and fortress (Ps 46:7) during times of loss, injustice and betrayal. It may be difficult for you to realize that God will punish those people who have hurt you (Ps 37:38; 62:12). When you are going through loss, injustice and betrayal, it is important that you pour your heart out to God (Ps 55:12; 62:8). This will make God your sustainer and refuge. It is important that you remember that God cares for you (1 Pet 5:7). Realize that Satan laughs at the righteous, because God laughs at the wicked (Ps 37:13).

One of the most profound verses in Scripture is also the shortest: "Jesus wept." — John 11:35. It shows how deeply Jesus is concerned about people and their suffering. Remember that Jesus and God are one, and therefore God cries (John 10:30).

One of the traits of God is that he sees our trials. Why did he not do anything to stop them? Satan knows that God watches the painful events that happen to you. He repeatedly told God that he could do nothing about it. The Bible teaches that Satan appears before the presence of God on a regular basis (Job 1:7-12; 2:1; Zech 3:1; Rev 12:10). It is also important that you recognize that God did not prevent the painful event that you have been through, but he did protect you through it. Prevent means to stop the event; protect means to allow the event, but to take care of you afterwards. Consider what the following verses say about God's protection: Psalm 12:7; 37:28; 41:2; 116:6; 140:1, 4. Matthew 12:20 gives a good illustration of how God sees you if you are a victim of some kind of abuse: as a bruised reed that he will not break!

Your picture of the emotions that God experiences during your pain is important to your healing. Do you see God as being faithful to people in painful events? Do you see God as being indifferent to your pain, apathetic to your needs, tolerant to evil, or consoled by your grief? If you do, how can you avoid becoming bitter towards God? It is important that you see God as having the power and ability to take the painful events of the past and make a ministry from them. This is a big step in the healing from bitterness (2 Cor 1:3-4; Rom 8:28). Realize that Paul did not say all things that happen to you are good; he said they all work together for good. If your goal in your Christian life is to be happy, then you are going to be bitter with God when pain happens. But, if your goal in your Christian life is to be holy, you won't be bitter when painful events happen. When you go through loss, injustice or betrayal you should not ask God, "When can I get out of this?" You should ask God, "What can I get out of this?"

17. **Let people love you, and allow yourself to love** (1 Pet 4:8). Bernie Siegal, M.D. in his book, *Love, Medicine and Miracles*, writes, "Unconditional love is the most powerful stimulant of the immune system. The truth is: love heals."[19] Bitterness is best maintained during periods when you feel unloved. David writes in Psalm 25:16-18, "Turn to me and be gracious to me, for I am lonely and afflicted. The troubles of my heart have multiplied; free me from my anguish. Look upon my affliction and my distress and take away all my sins." David felt unloved by others.

Remember that God loves you (John 3:16). His love is unconditional. Paul wrote about God's love in Romans 5:8, "But God demonstrates his own love for us in this: While we were still sinners, Christ died for us." Remember that you are never alone. Jesus promised he would be with us always (Matt 28:20). You may have difficulty receiving love from others because you are afraid it won't last, or that love eventually causes pain. You need to change your definition of love if it's negative before you can receive love from others.

Being alone and unloved allows people to hold onto grudges and create ways of seeking revenge. Genesis 2:18 confirms it is not good for man to be alone. It is important to have people around you to fight against bitterness. The mutual sharing you do with them, and they with you, is beneficial. It gives a sense of accountability.

18. **You must have goals and a future that can be reached** (Joel 2:25, 28). Without goals people go through life without purpose or aim. It is goals in life that frequently give people the reason to keep on living. Thomas Edison said, "Show me a satisfied man, and I will show you a failure." Let me change this slightly: show me a man who has no goals, and I will show you a bitter man. Accomplishing goals gets rid of bitterness. The word "vision" appears 70 times in the NIV, and the word "visions" appears 37 times. Being a dreamer is what kept Joseph from being bitter at his brothers (Gen 37:5-10). It was the same with Daniel (Dan 7:1). According to Proverbs 29:18, "Where there is no vision, the people perish" (KJV). Psalm 126:1 tells about having dreams restored.

Ask God to give you a ministry through the pain you have endured. Ask God to give you his vision through your suffering (Isa 46:11). A simple prayer might be this: "Father, with what I have been through use me to further your kingdom. Lead me to people who need to be led to you."

One of the ways to obtain hope is to have goals! To overcome bitterness you must have goals that can be reached with perseverance (Heb 10:35-36). Consider this famous man who persevered and reached his goal:

1831 – He failed in business.
1832 – He was defeated for the legislature.
1833 – He failed at business again.
1834 – He was elected to the legislature.
1835 – His wife-to-be died.

1836 — He had a nervous breakdown.
1838 — He was defeated for Speaker of the House.
1840 — He was defeated for Elector.
1850 — A son died.
1854 — He was defeated for the Senate.
1856 — He was defeated for Vice President.
1858 — He was defeated for the Senate.
1860 — He (Abraham Lincoln) was elected President.[20]

19. **You must have hope, and trust God to heal you** (Prov 13:12). Without hope people perish, or become sick. Hope is what gives people the desire to get up in the morning. David writes in Psalm 118:24, "This is the day the LORD has made; let us rejoice and be glad in it." Hope is a good prescription to ward off bitterness. The word "hope" appears 166 times in the NIV; "hoped" appears 8 times; "hopes" appears 7 times. (It is interesting that the word "hopeless" occurs only once in the NIV —Isa 57:10.) Even this verse is positive, because it says that the people refused to use the word "hopeless."

Many passages in the Bible are excellent for people who are having trouble with life. Job 11:16-18 states, "You will surely forget your trouble, recalling it only as waters gone by. Life will be brighter than noonday, and darkness will become like morning. You will be secure, because there is hope; you will look about and take your rest in safety." Other passages about hope are: Ps 26:1; 31:24; 52:7-8; 130:5, 7; 146:3; 147:11, Prov 13:12; Jer 17:5-8; 29:11; Rom 5:5.

Dr. Harold G. Wolff, a research scientist who did extensive studies about prisoners of war, wrote: "In short, prolonged circumstances which are perceived as dangerous, as lonely, as hopeless, may drain a man of hope and of his health. But he is capable of enduring incredible burdens and taking cruel punishment when he has self-esteem, hope, purpose and belief in his fellows."[21]

Healing for a Bitter Heart

Timothy Elliot, Ph.D., a psychologist at Virginia Commonwealth University, interviewed 57 young victims of spinal cord injuries. All 57 were paralyzed for life. He discovered victims who had hope were less depressed, and gained greater physical mobility. Those who had hope were also more socially active.

20. **Pray daily for yourself** as well as the person with whom you are bitter (Matt 5:44; 1 Sam 12:23). Much research has been done on the healing effects of prayer. Dr. Herbert Benson of Harvard Medical School was one of the first people to do research on the health benefits of prayer. He found that prayer stimulated physiological changes in the body that made it healthier. He termed these healthful changes in the body the "relaxation response."[22]

In the longest recorded prayer of Jesus, found in John 17, the first person he prays for is himself (17:1-5). Prayer allows bitterness to be expressed to God. This will encourage forgiveness. Pray also for the person who harmed you (Matt 5:44; Luke 6:28). Consider the following prayers found in the Bible:

Moses — Numbers 11:11-15
Joshua — Joshua 7:6-9
Elijah — 1 Kings 19:4
Job — Job 3:3-12; 10:18-22
Jeremiah — Jeremiah 4:10; 20:7-13
Habakkuk — Habakkuk 1
David — Psalm 42:43; 102:1-11

Look at what Romans 8:26, 34 say about prayer. Both the Holy Spirit and Jesus pray for you: what a motivation to pray!

Prayer is important to any task. Nehemiah continually prayed to God during his job of rebuilding the wall (Neh 1:5-11; 4:4-5, 9; 5:19; 6:9, 14; 13:14, 22, 31). You need to continually pray for your healing from bitterness!

152

You can also ask others to pray for your healing from bitterness. Cardiologist Dr. Randolph Byrd in 1988 published a study on the effects of people's prayers to heal others. He assigned 393 people from the coronary care unit of San Francisco General Hospital into two groups. One group was not prayed for and the other group was prayed for daily by name. The ten month study revealed that of the group that was prayed for daily:

They were five times less likely to require antibiotics than the non-prayed-for group.

They were 2.5 times less likely to have congestive heart failure.

They were less likely to have a cardiac arrest.[23]

You should also pray a blessing for the person that hurt you. In Matthew 5:43-44 Jesus taught, "You have heard that it was said, 'Love your neighbor and hate your enemy.' But I tell you: Love your enemies and pray for those who persecute you...." Pray daily for yourself and for the person that you need to forgive (1 Thess 5:17). A good prayer would be: "Lord, let the things that anger you, anger me. Lord, let the things that make you laugh, make me laugh!" W.T. McElroy said, "If you find yourself growing angry at someone, pray for him—anger cannot live in an atmosphere of prayer."

21. Learn to say "No" without feeling guilty (Matt 5:37). Many people have a hard time saying "no" to a request, and they end up doing something they don't want to do. This is due in part to low self-esteem and a fear of rejection. It is important to say "no" to things you don't feel you should do. If you do them, you will feel used and bitter. Josh Billings said, "One-half the troubles of this life can be traced to saying yes too quickly and not saying no soon enough."

22. Become more like a child (Matt 18:3). Adults tend to distrust, are future oriented, work seriously, doubt, and ask "why" when given gifts. Children tend to trust others, take one day at a time, play and have fun, have faith without sight, and say "thank you" for gifts. Bitterness in adults is very common, but in children it is very rare unless they have learned it from adults (Prov 22:24-25). Consider the following quote:

> Children have a remarkable talent for not taking the adult world with the kind of respect we are so confident it ought to be given. To the irritation of authority figures of all sorts, children expend considerable energy in 'clowning around.' They refuse to appreciate the gravity of our monumental concerns, while we forget that if we were to become more like children our concerns might not be so monumental.[24]

Dr. O. Carl Simonton writes that "...play is essential for life...It is not selective, it is mandatory."[25]

Jesus teaches that you must become like children, or you will never enter the kingdom of God (Luke 18:15-17; Mark 10:15; Matt 18:3). God wants us to make him our Daddy! (Rom 8:15; Gal 4:6) Look at some differences between children and adults:

Traits of Adults and Children

Adults	Children
Knowledge of evil and reality.	Sense of innocence.
Life is serious business.	Life is play.
Time runs their lives.	Little or no awareness of time.
Sense of humor, but not always laughter.	Laughter comes easily.
Sometimes it is hard to forgive.	Don't hold grudges.
Sometimes they lose who they are.	Know who they are.
Cynical.	Trust unconditionally.
Conditional love.	Love unconditionally.
Many fears and worries.	Few fears and worries.
Great concern about the future.	Concerned about today.
Independence.	Dependent on others.

154

Controlled by other adults.	Controlled by adults.
Dulled creativity.	Imaginative.
Loss of hope.	Hope.
Doubting, analytical.	Faith in believing what was said.

Can you see why God wants us to be like children?

23. **Recognize who Satan is**. He likes you bitter. George Barna, in his report *What Americans Believe*, gives some startling findings about Satan. He reports that among people associated with evangelical churches 49% believe Satan is a living being, but 47% believe Satan is only a symbol of evil. Among people who call themselves "born again," 52% believe Satan is a living being and 43% see him as a symbol for evil.[26] Keith Green, a contemporary Christian singer who has gone to be with the Lord, sang a song titled, "No One Believes in Me Anymore." It tells how no one believes in Satan, so he can do what he wants.

After you have been through loss, injustice or betrayal it is very likely that the person who caused them will be seen as an enemy. One of the Hebrew words for enemy is **oyeb** which, like the word **eybah** meaning enmity (Gen 3:15) is a derivative of the verb **ayab**, to hate. The New Testament Greek word enemy is **echthros** which also indicates hatred and hostility.

If you have declared people your enemy, then you hate them. One of the problems with declaring people as enemies is that you have to be at war with them. Bitterness is the war! The Christian only has one enemy, that being Satan (1 Pet 5:8; Matt 13:28, 38-39). As it will be discussed later, this enemy will use others around you to attack you, but these people are not enemies. When you have declared others as enemies, you have identified the wrong enemy and this will destroy you. Bitterness is Satan's favorite way of controlling people. When you are bitter you are following the will of Satan and not God. This should be a very

155

scary thought (2 Cor 2:11; Dan 7:25). One of the best ways to overcome Satan is to avoid becoming bitter! A biblical definition of Satan would be: the great opposer, or adversary, of God and man; the personal name of the devil. His goal is to establish a stronghold, an area he can operate from, in our lives.

How Satan develops a stronghold:

1. He needs evidence of sin. It can be yours or the sin of someone else that has affected you. (This is why he likes the past.)
2. He needs for a person to have a weak understanding of forgiveness. (This is why he tells lies about forgiveness.)
3. He then accuses the person (Zech 3:1; Rev 12:10; Col 1:22).
4. The person believes the accusations (Prov 23:7 KJV).
5. Those beliefs have consequences (Matt 12:34, 15:16).
6. Those consequences detain the person, creating a stronghold (Dan 10:13).

Satan's favorite and greatest tool is lies. He wants to create four types of separation!

1. **separation by guilt and shame** (Gen 3:7).
2. **spiritual separation** (Gen 3:8-10, 23-24).
3. **separation between people** (Gen 3:12).
4. **environmental separation** (Gen 3:17-19).

Many people have separated themselves from God without Satan doing anything. One major reason for this is that they blame God for painful events that have happened. Naomi is an example of this. Satan tries to do the same thing to people today. He tries to get people to listen to his lies. Paul writes in Philippians 4:8 "whatever is true, whatever is noble, whatever is right, whatever is pure, whatever is lovely, whatever is admirable — if anything is excellent or praisewor- thy — think about such things." This verse gives eight reasons why Satan lies. The lies that he tells are *not* true, noble, right, pure, lovely, admirable, excellent, or praiseworthy. Satan lies to control people's thought patterns.

He does not come to us with a forked tail and pitch- fork. Satan likes this description of himself because it gives people a cartoon image of what he really is. In contrast, the Bible says he is a roaring lion looking for someone to devour, (1 Pet 5:8) and he masquerades as an angel of light (2 Cor 11:14). No, Satan is not a cartoon character!

Satan knows that bitterness separates man and God! What is the advantage of Satan separating Christians from God? Five reasons are found in John 15:4-9. Satan will do anything to make Christians feel or believe they are far away from God. He would ransom his soul to send people to hell!

1. John 15:4 — **Christians cannot bear fruit by them- selves**. Back in Genesis, God's first command to man was to be fruitful and multiply (Gen 1:28). In Luke 13:6-9 Jesus tells about a fig tree that did not bear any fruit. It was to be cut down! Satan wants Christians to be cut down. He wants them to not prosper or increase the kingdom of God.

2. John 15:5 — **Apart from God Christians can do nothing**. Satan knows Philippians 4:13 says Christians can do anything with God's help. For him to have any effect, he has to pull Christians away from God. This causes Christians to lose the power source. Satan will also attempt to pull us apart from fellowship. Ecclesiastes 4:9 says two are better than one because they have a good return for their work. Satan knows one of the ways to make sure there is no return for their labor is to pull them away from God.

3. John 15:6 — **Christians wither and are thrown in a fire apart from God**. Satan likes this one best. He would like nothing better than to have Christians burn in the fire of hell. Satan realizes he can also create an earthly hell if successful in pulling Christians away from God. Since Satan is bound for hell, he would like nothing better than to take some of the most precious possessions of God to hell with him. This would greatly wound God.

People who live apart from God have no one to rely on in times of trouble except themselves. This is a very frustrating experience. They can only rely on their own strength. Proverbs 28:26 teaches, "He who trusts in himself is a fool, but he who walks in wisdom is kept safe." Proverbs 25:19 instructs, "Like a bad tooth or a lame foot is reliance on the unfaithful in times of trouble."

4. John 15:7 — **Prayers will not be answered**. This effect is devastating. Many people don't realize prayer is part of the full armor of God. Ephesians 6:18 tells us that Christians should pray in the Spirit on all occasions. Without a productive prayer life, a Christian is not ready for battle against Satan. Prayer is the supply line between God and Christians during times of war with Satan.

5. John 15:8 — **Christians will not glorify God apart from him**. Glorifying God in everything should be the goal for Christians. Isaiah 43:21 says God formed us so we might proclaim his praise. Psalm 102:18 says even those who are not created yet may praise the Lord. 1 Peter 2:9 says we should declare the praises of him who called us out of darkness into his wonderful light. Psalm 150 says all things that have breath should praise the Lord. Praising God is a battle plan that has defeated Satan over and over again. The walls of Jericho came tumbling down because of praise. Satan knows nothing could glorify and praise God less than a Christian being away from God.

24. **Get rid of the fear you have in your life** (1 John 4:18; 2 Tim 1:7). Fear is the breeding ground for bitterness. A couple of "benefits" of fear are bitterness and anger. Isaiah contains many passages declaring, "Do not fear" (35:4; 41:10; 13-14; 43:1; 44:8; 54:12-15). These traits should remind you of the Fruit of the Spirit. The opposite of bitterness and fear is **Peace** (Jer 30:5); **Security** (Jer 46:27); **Faith** (Mark 4:40); **Confidence** (Isa 35:4; Ps. 27:3); **Trust** (Prov 29:25; Isa 12:2); **Boldness** (Prov 28:1); and **Joy** (Prov 14:10).

As we conclude this chapter on 24 steps to get rid of bitterness, we will move next to one of the major reasons why it is so difficult to forgive. The first reason why forgiveness is so difficult is because we have been hurt by a person we know.

Source Notes

1. James D. Mallory Jr., M. D., *The Kink and I*, p. 53.

2. Dr. Sadler, *The Practice of Psychiatry*.

3. Paul Tillich, *The Eternal Now* (New York: Charles Scribner's Sons, 1963), pp. 150-151.

4. Robert L. Veninga, *A Gift of Hope* (Boston: Little, Brown, 1985).

5. M. Scott Peck, *People of the Lie* (New York: Simon and Schuster, 1983)

6. Don Polson, *Living Without Losing* (Eugene, OR: Harvest House Publishers, 1975), p. 23.

7. Neil T. Anderson, *The Bondage Breakers* (Eugene OR: Harvest House Publishers, 1990), pp. 195-196.

8. C. H. Spurgeon, *Day by Day* (Grand Rapids: Kregel, 1992).

9. W. Phillip Keller, *A Gardener Looks at the Fruits of the Spirit* (Waco, TX: Word Books, 1979), pp. 111.

10. Harriet Goldhor Lerner, Ph.D., *The Dance of Anger* (Harper and Row, 1985), p. 9.

11. Stephen F. Arterburn, M.Ed. and David A. Stoop, Ph.D., *When Someone You Love Is Someone You Hate* (Waco, TX: Word Publishing Co., 1988), p. 25.

12. Friedman, M.D. and Rosenman, M.D., *Type A Behavior and Your Heart* (New York: A Fawcett Crest Book), pp 199-206.

13. Hemfelt, Minirth, and Meier, *We Are Driven* (Nashville: Thomas Nelson, 1989), p. 137.

14. *Harper's Magazine*, January 1993, via *Youthworker Update*, March 1993.

15. Allen Klein, *The Healing Power of Humor* (Los Angeles: Jeremy P. Tarcher, Inc., 1989), pp. 4-6.

16. *Psychology, Religion, and Human Need* (Great Neck, NY, Channel Press, Inc., 1957), p. 210.

17. Erich Fromm, *Art of Loving*, (New York: Harper and Row, Colophon Books, 1956).

18. Patrick M. Morley, *Walking with Christ in the Details of Life* (Nashville: Thomas Nelson Publishers, 1992), p. 67.

19. Bernie Siegal, M.D., *Love, Medicine and Miracles* (New York: Harper and Row, 1990), back cover.

20. Alan L. McGinnis, *Bringing Out the Best in People* (Minneapolis, MN, Augsburg, 1985), p. 76.

21. "What Hope Does for a Man," *Saturday Review*, 5 January 1967.

22. "Does Prayer Heal," *Reader's Digest*, March 1996, p. 118.

23. Ibid., p. 117.

24. Conrad Hyers, *Comic Vision and the Christian Faith* (New York: Pilgrim Press, 1981).

25. O. Carl Simonton, Stephanie Matthews-Simonton, James Creighton, *Getting Well Again*.

26. George Barna, *The Barna Report: What Americans Believe* (Ventura, CA: Regal Books, 1991), p. 205.

6

The Hardest Person to Forgive

"The Bible tells us to love our neighbors, and also to pray for our enemies; probably because they are generally the same person."
— G.K. Chesterton

Recently while flying the friendly skies to Salt Lake City, Utah, to speak I ran across an article in a business magazine that talked about ways to avoid being audited by the IRS. It said that the number one source of information the IRS receives about people filing fraudulent tax forms is ex-spouses and spurned lovers. This fascinated me. What would prompt a person to turn someone in to the IRS? There could be a variety of answers, but the most likely answer would be revenge or retaliation for the break up. Satan loves this type of betrayal because it is costly and effective. This might be a good theme for some of the daytime talk shows, "My ex turned me in to the IRS."

Why would Satan use an ex-lover to betray someone? It is because there are at least six traits in people that Satan is likely to use in an attack. These traits are ingredients that comprise the hardest person to forgive. Satan will attempt to embitter people using these traits. The traits that he uses are done by design (DBD). Satan looks for the "GO" before he attacks–"Golden Opportunity" (Luke 4:13).

Satan will weave his way into relationships any way he possibly can. He is public enemy number one when it comes to relationships. In 1 Peter 5:8 it reads, "Be self-controlled and alert. Your enemy the devil prowls around like a roaring lion looking for someone to devour." There is enmity between him and the human race (Gen 3:15). Enmity is a feeling of hostility, hatred, ill will, animosity, and antagonism.

Satan, when attacking, is going to ask three strategic questions. Who can I use to cause hurt? (This is the "R" below.) What can I get them to do? (This is the "I" below.) When can I get them to do it, and for how long? (This is the "D" below.) So, there are three ingredients which determine the ease of forgiveness:

1. **Relationship**: The closer the relationship to the person that hurt you, the more difficult it is to forgive. A stranger can make a very cutting remark and it can be easily shrugged off. But, if a close friend makes the same statement it can really hurt (Prov 19:7). I came across a quote from a Focus on the Family Broadcast with Dr. James Dobson, "Satan's most successful maneuver in churches and Christian organizations is to get people angry at one another, to attack and insult our brothers and sisters, thus splitting the body of Christ."[1]

It is a sad fact that 80% of all reported cases of sexual abuse involved relatives, friends or neighbors. According to the 1979 FBI Uniform Crime Reports, 40% of female homicide victims are killed by a family member or boyfriend. Up to 60% of all married women experience physical violence by their husbands at some time during the marriage.

Time magazine did an article on abuse. The article said that 6 out of 10 women killed in 1991 were killed by someone they knew. Half were killed by a spouse or by some-one with whom they were intimate. Psychologist Angela Browne in the article said, "Women are more at risk of being killed by their current or former male partners than by any other kind of assault" (4 July 1994, pp. 18-25).

Several studies have been done on the topic of rela-tionship abuse. In one study, over a three year period, 6,100 undergraduates from 32 colleges reported the fol-lowing information.

25% of the women were victims of rape or attempted rape.

84% of those raped knew the attacker.

57% said the rape happened on a date.

42% of the victims told no one about the rape.[2]

The Bible teaches a lot about relationships and how they can be hurt. Consider the following verses:

❖ **Jeremiah 12:6:** "Your brothers, your own family — even they have betrayed you; they have raised a loud cry against you. Do not trust them, though they speak well of you."

❖ **Micah 7:6:** "For a son dishonors his father, a daughter rises up against her mother, a daughter-in-law against her mother-in-law — a man's enemies are the members of his own household."

❖ **Matthew 10:35:** "For I have come to turn 'a man against his father, a daughter against her mother, a daughter-in-law against her mother-in-law....'"

❖ **Luke 12:52-53:** "From now on there will be five in one family divided against each other, three against two and two against three. They will be divided, father against son and son against father, mother against daughter and daughter against mother, mother-in-law against daughter-in-law and daughter-in-law against mother-in-law."

2. **Intensity**: The worse the offense that took place, the harder it will be to forgive. The more severe, cold, cruel or harsh the injury, the more difficult it is to forgive.

3. **Duration**: The earlier the harmful event started, and the longer it lasted, the harder it will be to forgive. A constant, continuing attack is more difficult to forgive than a one-time event.

Let's look with greater detail into the relationship ingredient. Below is a profile of the person(s) Satan likes to use to attack you. There are at least two reasons Satan will use these people: 1. When this person hurts you, you are more likely to blame yourself. 2. This person is also the hardest person to forgive and confront. I will promise you Satan will attempt to use at least one of these six characteristics against you. He is actually hoping all six of these characteristics are found in the same person. He knows if all six are met, then your chance of becoming bitter is much better. It is important that you keep your mind off of who is attacking you and look at who is *behind* the attack (Eph 6:12; 1 Pet 5:8).

David wrote about the hardest person to forgive. In Psalm 55:12-14, 20-21 David wrote that he is not an enemy or a foe, but a man like himself, his companion and close friend. It is a man with whom David once had sweet fellowship. It is a man with whom David went to the house of God. It is a man who does not keep his word, and uses his words as a weapon. It is a man who attacks his friends. David in Psalm 41:9 wrote, "Even my close friend, whom I trusted, he who shared my bread, has lifted up his heel against me." The word that sticks out in this passage is "trusted." Notice the verb is in the past tense; he trusts this person no longer. Solomon wrote in Proverbs 19:4 about friends, "Wealth brings many friends, but a poor man's friend deserts him." Jeremiah wrote in Jeremiah 20:10

164

about friends, "I hear many whispering, 'Terror on every side! Report him! Let's report him!' All my friends are waiting for me to slip, saying, 'Perhaps he will be deceived; then we will prevail over him and take our revenge on him'."

What are the six characteristics possessed by the hardest person to forgive? Who is Satan most likely to use to attack you? Who is the person who could make you the most bitter if they hurt you? This person is likely to be:

1. **A Christian**: (Ps 55:14) People believe that "Christians should know better" because of what they believe about Christ. They are supposed to be "an example of Christ." In Galatians 6:9-10 Paul tells how Christians should treat each other. Paul writes, "Let us not become weary in doing good, for at the proper time we will reap a harvest if we do not give up. Therefore, as we have opportunity, let us do good to all people, especially to those who belong to the family of believers." If a Christian fails to treat us kindly, it is easy to understand why this is the hardest person to forgive.

One reason Satan will use a Christian is that he is hoping we will lose faith in God and the Church. He hopes people leave the fellowship that they are in. Satan knows, when a Christian is involved in fellowship, he is more difficult to overcome! This is one of the reasons Satan would like Christians to withdraw from fellowship.

Another reason Satan will use Christians is that hurtful behavior is not expected from them. Christians should be loving and supportive. King David would hate to admit it, but he would agree that non-Christians often treat Christians better than Christians do at times. David would also agree that Christians don't always heal the wounded — sometimes they "kill" them. I am greatly grieved when I hear that a non-Christian has ministered more to a hurting individual than a Christian has. This is a slap in the face!

2. **A family member**: (Ps 50:20; 55:13; Jer 12:6; Mic 7:6; Matt 10:35) Bitterness grows best when friends treat us better than family members. In times when we need our family's support and it is just not there, Satan will use this occasion to create a bitter, frustrated heart. Let's look at the relationships in the above five verses. They are: brother, family, son, father, daughter, mother, daughter-in-law, and mother-in-law. This pretty much hits all close relationships.

I had a client who had an abortion nine years ago. Now when she and her husband get into a fight he says, "At least I did not murder anyone." He brings this up because he knows it hurts her. This is exactly what he wants to do. This makes this relationship difficult to forgive. She told me recently that she wishes she had never confessed this to him. He knows too much about her past, and has an arsenal with which to attack. He is not mentioned in the above five verses, but he is definitely being used by Satan to attack her.

She is not alone in this attitude of wishing she had never told him her past secrets. Many people are hurt by family members in whom they confided. People may take what is said and use it against the person. This definitely causes a communication breakdown. In Job 19:4 Job says that people have used his humiliation against him. This separates lots of people. This is "miranda" communication, "You have the right to remain silent; anything you say can and will be used against you." This can cause separation, both emotionally and physically, in many relationships.

It is a sad thing that some people don't have family reunions, they have family feuds. People within the family have done or said things that have hurt other family members. These feuds may span several generations. The Bible speaks about these feuds. Look at Genesis.

Consider the fact that there are many "brother vs. brother feud" stories in the Bible. Some of them are:

Prodigal son and the elder brother — Luke 15:28
Abimelech and his brothers — Judges 9:1-5
Jephthah and his stepbrothers — Judges 11:1-2
Jacob and Esau — Genesis 27:41
Moses and Aaron — Exodus 32:19-22
Cain and Abel — Genesis 4:8
Absalom and Amnon — 2 Samuel 13:22
Joseph and his brothers — Genesis 37:4
David and his oldest brother Eliab — 1 Samuel 17:28-30

There are many relationships mentioned in the Bible where there is harm being done. Two father/son stories come to mind: Jacob versus his sons because Jacob loved his son Joseph more than the others, and they knew it (Gen 37:3-4). Abraham also had a conflict with his sons. Genesis 25:1-5 lists all the sons he had. Genesis 25:5 declares, "Abraham left everything he owned to Isaac." This must have made the sons of Abraham angry with Isaac as well as Abraham.

Two father and son-in-law stories stand out in Scripture where injury was done. The most obvious is Laban and Jacob. Laban promised Jacob he could marry his daughter Rachel if he worked seven years for him. After the seven years were up Laban made it so Jacob married Leah (his other daughter). Jacob then had to work another seven years to pay for Rachel (Gen 29:14-30). It was also a strange twist that Laban who became Jacob's father-in-law was also his uncle, the brother of his mother Rebekah (Gen 27:42-43). Another famous son and father-in-law story is King Saul and David. Saul was very jealous and bitter at David for killing Goliath. Saul even attempted to kill David several times.

Mothers were not immune to the virus of bitterness in the Bible either. Rebekah helped her younger son Jacob deceive his father Isaac and get the blessing that belonged to Esau. It was her plan and plot that helped deceive Isaac when he was old and almost blind. She prepared a meal for

Healing for a Bitter Heart

Jacob to give to Isaac and helped him with the hairy coverings that were put on Jacob's neck and hands, to convince Isaac that Jacob was actually Esau (Gen 27:5-19). This, of course, made Esau murderously mad at his brother, and perhaps his mother as well!

I ran across the following story about what friends can do when they get mad at each other.

EX-FRIENDS SHOOT IT OUT WITH SHOTGUNS Tucson, Ariz. (AP) *The Muncie Star*, June 8, 1994, p. 1.

Tristan Rossum and Jonathan Brown, Jr. won't win any awards for marksmanship. But how about luck.

The ex-friends decided to solve their dispute with a 12-gauge-shotgun shootout at 10 paces, authorities say. Fortunately, neither could hit the other.

Consider the following story from the *Lexington (Kentucky) Herald Leader*, 24 April 1992.

STUDY: 60% OF RAPE VICTIMS UNDER 18 Knight-Ridder News Service.

"....Although 22 percent of the victims said a stranger attacked them, the vast majority said they knew their attacker. Nine percent said they were attacked by a husband or ex-husband, 11 percent by a father or stepfather, 10 percent by a boyfriend or ex-boyfriend, 16 percent by other relatives and 29 percent by other familiar nonrelatives such as neighbors." This means that 75% of rape victims knew their attackers!

I found an article written by Michael J. Sniffen (AP writer) titled MORE THAN HALF OF RAPES INVOLVED UNDER 18 GIRLS in the *Johnson City (Tennessee) Press*, 23 June 1994. In the article the author says that family members or acquaintances accounted for 96% of the rapes of girls under 12 years of age.

Jesus talked about relatives hurting other relatives and friends. Jesus said in Luke 21:16, "You *will* be betrayed

168

even by parents, brothers, relatives and friends, and they will put some of you to death" (emphasis added). Jesus said in Luke 12:52-53, "From now on there will be five in one family divided against each other, three against two and two against three. They *will* be divided, father against son and son against father, mother against daughter and daughter against mother, mother-in-law against daughter-in-law and daughter-in-law against mother-in-law" (emphasis added). Jesus said in Luke 4:24, "No prophet is accepted in his hometown." Jesus said in Mark 6:4, "Only in his hometown, among his relatives and in his own house is a prophet without honor." Why would a prophet not be accepted in his hometown? This is because they know all about him. They know his past. They know what he was like, and they cannot consider him anything else than what they all ready know.

Families should be a place of love. They are not supposed to do things that hurt. It is this lack of love that is replaced by hurt that causes bitterness. In 1 Thessalonians 2:7-8, 11-12 Paul wrote that family members should be gentle, comforting, urging and encouraging to each other. Paul, in 1 Timothy 5:8, writes, "If anyone does not provide for his relatives, and especially for his immediate family, he has denied the faith and is worse than an unbeliever." When these "expectations of others" are not met, it is easy to understand why it would be difficult to forgive them. Being attacked by a family member is exactly the opposite of what God wants. In Malachi 4:6 we read that, "He will turn the hearts of the fathers to their children, and the hearts of the children to their fathers; or else I will come and strike the land with a curse."

There are several reasons Satan will attempt to use a family member or companion to attack you. One reason has to do with the emotional attachment (bonding) within families. When it is a family member who hurts you, the family may be split over who they believe. They may also be split over what should happen to the perpetrator. Some of the family will believe the victim and want the perpetrator punished, but others will believe the perpetrator and think that the victim is lying. Another reason Satan will attack you with a family member is to exploit the wide variety of "weapons" they carry from the past. They know all of the mistakes you have made. They also know the "hidden sins" that no one else knows. When they attack by bringing up the past, trust will be broken and defenses will be raised.

Another reason Satan will use family members or companions is that children draw their impressions of God through their families. If the family has been very forgiving, it is easy for a child to understand and accept forgiveness from God. But, if the family has not been a good model of forgiveness (especially from the father), a person from this family will have a hard time understanding and accepting forgiveness. They will frequently have a distorted image of God. Family members might tell you they forgive the mistakes and sins of your past, but in times of conflict they bring up those hurts. Children frequently believe God does the same thing. Job 9:17 gives the consequences when the past hurts are brought up; "He would crush me with a storm and multiply my wounds for no reason." Job gives two effects of bringing up a person's past: 1) it crushes the spirit of the person, and 2) it multiplies the wounds. In other words, it makes the matter worse.

When attacked by a family member or companion, one of the emotions you frequently feel is surprise! 1 Peter 4:12 says, "Dear friends, do not be surprised at the painful trial you are suffering, as though something strange were happening to you." I believe Peter would also say not to be surprised at who attacks you. Jesus is an example of a person being attacked and betrayed by his family. In Mark

3:21, he was criticized by his family for his teaching and preaching. They thought Jesus was out of his mind. They attempted to put him away. It is very possible even Mary, his own mother, thought Jesus was out of his mind. Jesus said in Luke 4:24, "I tell you the truth, no prophet is accepted in his hometown." John 1:11 reports, "He came to that which was his own, but his own did not receive him." I wonder how Jesus felt when even his own family would not believe or receive him. This surely hurt.

Jesus frequently speaks about the fact that family members will hurt each other. In Matthew 10:21 Jesus said, "Brother will betray brother to death, and a father his child; children will rebel against their parents and have them put to death." In Luke 21:16 Jesus warns the disciples, "You will be betrayed by parents, brothers, relatives and friends, and they will put some of you to death." Being hurt and betrayed by a family member is not a New Testament concept only. Jeremiah writes in Jeremiah 12:6, "Your brothers, your own family – even they have betrayed you; they have raised a loud cry against you. Do not trust them, though they speak well of you." Jeremiah 9:4-5 says, "Beware of your friends; do not trust your brothers. For every brother is a deceiver, and every friend a slanderer. Friend deceives friend, and no one speaks the truth...." In Isaiah 2:22 we read, "Stop trusting in man, who has but a breath in his nostrils. Of what account is he?" A common statement comes to mind: "With friends like that, who needs enemies?"

What happens when you put trust in people?

1. You become disappointed when it did not work out as expected.
2. Then you become angry at them and yourself for trusting them.
3. If this anger is held in, bitterness and depression develop.

Can you see why Esau had a hard time forgiving Jacob for stealing his birthright and blessing? Can you see why Joseph might have had a hard time forgiving his brothers for selling him into slavery?

3. **Someone you see often**: (Ps 55:12, 14) David wrote that he walked to the house of God with the person who hurt him. He said that he could not hide from this person. David saw this person a lot. Because of constant contact, there is a constant remembrance of the pain. Contact with the person who hurt you reopens the wounds that might have started to heal.

Satan knows two damaging things about people, their past and their weaknesses (limitations). 1 Peter 5:8 warns, "Be self-controlled and alert. Your enemy the devil prowls around like a roaring lion looking for someone to devour." This lion is going to attack Christians with his PAWS (Past And Weaknesses). His favorite game he plays with the human mind is "Flashbacks," using his knowledge of the past. Satan has an incredible memory when it comes to the pain people have experienced. Psychology frequently labels flashbacks as "post traumatic stress syndrome."

A flashback is an unwanted memory of a bad event that comes back into the mind. Flashbacks are things in our past that are remembered through present events. They are usually very graphic. Flashbacks can occur in a variety of ways. If they occur while sleeping, they are called nightmares. As the painful past event is replayed — as if in slow motion, repeatedly, frame by frame — people stare at it to decide how much they were at fault. Imagine how *you* would feel if you were the skier on the opening of ABC's "Wide World of Sports." You would constantly be reminded of your fall. You might demand residuals or sue for emotional suffering! Even then, you could turn bitter if you dwelt on it. An acrostic definition will help you understand what flashbacks are, and what Satan tries to accomplish through them:

Frequent
Looks
At
Satan's
Hope to
Break
A
Christian's
Kinship
Spirit with God

It is natural for people who experience flashbacks to have trouble sleeping. Flashbacks disrupt the whole sleep cycle. This lack of sleep creates stress and anxiety, making them very tense and depressed. Job 3:25-26 lists some of the "benefits of fear" Satan enjoys: "What I feared has come upon me; what I dreaded has happened to me. I have no peace, no quietness; I have no rest, only turmoil." Flashbacks are often in the subconscious mind, but they overshadow even conscious thought.

Satan uses the five senses to bring on flashbacks, remembering and re-creating pain. The five senses are actually linked to five memory sources in the brain where information is stored. Flashbacks can occur through:

Sight: seeing someone who reminds you of the event or person who hurt you.

Hearing: hearing a voice, song or noise that in some way reminds you of the event or person who hurt you.

Smell: smelling something that reminds you of the event or person who hurt you. This may be food or cologne, etc. I recently heard on a commercial for an allergy medication that your nose can smell 4000 different smells; that is a lot of flashback potential!

Touch: many times touching something, or being touched, can remind you of events that have happened to you.

Taste: tasting something that reminds you of a painful event.

Consider this example. Your fiancée wears a certain type of perfume, has a very unusual hair style and an uncommon laugh, and likes music by the Beach Boys. She breaks up with you, making very hateful remarks before the breakup. Five years later you are walking in a mall and you hear the Beach Boys. What do you think about? A little while later, you smell the same perfume your ex-fiancée used. What do you do? If you see her hair style, what do you do? If you hear someone who laughs like her, what do you do? You begin to think of the person and the injuries she caused you. You leave the mall. You might even give me a call and make an appointment to talk to me.

If you have problems with flashbacks, I would encourage you to do something that you enjoy, after having a flashback. One of my clients was molested by her grandfather who lives right next door. She sees him once a week at least, and it really bothers her when she sees him. I have encouraged her to do something she enjoys after seeing him. She told me that she likes brownies, so I told her that whenever she sees him she can have a brownie. This has taken away some of the power of the flashbacks, and she often forgets to eat the brownie! I have told other clients to get manicures or see a funny movie after they experience flashbacks. This greatly reduces the pain of flashbacks.

4. **Someone with whom we have shared our pain, past and lives**: (Ps 41:9; Dan 11:26-27; Obad 7) It is always harder to forgive when the person who hurt you is someone with whom you have shared your life. If this occurs a couple of times, you will have trouble letting anyone get close again. People who have a hard time open-

ing up to others often have been betrayed by someone with whom they have been close. This might be one reason for shyness. This might be one reason people have a hard time saying, "I love you." People who have been hurt by this type of person frequently spell "love" as "leave" instead! People who have experienced loss frequently do the same thing. They promise themselves, "No one is going to ever get close to me again." They believe this promise will keep pain away from their life. A promise like this promotes loneliness, pain and bitterness. If this promise is kept, they will be lonely; but if they break this promise, they will be afraid. Both loneliness and fear can create bitterness. Consider Obadiah 7: "All your allies will force you to the border; your friends will deceive and overpower you; those who eat your bread will set a trap for you, but you will not detect it." This verse relates very well to Psalm 41:9 which reads, "Even my close friend, whom I trusted, he who shared my bread, has lifted up his heel against me."

5. **Someone you have trusted and respected**: (Ps 41:9) When you get hurt by this person, it is difficult to trust and respect again. How many people do you know who have been betrayed by a minister or a close personal friend? What happens to the betrayed person? They frequently become embittered. They tend to transfer their bitterness to other relationships. Billy Graham wrote, "Forgiveness does not come easily to us, especially when someone we have trusted betrays our trust. And yet if we do not learn to forgive, we will discover that we can never really rebuild trust."[2]

Consider these two verses about trust:

Jeremiah 38:22 "...They misled you and overcame you — those trusted friends of yours. Your feet are sunk in the mud; your friends have deserted you."

Micah 7:5 "Do not trust a neighbor; put no confidence

in a friend. Even with her who lies in your embrace be careful of your words."

Paul, in 1 Thessalonians 2:8, tells us that people should share with each other: "We loved you so much that we were delighted to share with you not only the gospel of God, but our lives as well, because you had become so dear to us." This type of sharing encourages Christian growth. Gossip (which is a form of betrayal and injustice), on the other hand, separates close friends (Prov 16:28).

In a Harris Poll 1256 adults were asked whom they trust.

64% said small business owners; 39% said journalists; 31% said business executives; 25% said lawyers; and 19% said members of Congress.

I wonder if the percentages would be inverted if they asked who they believed is likely to betray them? The Bible teaches that liars will be silenced and that the Lord detests lying lips. It sounds like the people in this poll felt the same way.

6. **Someone with whom you have a lot in common**: (Ps 55:14; Jer 20:10) David wrote that the person who hurt him once enjoyed sweet fellowship with him. What did David have in common with King Saul? They were both army men, they had someone they both loved (David's wife was Saul's daughter, Michal — 1 Sam 18:27). They appeared to have a common enemy in the Philistines. Having several things in common brings about close relationships, but a common interest such as hobbies, music, or sports might actually be used as a weapon later. The more you have in common before the hurt, the more difficult it is to forgive. "The more intimate the friendship, the more deadly the enmity" (West Africa, Yoruba tribe proverb). Consider the following story:

The Hardest Person to Forgive

TEACHER SLAIN AS SMALL KIDS WATCH *The San Diego Union-Tribune*, Friday, July 29, 1994, p. A-12. Ardmore, PA. (AP)

A woman walked into a daycare center filled with children yesterday and shot the teacher to death, police said.

None of the youngsters was wounded at the Ardmore Child Care Center, west of Philadelphia.

Arcelia Trumaine Stovall, 36, was arrested at her home and confessed to the shooting, Lower Merion Township police said.

Relatives said the teacher, 40-year-old Diane Morse, had known Stovall since childhood.

"We've known her for years," said Lesa Pierce, 30, Morse's sister-in-law. "We all grew up in the same area."

The Bible says a lot about friends and friendships. In Ecclesiastes 4:9-12 we read, "Two are better than one, because they have a good return for their work: If one falls down, his friend can help him up. But pity the man who falls and has no one to help him up! Also, if two lie down together, they will keep warm. But how can one keep warm alone? Though one may be overpowered, two can defend themselves. A cord of three strands is not quickly broken." In this verse, notice three things a friend should do: 1. help people up when they fall, 2. keep people warm, and 3. defend people who need help. Betrayal is not one of the things friends should do! Proverbs 31:8-9 tells us what people should do, "Speak up for those who cannot speak for themselves, for the rights of all who are destitute."

The book of Job says a lot about friends (people with whom you have a lot in common). Remember who came to "minister" to Job in his time of need? According to Job 2:11, "When Job's three friends, Eliphaz the Temanite, Bildad the Shuhite and Zophar the Naamathite, heard about all the troubles that had come upon him, they set out from their homes and met together by agreement to go and sym-

pathize with him and comfort him." Here is a sampling of
verses from Job about friendship gone sour:

❖ Job 6:15: "But my brothers are as undependable as
  intermittent streams...."
❖ Job 12:4: "I have become a laughingstock to my friends,
  though I called upon God and he answered — a mere
  laughingstock, though righteous and blameless!"
❖ Job 17:5: "If a man denounces his friends for reward,
  the eyes of his children will fail."
❖ Job 19:14: "My kinsmen have gone away; my friends
  have forgotten me."
❖ Job 19:19: "All my intimate friends detest me...."
❖ Job 19:21: "Have pity on me, my friends, have pity, for
  the hand of God has struck me." Job says this because
  his friends were pitiful, but had no pity for Job.
❖ Job 32:3: "He was also angry with the three friends,
  because they had found no way to refute Job, and yet
  had condemned him." This quote is from Elihu, probably one of Job's best friends, who was not one of the
  original three friends. He is angry with Job, but he is
  also angry with the three friends (32:2). Notice in 32:4
  he is younger than the other three friends of Job.
❖ Job 42:10: "After Job had prayed for his friends, the
  LORD made him prosperous again and gave him twice
  as much as he had before."

Look at Job's forgiving attitude and the recognition he
received from God for it (Job 42:7): "After the Lord had
said these things to Job, he said to Eliphaz the Temanite, 'I
am angry with you and your two friends, because you have
not spoken of me what is right, as my servant Job has.'"

Consider these other Bible passages that deal with friendships and how they might turn out badly:

❖ Lamentations 1:2 "Bitterly she weeps at night, tears
  are upon her cheeks. Among all her lovers there is

none to comfort her. All her friends have betrayed her; they have become her enemies."

❖ Zechariah 13:6 "If someone asks him, 'What are these wounds on your body?' he will answer, 'The wounds I was given at the house of my friends.'"

Who are the people you have a hard time forgiving? It is my belief they have at least two of the above characteristics! This is "done by design"! Satan is hoping that after you have been hurt by these people, you learn to stay away from all people. If these traits are true, then the hardest person to forgive might be yourself! How many of these characteristics do you meet? An old saying comes to mind, "If I can stand me, I can stand anything." The hardest things to forgive yourself for are things you have done after you became a Christian! What does a person do when they can't forgive themselves? Self-abuses of many kinds are caused by people not forgiving themselves. Frequently people have a hard time forgiving themselves for what they were, when what they "were" does not exist anymore (2 Cor 5:17; Gal 2:20). Love yourself for who you are becoming; forgive yourself for who you were.

What is the hardest thing for you to forgive yourself for? Is there a list of them? Are they constantly in your mind? This is what Satan will use to attack you! If he knows something in your past bothers you, he will continually bomb you with it. It is important for you to forgive yourself for any event that hinders and entangles you (Heb 12:1). If you cannot forgive yourself, you will *never* find peace. It is equally important that you also quit beating yourself up because of your sins. Your sins are no different in God's eyes than any other sin. As a Christian you are not under a curse because of your sins!

One reason Satan will attack you with these six traits is because after you have been hurt by them, you have a difficult time trusting. This makes it difficult for you to share your burdens with others. This is a command from the Lord (Gal 6:2). When one carries his burdens alone, he will eventually fall because of exhaustion. When people carry their burdens alone, they are going to fall and have no one to help them up; they are going to get cold and have no one to warm them; they are going to be overpowered by Satan (Eccl 4:9-12).

If these six traits are true about the hardest person to forgive, who would be the easiest people to forgive?
1. *Non-Christian.*
2. *Non-family member.*
3. *Someone you see hardly at all.*
4. *Someone with whom you have not shared your past and pain.*
5. *Someone for whom you have no respect or trust.*
6. *Someone with whom you have nothing in common.*

This person does not even exist in your world! This person is not going to hurt you.

As we move away from who is the hardest person to forgive, let's turn our attention next to why Satan is a liar and the lies he tells about forgiveness. This chapter will give you another reason why it is hard to forgive.

Source Notes

1. From a broadcast titled "Fighting Satan in Today's World."

2. Josh McDowell and Bill Jones, *The Teenage Q/A Book* (Dallas: Word Publishing Co., 1990), pp. 183-184.

3. Billy Graham, *Answers to Life's Problems* (Minneapolis: Grason Publishing Co., 1988), p. 40.

7

Lies that Satan Tells
about Forgiveness

"Two things I ask of you, O Lord; do not refuse me before I die: Keep
falsehood and lies far from me; give me neither poverty nor riches, but
give me only my daily bread."
Proverbs 30:7-8

Lying, and believing lies, has consequences. There
was recently a beauty queen who was dethroned amid
claims that she exaggerated on her resume about her high
school and college academic credentials. She also apparently introduced herself to the audience at the competition
as "a first-year law student." Two television stations reported
stories in which pageant officials learned that she was not
accepted to the law school as she claimed to have been.
This is what lying can do to people. But, what about believing lies? This chapter will discuss in great detail what
believing lies will cause.

Of all the definitions Jesus could have given for Satan,
why did he refer to him as the "father of lies"? Jesus said in
John 8:44-45, "You belong to your father, the devil, and
you want to carry out your father's desire. He was a mur-

derer from the beginning, not holding to the truth, for there is no truth in him. When he lies, he speaks his native language, for he is a liar and the father of lies." This used to puzzle me until I learned about the power of lies.

Power of lies

One of the major powers that lies have is they come from, and create, wickedness (Prov 29:12). Wickedness is part of Satan's nature, so I can understand why Jesus called him the "father of lies."

One of the reasons people tell lies is to cause confusion. This is another ultimate power of lies. Satan has a great understanding of this power. Satan knows that a person's beliefs (whether true or false) form the foundation of that person's life. In Proverbs 24:3-4 we read, "By wisdom a house is built, and through understanding it is established; through knowledge its rooms are filled with rare and beautiful treasures." Believing the truth puts the foundation of the "house" on the rock. Believing lies puts the foundation on the sand. Where the foundation is set determines the outcome of the structure (Matt 7:24-27). Jesus says the person who built his house upon the rock (Jesus' truth), had a house that did not fall when the winds, water and rain beat against it. Jesus said the man who built his house on the sand (Satan's lies), had a house that fell with a great crash. Jesus calls this man "foolish" (verse 26).

There are many liars found in the Bible:

The Elder Brother – Luke 15:11-12, 28-29
Aaron – Exodus 32:2-4, 22-24
Cain – Genesis 4:8-9
Jacob – Genesis 27
Laban – Genesis 29
Satan – Genesis 3:1-5
Ananias and Sapphira – Acts 5:1-9
Potiphar's wife – Genesis 39

Gehazi – 2 Kings 5:20-23
Jezebel – 1 Kings 21
Abraham – Genesis 20:11-13
Isaac – Genesis 26:6-7.

According to John 8:44 Satan is a liar, the father of lies. Lies are Satan's native language, but Satan never tells 100% lies because no one would believe them. He tells partial lies, making them easy to believe and accept. Mark Twain said, "A lie can travel half way around the world while the truth is putting on its shoes." Edgar J. Mohn is quoted to have said, "A lie has speed, but truth has endurance." H.G. Adams said, "Hell is truth seen too late." These three quotes might give us a clearer picture of why Satan tells lies.

One reason Satan lies is to put people into bondage. John 8:32 says truth causes freedom. Lies therefore cause bondage! Lies are bondage beliefs that Satan teaches. This bondage is what God wants to free us from (Isa 9:4; 10:27; 14:25).

In 1 Timothy 4:1-2 we read, "The Spirit clearly says that in later times some will abandon the faith and follow deceiving spirits and things taught by demons. Such teachings come through hypocritical liars, whose consciences have been seared as with a hot iron." The root word for hypocritical is the Greek word **hypokrites** meaning actors. Satan has lying actors who teach lies to lead people astray. Satan hopes people will believe these lies and abandon their faith! Jesus spoke about this in Matthew 24:4, "Watch out that no one deceives you." Later in this chapter Jesus said, "For false Christs and false prophets will appear and perform great signs and miracles to deceive even the elect – if that were possible" (v. 24).

In Matthew 4 Satan quotes Scripture to Jesus. This is a clear indication that Satan knows the Bible. In Genesis 3 when Satan dealt with Adam and Eve, Satan knew what

Healing for a Bitter Heart

God said. He simply twisted it. It is from the Bible that Satan will conceive most of his lies that will lead Christians astray! It is interesting to realize that Satan's first word to Eve was "Did" (Gen 3:1) and his first word to Jesus was "If" (Matt 4:3). Both of these words were used to create doubt. Doubt is another outcome of listening to lies.

There are two basic ways Satan tells lies using Scripture:

1. **Taking verses out of context and making inaccurate life applications with them.** An example of this type of lie could be made from Isaiah 56:12. Using just this verse, what does the Bible say people can do? It suggests they can get drunk and have their fill of beer, and doing this will make tomorrow like today, only far better. See how easy this type of lie is? Satan is a master of this.

2. **Twisting a verse around.** This involves changing slightly, but severely, its meaning. An example of this is found in Genesis 3:1-5. What did Satan ask Eve? He said, "Did God really say....." The whole purpose of this was to create doubt in Eve's mind. What Satan did was to change a couple of God's words. This was really subtle but effective. By doing this he helped Eve fall into sin. What did God tell Eve she could not do? (Gen 2:17) God did not tell Eve that she could not touch the tree or eat from any of the other trees, but by Satan's question he made it seem so. God told her she could not eat from one certain tree. Anyone who debates with the devil loses!

What are lies exactly? What is his goal when he lies? Two acrostics will answer both of these questions.

L ucifer's	**L** ucifer
I nitiative	**I** nstructor
E ncouraging	**A** dvancing
S eparation	**R** ebellion

184

Below is a list of some of the outcomes of believing lies. These show the power of lies!

❖ **Jeremiah 9:5**: This verse tells us that people have taught their tongues to lie. Lies reside in the heart of man. Matthew 12:34 links the heart with the mouth. Lies also weary a person with sinning. I would encourage you to also look up Jeremiah 12:6 and Daniel 11:27.

❖ **Jeremiah 23:14**: People can live a lie. Lies strengthen the hands of evildoers. Lies cause a person not to repent. If the lie is believed, they become like Sodom and Gomorrah. At the time Jeremiah wrote this verse, both of these cities had been destroyed (Gen 19)! Believing lies brings destruction to a person's life (Isa 32:7).

❖ **Jeremiah 23:32:** Satan's purpose for telling lies is to lead people astray. Revelation 12:9 tells us that Satan leads people astray. This happens because they believe his lies. A good example of the effects of lies is found in Genesis 3:1-5. Satan tells Eve she will not die; she will become like God if she eats of the tree. It is too bad Eve did not recognize she was already like God (Gen 1:27). The purpose of Satan's lying to Eve was to lead the whole human race out of the physical presence of God. Satan remembered what God did to him when he sinned – he was kicked out of heaven (Rev 12:7-12). He was hoping God would kick the man and woman out of their "heaven." He was hoping he would doom the human race to hell! Satan did not realize that God would make a way for people to come into heaven. In John 14:6 Jesus declares, "I am the way and the truth and the life. No one comes to the Father except through me." Zechariah 10:2 relates to lies leading people astray. It comments, "The idols speak deceit, diviners see visions that lie; they tell dreams that are false, they give comfort in vain. Therefore the people wander like sheep oppressed for lack of a shepherd."

❖ **Jeremiah 29:31-32:** This verse gives evidence that people are led to believe lies. One of the outcomes of believing a lie is rebellion against God. In Israel's history, the people of the Exodus were not allowed to go into the promised land because they believed the lies of the ten spies and refused to believe the truth of the two spies. Numbers 13:26-33 gives the account of this. The "bad reports" spread by the ten spies (verse 32) were lies! The book of Jeremiah tells of many times when people prophesied lies (bad reports) (5:31; 14:14; 23:25; 27:10; 14-16; 29:9, 21). Chapter 14 of Numbers records the people's rebellion against God. Deuteronomy 1:19-46 gives another picture of this event. It is sad that ten people can literally lead millions into rebellion. If ten can lead millions astray and into rebellion, how many would it take to lead one astray? Disobedience is one of Satan's goals for telling lies. Ephesians 2:2 says that Satan is at work in people who are disobedient.

❖ **Jeremiah 6:10** lists two outcomes of listening to and believing lies: 1. ears closed to the truth: so they cannot hear it. 2. the words of the Lord are offensive to them.

❖ **Jeremiah 8:9** asks an interesting question: If people reject the word of the Lord (and believe lies), what kind of wisdom do they have? They have no wisdom at all.

What can be done to the truth?

Acts 20:30 — It can be *distorted*. This will draw disciples away from the Lord. In Jeremiah 23:36 we read that the words of the Living God can be distorted. This is exactly what Satan does.

Romans 1:18 — Truth can be *suppressed* by wickedness.

Romans 1:25 — The godless *exchanged the truth of God for a lie.* Doing this causes them to serve created things rather than the Creator. This is one of the most dangerous results of believing lies.

186

Romans 2:8 — The truth can be *rejected*, causing people to follow evil.

2 Thessalonians 2:10 — The truth can be *refused*. People can refuse to love the truth. In doing so, they perish and are not saved.

2 Thessalonians 2:12 — The truth can be *denied* or not believed. The outcome of this is condemnation.

2 Timothy 2:18; James 5:19 — People can *wander* from the truth, destroying the faith of some.

2 Timothy 3:7-8 — The truth is something that is *not always acknowledged*. Truth can be opposed. Look at two strong descriptions (depraved minds and rejected) of people who turn away from the truth!

2 Timothy 4:4 — People can *turn away* from the truth.

1 John 1:6 — The truth is something people can *choose not to live by*.

The power of the truth:

Jesus understood the power of truth! This is why he said, "I am the way and the truth and the life. No one comes to the Father except through me" (John 14:6). Truth is the opposite of lies; it causes people to be set free from the bondage of bitterness (John 8:32). What does the Bible say about the truth?

Acts 24:8 — Truth is learned.

1 John 2:21 — No lie comes from the truth.

1 John 3:19 — People can belong to the truth.

2 John 4; 3 John 3-4 — People can walk in the truth. This is a command from God.

Isaiah 45:19 — Truth is found in the Lord.

When you tell people the truth about forgiveness, you might become an enemy to them (Gal 4:16). The reason truth becomes an enemy is because it challenges people to change. People hate the truth; remember they killed it (John 14:6). Isaiah 59:14-15 makes some statements about truth. It says that it can stumble in the streets, and that truth at times is nowhere to be found.

How are lies and forgiveness connected?

In Matthew 13:24-30 Jesus told the parable of the weeds. The weeds were sown by the enemy into the field that just had good seed planted in it. I believe that the weeds could refer to lies. In verse 25 Jesus said that the weeds were sown when everyone was sleeping. This is usually when Satan does his best work. Darkness is one of the best times for Satan to move because he cannot be seen. Lies grow best in the dark, not being exposed to the light (truth).

C.S. Lewis wrote,

> Everyone says forgiveness is a lovely idea, until they have something to forgive, as we had during the war. And then, to mention the subject at all is to be greeted with howls of anger. It is not that people think this is too high and diffi-cult a virtue: it is that they think it hateful and contempt-ible. "That sort of talk makes me sick," they say. And half of you already want to ask me, "I wonder how you'd feel about forgiving the Gestapo if you were a Pole or a Jew?"[1]

One reason it is difficult for people to forgive is that Satan tells at least twelve basic lies about forgiveness. These lies make it almost impossible to forgive ourselves, as well as others. Remember, when Satan lies, he speaks his native tongue. He is a liar and the father of lies (John 8:44). Jesus did not tell us what Satan lies about. It only makes sense he lies about everything, including forgive-ness. If the Bible speaks about a subject, you had better believe Satan has a lie about it!

The big lie about God and forgiveness:

God is so loving he would not send anyone to hell. Read 2 Samuel 6:6-7. But this is from the Old Testament! Read Matthew 5:17. God's forgiveness is not unconditional! He extends forgiveness to everyone, but not everyone receives it. Forgiveness requires repentance and baptism (Acts 2:38). The **Truth** is God does not send anyone to hell, but the person sends himself to hell!

Believing any of the following lies will keep a person in bondage to bitterness and rage (Acts 8:23). It is important that you spot and stop the lies that people believe about forgiveness before you teach them what forgiveness is and how to forgive! You might be surprised how many of these lies you have heard. These lies are very prevalent in society today. You might be surprised how many of the lies you believe yourself. The lies about forgiveness are:

1. **LIE**: If I forgive, I am saying what has happened to me is no big deal and it is OK. This lie also says there is a thin line between forgiving and making excuses.

TRUTH: Jesus did not die for something that was no big deal. Since God and Jesus believe sin's only payment is death, sin has to be very serious in God's eyes. Sin was the reason Jesus came to earth to die in our place (John 3:16-17; 2 Cor 5:21). Forgiveness was almost impossible for God to do. This is why it took such a drastic step as having his only Son die on Calvary to create forgiveness!

2. **LIE**: If I forgive, I am being weak, a doormat, or a fool.

TRUTH: The strongest picture in the world is Jesus on the cross. He didn't cry (but Matthew 27:46 comes close) or show any form of bitterness or revenge. How can we call him weak, a doormat or a fool? (Isa 53:7). He is the picture of strength, because he could have chosen not to die. John 10:18 speaks of his choice, "No one takes it [life]

189

from me, but I lay it down of my own accord. I have authority to lay it down and authority to take it up again. This command I received from my Father."

3. **LIE**: If I forgive, I am giving permission for the person to hurt me again. Proverbs 26:11 is the verse Satan bases this lie on! Consider this story:

> ILLINOIS MAN CHARGED WITH KILLING 'FORGIVING WIFE' *The Evening Press*, Muncie, Indiana, Tuesday, December 28, 1993, p. 3.
>
> Naperville, Ill. (AP) Soon after Marsha Brewer-Stewart's husband was accused of trying to stab her to death seven months ago, authorities began pleading with her to leave him and get help.
>
> Their advice went unheeded.
>
> Not only did she stay with her husband, she posted his $10,000 bond and moved back in with him. On Sunday, Gregory Stewart again attacked his wife, and this time he killed her, police said.
>
> "It's very, very tragic," said DuPage County State's Attorney James Ryan.
>
> Stewart, 38, was charged Monday with murder and ordered held without bond.
>
> His 44-year-old wife called police Sunday night from her home, saying she was being threatened with a knife, Ryan said. She hung up quickly and when they called back, Stewart answered, saying there was nothing wrong.
>
> Squad cars were dispatched, but it was too late. Police found Brewer-Stewart's body with a knife in her chest, Ryan said. She was pronounced dead at the scene.
>
> In May, Ryan's office charged Stewart with attempted murder after Brewer-Stewart's throat was slit.
>
> Ryan said his office had sought a court order barring Stewart from having contact with his wife, but she objected and no order was entered.
>
> "We asked her several times to get orders of protection," Ryan said. "But she just didn't want them."

Police also were unsuccessful in getting Brewer-Stewart to seek help.

"We offered help and we tried to get her to go along with orders of protection from her husband, but she would never agree," said police Capt. Paul Shafer.

TRUTH: Jesus said to go and leave your life of sin (John 8:11). Jesus never gave anyone permission to sin. Look at what he told the man in John 5:14, "Stop sinning or something worse may happen to you." This man had been paralyzed for 38 years. Forgiveness does not mean giving permission for people to continue to harm you. Forgiveness is not the same as trust. Trust has to be earned, or re-earned. The above story will only make people think that forgiveness is a human flaw.

4. **LIE**: I have to forgive only after the person asks for forgiveness and shows signs of repentance. Luke 17:3 is the verse on which Satan bases this lie!

TRUTH: Jesus forgave the woman caught in adultery even though she did not ask for forgiveness, so we see how willing Jesus is to forgive sin (John 8:1-11; Luke 7:41-48). There appear to be nonverbal signs to God which people use to ask for forgiveness. To be forgiven today, everyone has to ask for forgiveness and be baptized (Acts 2:38; Mark 16:16). This last sentence seems to contradict the previous one. It implies that people back in Bible times could give non-verbal signs that we can't today. The reason people have to ask today is because Jesus is not on the earth to "see" people ask for forgiveness!

In Luke 17:3-4 Jesus teaches that if a brother sins and repents you should forgive him up to seven times in one day. Does this mean a person must ask for forgiveness to be forgiven? To be on the safe side, forgive the person their sins whether they ask or not and whether they repent or not. Being willing to forgive a person before they ask creates an attitude of forgiveness that prevents bitterness!

5. **LIE**: I will forgive, but it will take a long time for the person to know it. The longer it takes for him to know it, the less likely he is to do it again.

TRUTH: It took Jesus hardly any time at all to forgive the woman caught in adultery (John 8:1-11). Bitterness develops during the delay of forgiveness. The longer forgiveness is delayed, the less likely it is to occur, and the more bitter a person is likely to become. The longer it takes for you to forgive a person, the more likely you are to forget to forgive.

6. **LIE**: Forgiveness is for the benefit of the person who hurt you. It does not affect you at all if you don't forgive.

TRUTH: Forgiveness sets the forgiver free to be forgiven by God (Matt 6:14-15; 18:21-35). If you do not forgive, God cannot forgive you!!

7. **LIE**: Forgiveness is only a spiritual exercise that has no practical applications.

TRUTH: Forgiveness is the major reason Jesus came to earth. If you believe this lie, you must also believe Jesus' life, teachings, and ministry have no practical applications to life (Luke 19:10; 1 Tim 1:15). Without the application of forgiveness in marriage, divorce is inevitable!

8. **LIE**: Forgiving and forgetting are the same thing.

TRUTH: If this is so, why does Isaiah 43:25 point out that God both forgives and forgets sin? If they were one and the same, this verse would be redundant. You frequently hear, "I can forgive, but I can't forget." What this statement is saying, is that I forgive you, but anytime I want to bring it back up to hurt you I will. This is not forgiveness. This is selected retention of memories to inflict harm. You frequently hear, "forgive and forget." This is totally impossible. This is one of the reasons why Satan wants us to try to do this.

9. **LIE**: If I don't forgive, I am punishing the perpetrator.

TRUTH: If you don't forgive them, they can still be forgiven by God, but what about your sins? (Matt 6:14-15; 18:32-35) Your lack of forgiveness would justify God in remembering your confessed, forgiven sins and reinstating the debt of sin owed to God (Matt 18:34; Rom 6:23). Look at what happened to the servant who chose not to forgive his fellow servant's debt in the parable in Matthew 18:21-35. This is what happens when you choose not to forgive.

10. **LIE**: Forgiveness should occur only after all of the effects of the event are over.

TRUTH: If this were true, then no one would ever be able to forgive. The effects of someone's sin never truly go away 100%. I work with many people who have been betrayed through adultery. One of the major struggles they face later is with the issue of trust. They trusted their spouse and then their spouse had an affair. The relationship ended with a divorce, and now the victim is dating again but has a lot of fears about getting hurt and trusting. (See Ps 41:9; Exod 20:4-5.)

11. **LIE**: If I forgive the person who hurt me, then God will forgive them. They will end up in heaven.

TRUTH: Your forgiveness of them does not mean God forgives them. They still have to ask God personally to forgive them. Your forgiveness allows God to forgive you, not them.

12. **LIE**: If I forgive, I am being self-righteous. It is only for "show."

TRUTH: When a person forgives, he is being obedient to God! It can appear to be self-righteous; it depends on how it is done. Forgiveness should be done in such a way as to not "parade" it so other people see and hear about it (Matt 6:1-4). Jesus told a great parable about self-righteousness found in Luke 18:9-14. The Pharisee prayed about himself. The tax collector prayed to God. The tax collector walked away forgiven by God.

I found a book entitled, *Courage to Heal*, by Ellen Bass and Laura Davis in some Christian bookstores. It has some statements on forgiveness I find very heretical. After reading this book I could hardly wait for my book to be published, so people will have another source of healing. Bass and Davis, in their book on "healing," spend some time talking about forgiveness. Consider the following quotes from their book:

> When talking about the stages in the healing process, the question is inevitably raised: What about forgiveness? The only necessity as far as healing is concerned is forgiving yourself. Developing compassion and forgiveness for your abuser, or for the members of your family who did not protect you, is not a required part of the healing process. It isn't something to hope for or shoot for. It is not the final goal.[2]

> When a friend inadvertently hurts our feelings and apologizes, we forgive her. We no longer blame her. The relationship is mended. We reconcile and we continue to trust and respect, without residual anger between us. This kind of forgiveness — giving up anger and pardoning the abuser, restoring a relationship of trust — is not necessary in order to heal from the trauma of being sexually abused as a child. You are not more moral or courageous if you forgive.[3]

> It is insulting to suggest to any survivor that she should forgive the person who abused her. This advice minimizes and denies the validity of her feelings. Yet the issue of forgiveness is one that will be pressed on you again and again by people who are uncomfortable with your rage or want to have you back under their control. While you don't have to stay angry forever, you should not let anyone talk you into trading in your anger for the "higher good" of forgiveness.[4]
> [NOTE from Charley: Not forgiving the person who hurt you will keep you angry and bitter at the world forever!]

194

If you have strong religious ties, particularly Christian ones, you may feel it is your sacred duty to forgive. This just isn't true. If there is such a thing as divine forgiveness, it's God's job, not yours. If feelings of compassion and forgiveness rise naturally and spontaneously during the course of healing yourself, fine. They can be a powerful part of your healing, but not if they're forced into being because you think you should forgive them.[5] [NOTE from Charley: These feelings don't arise naturally. They go against human nature!]

Healing depends a lot on being able to forgive yourself, not on being able to forgive your molester. I don't think any time spent trying to forgive your molester is worthwhile time spent. You don't try to forgive Hitler. You don't sit around and work on that. There are a lot of other things to be doing with a life.[6] [NOTE: Of course I don't sit around and try to forgive Hitler. He never hurt me. But if he had, forgiving him would be time well spent and would allow me to go to heaven!]

Forgiveness of yourself is what's important, and when you start to feel that forgiveness, it just naturally extends itself to other people in the world. You start to get an understanding of what humanity is all about. You become able to see when somebody does something right. You can respond to a humane, loving act. And that's what forgiveness is really about.[7]

Do any of these statements sound like the lies mentioned in this section? What would happen to people if they believed what these authors were writing? After reading this chapter of their book I was reminded of a couple of verses in the Bible. In Jeremiah 8:8-9 we read, "How can you say, 'We are wise, for we have the law of the LORD,' when actually the lying pen of the scribes has handled it falsely? The wise will be put to shame; they will be dismayed and trapped. Since they have rejected the word of the LORD, what kind of wisdom do they have?" In James 3:1 we read that "Not many of you should presume to be

teachers, my brothers, because you know that we who
teach will be judged more strictly." 1 Corinthians 4:6, "Do
not go beyond what is written...." Galatians 1:6-7, "I am
astonished that you are so quickly deserting the one who
called you by the grace of Christ and are turning to a different gospel —which is really no gospel at all. Evidently some
people are throwing you into confusion and are trying to
pervert the gospel of Christ." Forgiveness is God's only
solution to bitterness! Forgiveness is not man's solution.
Man's solution is revenge, retaliation and resentment. Forgiveness to man seems foolish, hard to accept and hard to
understand (1 Cor 1:18-25, 2:14).

Source Notes

1. C.S. Lewis, *Mere Christianity* (New York: Macmillan Publishing
Company, Collier Books, 1952), p. 104.

2. Ellen Bass and Laura Davis, *Courage to Heal* (New York: Harper
and Row, 1988), p. 149.

3. Ibid., p. 150.

4. Ibid., pp. 150-151.

5. Ibid., p. 151.

6. Ibid.

7. Ibid.

8

What Is Forgiveness Exactly?

"The voice of sin may be loud, but the voice of forgiveness is louder."
D.L. Moody

"As far as the east is from the west, so far has he removed our transgressions from us."   Ps 103:12

During a call to worship at the Church where I am a member, I was going to teach what worship was. I had brought with me two bags. One of the bags contained a ring, a pair of sandals, and a robe; and the other bag had a toy stuffed cow. I put all the objects on the pulpit for the congregation to see. Then I talked about how these objects were found in the prodigal son story. But then I asked them what was missing? None of them could tell me. When the prodigal son returned the father said, "Quick! Bring the best robe and put it on him. Put the ring on his finger and sandals on his feet. Bring the fattened calf and kill it. Let's have a feast and celebrate" (Luke 15:22-23). Now do you know what was missing from the top of the pulpit? It is the celebration. This is what worship should be — a celebration. This is exactly what forgiveness is, and should cause. Forgiven people should celebrate God's great gift of forgiveness. Forgiveness is a celebration and should cause a celebration. Jesus taught that when a sinner repents and seeks God's forgiveness, heaven has a celebration (Luke 15:7, 10).

There is tremendous power when we forgive people. In John 20:23 Jesus told his disciples, "Whose soever sins ye remit, they are remitted unto them; and whose soever sins ye retain, they are retained." (KJV) It is interesting to think about what it means to retain sin. It could be that when a person has sinned against us, and we refuse to forgive them, we retain their sin. When a Christian asks for forgiveness from a person he or she has wronged, and we refuse to forgive them, God has released them from that sin and given the consequences to the one who refuses to forgive. This idea is closely related to Proverbs 24:17-18 which says that when people gloat when an enemy falls, God turns his wrath from him. He actually might give his wrath to the one doing the gloating.

Is it God's will that we forgive the people that have harmed us? This answer is found in the Lord's prayer. In Matthew 6:10 we read, "your kingdom come, your will be done on earth as it is in heaven." Two verses later Jesus said, "Forgive us our debts, as we also have forgiven our debtors." It is God's will for us to forgive, so we can be forgiven by God. In Matthew 18:22 Jesus tells us how many times we should forgive, "I tell you, not seven times, but seventy-seven times." Some translations say seventy times seven. Later in the same passage Jesus calls the unforgiving servant wicked. Jesus also mentions that forgiveness must come from the heart for us to be forgiven (Matt 18:35). A heart that is full of bitterness can't be a forgiving heart!

Paul wrote to the Church at Ephesus that he insists on several things (Eph 4:17). Some of the things that he insists on are:

"In your anger do not sin" (Eph 4:26).

"Do not let the sun go down while you are still angry"
(Eph 4:26).

"Do not give the devil a foothold" (Eph 4:27).

"Get rid of all bitterness, rage and anger, brawling and
slander, along with every form of malice" (Eph 4:31).

"Be kind and compassionate to one another" (Eph
4:32).

"Forgive each other" (Eph 4:32).

These things that Paul insists on are for a Christian's own
protection and survival. If we would do these six things the
witness of the Christian community would be huge. These
six things also defeat the effects that Satan is trying to
establish.

Five basic concepts about forgiveness need to be
understood.
1. Without the shedding of blood there is no forgiveness
(Heb 9:22).
2. It is impossible for the blood of bulls and goats to take
away sin (Heb 10:3-4).
3. Jesus Christ is the only sacrifice for sin, once and for all
(Heb 10:10, 14).
4. Where there has been forgiveness, sacrifice is no longer
required (Heb 10:18).
5. Your forgiveness of others is nowhere near as difficult
when compared to what Jesus had to do to forgive
you (Heb 12:4).

Kenneth Kaunda, the first President of Zambia writes:

Forgiveness is not, of course, a substitute for justice.
Forgiveness is a gift, not something we earn, but to know
the reality of forgiveness we must be prepared to turn our
back on the things we have done which require us to seek
forgiveness in the first place. Justice and forgiveness are
related this way. To claim forgiveness whilst perpetuation

of injustice is to live a fiction; to fight for justice without also being prepared to offer forgiveness is to render your struggle null and void. Justice is not only about what is due to a human being; it is also about establishing right relationships between human beings.[1]

Leslie Weatherhead, a British clergyman once wrote, "The forgiveness of God is the most powerful therapeutic idea in the world. If a person can really believe that God has forgiven him, he can be saved from neuroticism."

Norman Vincent Peale suggests this visual image of forgiveness:

Try visualizing a blackboard with a jumble of disconnected words and phrases, or a tangle of scrawled mathematical problems with wrong answers—in short, a sorry record of mistakes. Then imagine a shining figure, the Lord Himself, sweeping a sponge or a damp cloth across that blackboard, wiping it clean, preparing it for another, stronger, better effort. The Lord has forgiven your sins and mistakes. Then forgive yourself, for if you don't the old guilt circle will repeat itself. Run this total picture sequence over and over in your mind. What you are imaging is forgiveness and acceptance, and if the vision is vivid enough, a great sense of peace and well-being will follow. (Source unknown).

Why did Jesus come to earth? (John 6:38) I like the passage in John where Jesus is on the cross and he tells his Father, "It is finished" (John 19:30). The "it" Jesus is referring to is the process of forgiveness that God sent his Son to fulfill and complete. Scripture teaches us that Jesus' mission of forgiveness was:

❖ **1 John 2:2** — To be the atoning sacrifice for the sins of the world.

❖ **Hebrews 13:20-21** — To equip Christians for doing every good work, and to glorify God.

❖ **1 John 3:5** — To take away sin. By Jesus having the

authority to remove sin, he proves he is God. Mark 2:7 asks the question, "Who can forgive sins but God alone?" Jesus forgave sin; therefore he must be God. Realize that when Jesus died he forgave past, present, and future sins. Why is it so difficult to understand that Jesus has forgiven your future sin? Remember that Jesus died for your sins a long time before you were born. He made forgiveness possible for you before you even existed! (Rom 5:8)

❖ **2 Corinthians 5:21** – To become sin for the world.

❖ **1 John 3:8** – To destroy the work of the devil.

❖ **John 3:16-17** – Jesus tells us why God sent his Son to the earth. Not to condemn the world, but to save the world. He sent Jesus to the earth because he loves people more than they can ever imagine. This is one of the reasons Paul wrote Ephesians 2:14-21. Paul wants people to understand the total depth and extent of God's love for us.

❖ **Mark 1:38** – To preach the good news.

❖ **Luke 19:10** – To seek and save that which was lost.

❖ **1 Timothy 1:15** – To save sinners.

❖ **Matthew 20:28** – To serve and give his life as a ransom for many.

❖ **Luke 4:18-19** – To preach good news to the poor; to proclaim freedom to the prisoners and recovery of sight to the blind; to release the oppressed; to proclaim the year of the Lord's favor.

❖ **Hebrews 2:17** – To become a high priest in service to God. To make a sacrifice atoning for the sins of the people.

❖ **Hebrews 7:25** – To intercede for the saints.

❖ **John 1:29** – To take away the sins of the world.

❖ **Luke 2:11** – To be the Savior of the world.

❖ **Matthew 1:20-21** – To save the people from their sins. Does the use of the word "their" denote personal responsibility for the sins people commit? Yes.

❖ **John 18:37** — To testify to the truth and establish God's kingdom.

❖ **Hebrews 9:26** — To be sacrificed once for all to take away the sins of the world (Heb 10:10).

❖ **John 10:10** — To give abundant life.

❖ **John 10:18** — To die willingly so that people could go to heaven.

❖ **John 13:15** — To be an example for people to follow (John 13:15). Jesus' example and teaching on forgiveness are wonderful to study. Jeremiah 5:7 states, "Why should I forgive you? Your children have forsaken me and sworn by gods that are not gods. I supplied all their needs, yet they committed adultery and thronged to the houses of prostitutes." Why did Jesus forgive? He chose to forgive because he loved the people of the world. Why did Jesus choose to be born? He chose to be born, so that he could die! Why did Jesus choose to die one of the most painful ways known to man? Because by his death he made it possible for the world to be forgiven for their sins.

There is a wonderful song called "There is a Savior" (Written by Greg Nelson, Sandi Patti Helvering, Bob Ferrell; New Wings Music, Greg Nelson Music, Sandi's Song Music, BMI, Summer Dawn Music, ASCAP). One of the verses says, "Are there burdens in your heart, is your past a memory that binds you? Is there some pain that you've carried far too long? Then strengthen your heart with His good news, there is a Savior and he has forgiven you." This song lists three reasons Jesus forgives:

❖ because of the burden of sin and guilt (Ps 38:4).
❖ because of past memories that bind (Ps 51:3).
❖ because of the condition of the heart (Prov 14:10).

202

Jesus has to be the ultimate role model for our forgiveness.

Following are 13 teachings on, or examples of Jesus' forgiveness.

(1) In John 6:64 we see that Jesus knew Judas was going to betray him. He could have had Judas walk on the water and let him drown. He could have asked him not to be a disciple. It is very difficult to forgive a person who betrays you; it is even more difficult when you know of the betrayal in advance of its occurrence. We will never have to forgive as much or as often as Jesus did! If you combine the Lord's Prayer with his teaching on forgiveness, here is what it would be like:

> "Our Father in heaven,
> Hallowed be your name,
> Your kingdom come,
> Your will be done,
> On earth as it is in heaven.
> Give us this day our bread.
> Forgive us our debts,
> as we forgive our debtors.
> For if we forgive men, when they sin against us, you will also forgive us. But if we do not forgive men their sins against us, you will not forgive us.
> And lead us not into temptation,
> But deliver us from the evil one."

(2) Luke 23:42-43 — Jesus was on the cross making forgiveness possible for the whole world. For one split second he looked at the thief on the cross next to him and said, "Today you will be with me in paradise." Realize that when Jesus was on the cross, he forgave the three dimensions of sin: the past sins, the present sins, and the future sins — praise God for this fact! My favorite verse in the Bible that deals with the past does not have the past mentioned in it. Romans 8:38-39 state, "For I am convinced that neither death nor life, neither angels or demons, neither the present nor the future, nor any powers, neither height nor depth, nor anything else in all creation, will be able to separate us from the love of God that is in Christ Jesus our Lord." The past is not mentioned in this verse, because the past is gone! Believe God and trust God that your past is gone!

(3) Luke 7:40-48 — Jesus forgave a sinful woman who washed his feet and dried them with her hair. The amazing thing about this story is the woman did not ask for forgiveness. How did Simon feel after Jesus had told him the story about forgiveness?

Reading Matthew 9:1-8 (Mark 2:10; Luke 5:24) we realize that Jesus forgave the sin of the man who had been paralyzed. It is interesting to note the possibility that the men who carried this man to Jesus had more faith than the paralyzed man. Jesus draws a comparison between sin and physical illness in John 5:1-6, 14. Jesus heals a man who had been paralyzed for 38 years. He then says a little later to the man, "See, you are well again. Stop sinning or something worse may happen to you." Could it be that there is a link between sin and disease, but the medical profession does not want to deal with it? This might be due to the fact they feel unprepared to work with the sin aspects of illness. (I am not advocating a person look for sin behind every sneeze!) Many doctors overlook the connection between the physical and the spiritual altogether. They must feel uncomfortable because spirituality is really not a "science" they have studied.

(4) Mark 16:7 — This is one of my favorite passages in the whole Bible because it shows the compassion Jesus has for ones who have fallen away. Jesus specifically names Peter in this passage. This shows Jesus is aware of individual needs when it comes to forgiveness. He knew exactly

what Peter needed! Peter needed to know that the Lord personally forgave him for his denials (Mark 14:66-72). It was Peter's knowledge of God's forgiveness that made him a bold preacher in Acts (Acts 2:14-40).

(5) Luke 23:34 – "Father, forgive them" are the three words that shook mankind to the core. Jesus shows his forgiveness here when he forgives the people who were crucifying him. These people did not ask to be forgiven. Jesus forgave them because he knew what was inside their hearts (Matt 9:4).

(6) John 4:1-26 – Jesus is with the woman at the well. He has compassion for her, and makes such an impact on her life that she goes back to her village and tells the people what Jesus did. Because of her testimony, many from the village believe Jesus was the Christ. Here we see what one simple act of forgiveness can mean to many people (John 4:39-41). This woman understood the teaching found in Psalm 107:2, "Let the redeemed of the LORD say this – those he redeemed from the hand of the foe." The word "this" refers to the fact they are forgiven.

(7) One of my favorite stories about forgiveness in the Bible is found in John 8:1-11. Jesus is confronted by the Pharisees who have a woman caught in act of adultery. The Pharisees want Jesus to condemn her. Jesus actually stands between this woman and guilt, fear, death, hell, the law, Satan, trouble and condemnation. This is exactly what forgiveness is: Jesus on Calvary stood between us and death. Jesus stands between us and Satan, death, hell, fear, condemnation and the law. His standing between us and God is what improves our standing with God and allows us to go to heaven. Ezekiel 22:30 tells about God not being able to find a man who could stand in the gap, until Jesus stood there allowing us to go to heaven.

In this passage (John 8:1-11) Jesus makes the statement, "If any of you is without sin, let him be the first to throw a stone." The only person in the group who could rightfully have thrown the stone at the woman was Jesus. But instead of throwing the stone, Jesus forgives her and tells her to leave her life of sin. I am interested in knowing what Jesus wrote on the ground with his finger. It could be he was listing the accusers' sins. Why did the older ones walk away before the younger? Jesus knew that one of the reasons the Scribes and Pharisees brought this woman to him was their hope that Jesus would condemn her. If he condemned her, Jesus would have lost some of his "popularity" because the people would have believed he was just like the Pharisees. Jesus was held in high esteem by the people not only because of what he taught, but also because of how he taught (Matt 7:28-29). The Pharisees knew if Jesus did not condemn the woman he would be breaking Old Testament law (Lev 20:10). This was one of many traps the Pharisees tried to set for Jesus.

(8) John 21:15-17 — Jesus, after his resurrection, meets Peter while he is fishing. Jesus asks him three times, "Do you love me?" He did this because Peter had to realize he was forgiven and reinstated as a disciple. What joy Peter must have felt after Jesus forgave him! He then would have realized what David meant when he wrote Psalm 51:12, "Restore to me the joy of your salvation and grant me a willing spirit, to sustain me." In the second chapter of Acts Peter is bold in his preaching of the gospel. It was Jesus' forgiveness and Peter's knowledge of this fact that made him bold.

(9) Matthew 18:21-22 — Jesus is asked a "numbers" question. Peter is trying to figure out the greatest possible number of times he has to forgive someone. Jesus gives an answer that means the number is unlimited. People today ask similar questions. In a society that stresses assertiveness as ours does, Jesus' answer would not be well received.

(10) Mark 11:25 — Jesus draws a comparison between prayer and forgiveness. Unforgiveness hinders prayers (1 Pet 3:7). He also reminds us that for us to be forgiven by God we must forgive others.

(11) Matthew 6:12 — Jesus said that God will forgive us our debts as we have forgiven others' debts. In Matthew 18:23-35 Jesus uses the same illustration of debt cancellation two more times.

(12) Matthew 6:14-15 — This is the strongest teaching of Jesus on the matter of forgiveness. He makes it plain that if people don't forgive others, they are preventing God from forgiving them. (A similar statement is found in Luke 6:37.)

(13) Luke 17:3-4 — Jesus teaches that if a brother sins and repents, you should forgive him up to seven times in one day. Does this mean a person must ask for forgiveness to be forgiven? To be on the safe side, forgive the person their sins whether they ask or not and whether they repent or not. Being willing to forgive a person before they ask creates an attitude of forgiveness that prevents bitterness! This passage could easily be used to rationalize not forgiving someone, but I have already shown that Satan likes to twist Scripture to lead people astray. Satan teaches that if a person did not ask for forgiveness or show the appropriate signs of repentance, you don't have to forgive them.

Jesus was so willing to forgive others! What about us? Colossians 3:13 tells us we should forgive just as Christ forgave us. Paul would not have written this if it were not possible. Jesus sacrificed for our sins; what can we sacrifice when others sin against us? One thing is our desire to punish them. Another sacrifice is giving up our right to be angry and bitter at the person who hurt us.

For greater detail about the teachings of Jesus on forgiveness see appendix A in the back of the book.

What is forgiveness according to Scripture?

Forgiveness is where Jesus has the opportunity to stone us because of our sin, and he chooses not to (John 8:1-11). One of my clients wrote "Forgiveness is one that I don't understand. I have too many questions and have no answers. Forgiveness in the Bible, is it a command? I want to forgive, but I cannot forgive him. Which is worse, me not forgiving or his sin? Which comes first, forgiveness or healing of the hurt? When I do forgive, I'll do it for me, not him."

Why would I have to spend some time in this book talking about what forgiveness is? This chapter is necessary because most people, even those who are Christian, have very little understanding of forgiveness. I have become aware of this fact in my working with people. I frequently ask my clients, who are Christian, what forgiveness is. Many have no answer at all!

When was the last time you heard a sermon on what forgiveness is? I am not saying a sermon on reasons to forgive, but one that discusses what forgiveness is. I have been a Christian for a long time and have been in a church most of my life, but I cannot remember even one sermon that explained what forgiveness is. This is a sad commentary on our churches today and is one of the major reasons I started writing this book. Knowing what forgiveness is does not mean that you forgive. Forgiveness has to be more than head knowledge! It has to be applied into every relationship you have.

If Christians don't know what forgiveness is, how can they talk about it? How can they teach others about it? It is not good enough to tell people they can be forgiven by God and go to heaven. You must be able to explain why they need forgiveness! You must be able to explain what forgiveness is in ways a non-Christian can understand! How much do you know about forgiveness? If you had to describe forgiveness to a person who had no Bible knowledge, how would you do it? How many verses do you know that speak about forgiveness? Knowing just John 3:16 is not enough! Am I making my point clear? It would be wise for seminaries to teach a course on forgiveness. A professor could easily come up with enough information to last a whole semester. One area where the knowledge of forgiveness is important is in the field of counseling. It bothers me, but does not surprise me, that many counselors have no idea what forgiveness is, how to teach it, or why it is even important.

Many people who come into my office have to forgive people from their pasts. I feel sorry for those who are burdened by the effects of sin and guilt and turn to non-Christian professionals! These non-Christian professionals will never bring up the idea of forgiveness. You may think that I am taking a tough stand, and you're right. Without knowing Jesus, counselors of all degrees (M.A., Ph.D., M.D.) know nothing of lasting eternal value! I grieve for people who need forgiveness but turn to sources that steer them away from it! I am not saying the whole process of counseling is one of forgiveness, but forgiveness is a crucial part of counseling for anyone who is dealing with issues from the past.

Paul wrote in 2 Corinthians 4:4, "The god of this age has blinded the minds of unbelievers, so that they cannot see the light of the gospel of the glory of Christ, who is the image of God." I believe this verse is appropriate when it comes to the topic of forgiveness and psychology. Only Christians can adequately teach people to forgive themselves and others. Non-Christians may be able to understand some aspects of forgiveness, but they are not able to understand in such a way that they can teach it to others. The only way you gain this understanding is through a personal relationship with Jesus!

To make my point more clear about psychology's lack of understanding of forgiveness, look in any abnormal psychology book's index under forgiveness. It is seldom found. Page after page is written about guilt and how to get rid of it. Forgiveness is not even mentioned as a way to get rid of guilt. Secular psychologists explain this lack of writing about forgiveness by saying they use the "medical model." If this is true, then this medical model is a non-Christian model, and inadequate to deal with many of the problems man has!

Why is it important to understand forgiveness? There will come a time in your life where you will need to forgive! There will come a time in your life when someone will ask you what forgiveness is. If you don't tell them, who will? 2 Corinthians 5:20 says, "We are Christ's ambassadors, as though God were making his appeal through us." God's appeal is for all people everywhere to accept Christ as Lord and Savior (John 6:40). If people don't understand forgiveness, then how are they going to accept God's salvation? As Christ's ambassadors we must learn as much about forgiveness as possible. This is one of the important reasons Christians need to read, study and know the Bible.

Most Christians do not study God's word the way they should (Josh 1:8-9). It should be studied day and night. Most Christians today are "Bible illiterates" spending almost no time in the word of God. This is the major reason Christians have a difficult time describing forgiveness. One of these days God will ask why we didn't read his word. God will not accept the fact we thought other things were more important; that there was no time in our schedule to read God's word; that we thought the Bible was too difficult to understand; that we thought the Bible was an outdated book.

Greek words used in the New Testament for forgiveness are:

aphiemi: To send forth, forsake, lay aside, leave, let (alone, be, go), omit, yield up, remit, put (send) away
apoluo: To free fully, relieve, dismiss, release, let die, pardon, divorce, set at liberty.
charizomai: To grant a favor, freely give (grant), deliver.

In the New International Version of the Bible the word "forgive" appears 74 times. The word "forgiveness" appears 14 times. The word "forgiven" appears 45 times. The word "forgave" appears 7 times. The word "forgiving" appears 7 times. The word "forgives" appears 3 times.

Walter Wangerin, Jr. writes:

> Forgiveness is a sort of divine absurdity. It is irrational, as the world reasons things, and unwise. But 'has not God made the foolish the wisdom of the world?' It is a miracle maker, because it causes things to be that, logically, empirically, have no right to be. For-give-ness is a holy, complete, unqualified giving.[2]

Let's begin our journey into understanding forgiveness by learning eleven simple definitions of forgiveness.

Simple Definition # 1: **Grace**
Proverbs 3:34

Paul is my favorite writer on grace in the New Testament. Consider two of the things he wrote about grace. "For it is by grace you have been saved, through faith — and this is not from yourselves, it is the gift of God — not by works, so that no one can boast" (Eph 2:8). "I thank Christ Jesus our Lord, who has given me strength, that he considered me faithful, appointing me to his service. Even though I was once a blasphemer and a persecutor and a violent man, I was shown mercy because I acted in ignorance and unbelief. The grace of our Lord was poured out on me abundantly, along with the faith and love that are in Christ Jesus" (1 Tim 1:12-14). An acrostic definition for grace is:

God's
Rare
And
Complete
Endowment (gift)

God: the author and provider of forgiveness (Exod 34:6-7).

Rare: because forgiveness is precious and not very abundant in this world (Eph 1:7).

Complete: because Jesus did everything needed to give man forgiveness from God (John 19:30).

Endowment: forgiveness is a gift from God that cannot be earned, or worked for (Rom 5:17; 6:23; Eph 2:8; Acts 5:31). The word "endowment" means "a gift that does not have to be repaid." It is vitally important for Christians to know what grace is so that when Satan comes to battle them, he cannot outwit them with his schemes (2 Cor 2:11).

The Greek word for grace is **charis**. It means to bestow pleasures on, delight or favorable regard. It is the root of **charizomai**, which means to show or grant kindness to. **Charizomai** is also one of the New Testament Greek words for forgiveness.

Grace is when God gives man what he does not deserve. Mercy is when God does not give to man what he does deserve! In Psalm 103:10 we read, "He does not treat us as our sins deserve or repay us according to our iniquities." Many places in Scripture describe God as gracious (Exod 34:6; Neh 9:17; Ps 86:15; 103:8; 145:8; Joel 2:13; Jonah 4:2). John 1:14 says Jesus was full of grace and truth. The word "grace" comes from the same root as the word "gracious." In Romans 5:20 Paul wrote, "The law was added so that the trespass might increase. But where sin increased, grace increased all the more."

Another definition of grace would be the undeserved love and salvation God gives to man. According to Romans 6:23 people deserve to die because of their sins. Instead of death God gives the gift of eternal life in Jesus Christ.

Grace is a teacher (Titus 2:11-12). "It teaches us to say "No"! to ungodliness..." Grace is what teaches people the value God has for them. Grace is one of the most misunderstood concepts about forgiveness. Many people say they don't think it is fair for people who have not been Christians very long to go to heaven. Their statements may sound like this: "I have been a Christian all of my life and I've worked very hard on my faith and salvation. It is just not fair for Joe, who has lived such a sinful life, to go to heaven too."

The diagram below will explain one of the confusing aspects of understanding grace.

Birth ▸————————▸ Baptism ▸————————▸ Death
   (Grace)   (Performance)
Ephesians 2:8-9   Matthew 18:32-35

Between birth and baptism, Christians accept the fact that their salvation rests solely on God's grace. They accept the fact that their past sins (those before baptism) have been forgiven by grace. They accept this belief because it is impossible to go back into the past and correct sins. Between baptism and death, a lot of people forget about grace and believe forgiveness now rests on performance. This "performance salvation" idea creates a lack of spiritual security. Its main belief is that after baptism, salvation now depends on performances and behaviors, not on God's grace. There is no manual to say what these performances are and if they change from day to day. So, in actuality, salvation then becomes a guessing game. These people hope they select and do behaviors that please God.

One major flaw in this theology is that if people are not pleased with their behavior, they assume God is not pleased. Their confidence in their salvation then is based on how they feel about their performance that given day. Feelings change all the time. Isaiah 32:10-11 states, "In little more than a year you who feel secure will tremble; the grape harvest will fail, and the harvest of fruit will not come. Tremble, you complacent women; shudder, you daughters who feel secure!..."

Satan uses the idea of performance salvation against us! Satan uses Bible verses to get people to believe in performance salvation. In Matthew 4:6 Satan quoted Scripture to Jesus. I am assuming he also knows the New Testament. Christians should hold on to what the Bible teaches so that Satan cannot come and steal it away.

Simple Definition # 2: **Voluntary Debt Cancellation**
Matthew 18:21-35; Luke 7:36-50; John 10:18

This is an easy way to understand forgiveness, because most people understand what debts are. To give you a graphic image of this kind of forgiveness, let me tell you what a mechanic did for me right after Christmas of 1989. I had just spent $900.00 fixing my car. I had put on new shocks and struts and replaced part of my transmission. Less than one week after this work had been done, my car was totalled in a wreck. When my mechanic, who is a strong Christian, found out what had happened to my car, he cancelled the debt on the labor part of the bill. I did not ask him to do this. I was quite surprised when he did. He "forgave" my debt because of the relationship we have and because he loves the Lord.

What is the debt Jesus paid for us? (1 Cor 6:19-20). He gave his life as the full payment for your debt of sin. The idea of "debt" coincides with Jesus' teaching in Matthew

214

6:12 (KJV) when Jesus prayed "forgive us our debts." The "year of cancelling debts" in Deuteronomy 15:1-3 relates to this definition of forgiveness. The creditor had to cancel the debts of a fellow Israelite every seven years. The "year of Jubilee" mentioned in Leviticus 25:8-54 emphasized the debt concept of forgiveness. Leviticus 25:10-12 states, "Consecrate the fiftieth year and proclaim liberty throughout the land to all its inhabitants. It shall be a jubilee for you; each one of you is to return to his family property and each to his own clan. The fiftieth year shall be a jubilee for you; do not sow and do not reap what grows of itself or harvest the untended vines. For it is a jubilee and is to be holy for you; eat only what is taken directly from the fields."

Simple Definition # 3: **Being Made Alive Again**
Ephesians 2:1-5; Luke 15:11-32

This simple definition of forgiveness is an easy way to understand forgiveness because all people are familiar with death and birth. John 5:24 mentions this same simple definition: "I tell you the truth, whoever hears my word and believes him who sent me has eternal life and will not be condemned; he has crossed over from death to life."

I have a personal story about this type of forgiveness. Back when I was in high school, I did something during Halloween that created a stir in my family. In fact, I was lucky that what I did was kept out of the paper. When my parents found out what I did, they made me go over to the police department to explain my actions. Confession is good for the soul! I went over on a Saturday morning, feeling sure I would be grounded for a long time when I got home. The day I told the police was also my bowling league day. I was sure I could forget bowling for the rest of the year. But, to my surprise, after I told the police what I did, my dad let me go bowling and my deed was never mentioned in the house again, though every family member knew about it. It was not even mentioned when I did other things wrong! This was my greatest forgiveness experience from human sources. Because of this I have never doubted the fact that my family loves me. 1 Peter 4:8 applies to me in this case: "Love covers a multitude of sins." I am glad it does! Because of the forgiveness I experienced from my family, it was easy for me to believe God could forgive me.

Simple Definition # 4: **Going Beyond What Was Expected**
Luke 10:25-37; 15:11-32

This is easy to relate to because we understand and want compassion. One more personal story will illustrate this style of forgiveness. My wife and I were traveling back from Lexington, Kentucky, to Indianapolis to visit her grandmother. Right before we entered Indiana my car had a flat tire. I tried, but I could not put the spare on. Janelle and I decided to walk to the nearest town, which was about five miles. Right after we started walking, an elderly couple stopped and picked us up. They told us they had never picked up anyone before. They drove us to a local convenience store. I made calls to get the tire fixed. The problem was we were in Indiana, my car was in Ohio and the tow truck was coming from Kentucky. A local policeman drove us back to the car even though he was not supposed to cross the state line. When we got to the car, the truck from the garage was already there and the tire was fixed. I had very little cash with me to pay the bill. When the time came to pay the bill, the repair man felt sorry for us and only charged us a very small amount.

In the parable of the good Samaritan (Luke 10:25-37), of the three people in the story, which one did the Jews expect to be called good? The Jewish people expected the good guy to be a Jew. It made them mad when Jesus made the hero a Samaritan. This story tells us that our neighbor is anyone who is in need or hurting.

216

In the parable of the prodigal son, the younger son expected his father to make him a hired servant, not reinstate him as a son (Luke 15:21). Even though the son had a good knowledge of the love his father had for him, this act of going beyond what was expected no doubt surprised the son. The older brother was angry at both his brother and father. He was angry at the brother for coming back. He was angry at his father for taking his brother back.

The above parables teach us that mercy needs to be extended even if the injury is caused by the person's own negligence! James 2:12-13 would back up this belief. These two examples of "simple definition # 4" of forgiveness have several things in common:

1) Both "forgivers" were compassionate.
2) Both "forgivees" were at the mercy of the forgiver.
3) Both "forgivers" had to take action to complete the act of forgiveness (John 19:30).
4) The "forgivees" had to be willing to let the "forgivers" help them.

Simple Definition # 5: **Peace and Rejoicing**
Galatians 5:22

Thomas á Kempis said, "First keep peace within yourself, then you can also bring peace to others."

Peace is what all people search for and want. It is what people are seeking through tranquilizers and alcohol. Isaiah 57:2 promises, "Those who walk uprightly enter into peace; they find rest as they lie in death." Look at what Isaiah 26:3, 12; 32:17; 48:18; and 54:10 say about peace. Ephesians 2:15 explains, "...His purpose was to create in himself one new man out of the two, thus making peace." In John 14:27 Jesus says, "Peace I leave with you; my peace I give you. I do not give to you as the world gives. Do not let your hearts be troubled and do not be afraid." What kind of peace does the world give? Not a very complete one. Forgiveness is peace between man and God. It is peace between man and man. This definition is easy to comprehend because we understand war!

In John 16:20, 22 Jesus is speaking about mourning turning to rejoicing. This is a great description of forgiveness. Ironically in John 16 during the same time Jesus mentioned peace, he also mentioned his death. It was through his death that Jesus brought about us having peace with God. How did Jesus' death bring peace? When Jesus died on Calvary he met the Old Testament's requirement for sins to be forgiven. His death made us alive. It is fascinating to realize that when God saw Jesus on the cross at Calvary, he saw us on the cross. Now when God looks at us today, he sees Jesus! Paul writes in Ephesians 2:14-15 that when Jesus died, he destroyed the wall of hostility between us and God.

Simple Definition # 6: **Love**
Galatians 5:22

Paul writes in Galatians 5:22 that love is part of the fruit of the Spirit. It is also a definition of forgiveness. Paul writes to the Corinthian Church, "If anyone has caused grief, he has not so much grieved me as he has grieved all of you, to some extent — not to put it too severely. The punishment inflicted on him by the majority is sufficient for him. Now instead, you ought to forgive and comfort him, so that he will not be overwhelmed by excessive sorrow. I urge you, therefore, to reaffirm your love for him" (2 Cor 2:5-8).

Christians have a rare opportunity to teach others about Jesus and God when they show love and forgiveness. Forgiveness means giving up your right to seek revenge or to get even for what the person did to you. You give up your right to seek what is "fair." If we received what was "fair" from God, we would all be headed for hell and Jesus would not have died on Calvary.

The most well known verse in the Bible is probably John 3:16 — "For God so loved the world that he gave his only begotten son, that whosoever believes in him should not perish but have everlasting life" (NKJV). Love is the reason Jesus died for our sins. Love is a simple definition of forgiveness. It was not nails that kept Christ on the cross — it was love!

In 1 Peter 4:8 it states that love covers a multitude of sins. This is what Jesus did on Calvary. He became our sin covering. In 1 John 4:16 we are told, "And so we know and rely on the love God has for us." It is through his love that God forgave us, and we must learn to trust and rely on God to forgive us.

Simple Definition # 7: **Justified**
Romans 3:21-24

Justified: Definition — To be declared innocent; being made right before God; declared completely righteous in God's sight; "Just if I'd" never sinned. It is God making us acceptable to him. According to verse 24, grace is what justifies people! In Romans 4:25 we read, "He was delivered over to death for our sins and was raised to life for our justification." Acts 13:39 is my favorite verse about justification. It shows us the power that Jesus has to forgive: "Through him everyone who believes is justified from everything you could not be justified from by the law of Moses."

Paul, in Romans and Galatians, writes a lot about justification.

He claimed we are justified freely (Rom 3:24), that we are justified by faith (Rom 3:26), that we are justified by faith without observing the law (Rom 3:28), that Christians are justified by faith and we have peace with God (Rom 5:1). He wrote that Christians are justified by Jesus' blood (Rom 5:9). In Galatians 2:16 Paul declared Christians are justified through faith in Jesus. He also stated we are justified in Christ (Gal 2:17). He further maintained we are not justified by observing the law (Gal 3:11). Paul also taught that the law was there to lead us to Christ, so we could be justified through faith (Gal 3:24).

Simple Definition # 8: **Righteous**
Romans 4:24; Psalm 85:10-13

What does it mean to be righteous? Look at the first five letters of the word for a clue. It means to be "right" before God. The word "right" can be translated "correct." The Greek word for righteousness is *dikaiosune*, meaning a character or quality of being right or just.

In Romans 4, Paul uses the word *credited* linked to righteousness. The Greek word for credit is *logizomai*, meaning "to reckon." It is an accountant's term meaning "to make an entry in the account book." Looking at Romans 4:3, 4, 5, 9, 10, 11, 22, 23, 24, you will find that all of these verses deal with "credited righteousness."

Much is written in the Bible about righteousness. Paul writes to the Church at Rome, "For it is not those who hear the law who are righteous in God's sight, but it is those who obey the law who will be declared righteous" (Rom 2:13). This declaration, like the Declaration of Independence the United States signed against Britain, created a war. After a Christian is declared righteous by God, there is going to be a war with Satan!

It is only by God that people are declared righteous. Paul writes in Romans 3:10, "There is no one righteous, not even one." This is very similar to what God said through Isaiah in Isaiah 64:6, "All of us have become like one who is unclean, and all our righteous acts are like filthy rags; we all shrivel up like a leaf, and like the wind our sins sweep us away." According to this passage, man's righteous acts are dirty to God.

Isaiah 42:6 speaks about righteousness when it says, "I, the Lord, have called you in righteousness; I will take hold of your hand. I will keep you and will make you to be a covenant for the people and a light for the Gentiles." Later in Isaiah 61:10 Isaiah says, "I delight greatly in the Lord; my soul rejoices in my God. For he has clothed me with garments of salvation and arrayed me in a robe of righteousness...." Christians need to remember continually that they have been clothed in Christ and they are righteous in God's sight (Gal 3:27; Rom 13:14). Righteousness has several fruits. Some of them are peace, quietness and confidence (Isa 32:17).

Solomon wrote in Proverbs 28:1 that "the righteous are as bold as a lion." We should be bold because we have God on our side. Solomon wrote in Proverbs 11:6 that "The righteousness of the upright delivers them, but the unfaithful are trapped by evil desires." He also wrote that righteous people will be rescued from trouble (Prov 11:8).

Simple Definition # 9: **Reconciliation**
2 Corinthians 5:18-21

There are two Greek words for reconcile in the New Testament. One Greek word for reconcile is *allasso* (found 6 times in the New Testament), which means "an alteration or change." The Greek word *apokatallasso* stresses the meaning of a complete restoring (Eph 2:16; Col 1:20, 21). Reconciliation means the restoring of peace and friendship by settling any differences. Reconciliation can also be defined as "to change or make an adjustment."

In banking terms reconciliation means to balance. Reconciliation is being drawn back into an acceptable (balanced) relationship with God! Reconciliation was prophesied in Daniel 9:24 — "Seventy 'sevens' are decreed for your people and your holy city to finish transgression, to put an end to sin, to atone for wickedness, to bring in everlasting righteousness..."

Paul wrote in 2 Corinthians 5:18 about reconciliation, "All this is from God, who reconciled us to himself through

Christ and gave us the ministry of reconciliation. Paul describes reconciliation as God not counting man's sins against him (2 Cor 5:19). Jesus taught that reconciliation between brothers should occur before an offering is given to God (Matt 5:24).

In Romans 5:10 Paul wrote, "For if, when we were God's enemies, we were reconciled to him through the death of his Son, how much more, having been reconciled, shall we be saved through his life!" The cross was the instrument of God's reconciliation (Eph 2:16). It was the shed blood of Jesus that brought peace and reconciliation between God and man (Col 1:20).

Most of these verses have a common phrase, "through Christ" or "in Christ." This is how reconciliation occurs. It is through Christ that we are saved. Jesus said in John 14:6, "I am the way and the truth and the life. No one comes to the Father except **through** me." Jesus is the gateway to salvation and reconciliation (John 10:7).

Simple Definition # 10: **Atonement**
Romans 3:25; 1 John 2:2; 4:10; Exodus 30:15; 2 Chronicles 29:24; Daniel 9:24

At times the word "atonement" is used in some translations to mean reconciliation or propitiation. In the Old Testament the Hebrew word for atonement is *kippur*. This word and related words are found over 150 times in the Old Testament. The Arabic root of this word means "to cover or conceal." (See Leviticus chapters 4, 14 and 16.) Atonement is an act of making amends, restoring harmony or making a payment for wrongs between people who are at odds. The Hebrew word "Kippur" literally means covering. (See Leviticus 4:26.) Psalm 85:2-3 says, "You forgave the iniquity of your people and covered all their sins. You set aside all your wrath and turned from your fierce anger." This is atonement.

The New Testament uses the same word for atonement, reflecting the Old Testament meaning (Rom 3:25; Heb 2:17; 9:5; 1 John 2:2, 4:10). A good definition of atonement is "At-One-Ment," or being united with Christ again. In some translations the word "propitiation" is used instead of atonement. In Greek culture this word conveyed the idea of acting in such a way as averting the terrible destruction of God. Possibly even winning God's favor. Propitiation means the turning away of wrath with a gift of offering (Prov 21:14). Each year there was a set Day of Atonement (Lev 16:29). In this chapter the "scapegoat" is mentioned. Another name for this goat was, "the goat of removal" (Lev 16:8, 10, 20-22, 26). This goat was to symbolically carry all of Israel's sins into the desert. What did the priest have to do after he performed this ceremony with the goat? He had to wash his clothes and bathe himself with water (Lev 16:26). This sounds like baptism.

Paul, in 2 Corinthians 2:12-3:18, wrote that Christians are ministers of the new covenant. This new covenant is a new way of gaining forgiveness. Blood is required in both of these covenants (Heb 9:14, 22; Eph 1:7; 1 John 1:7; Rev 1:5). The difference in the covenants is the frequency of sacrifice, as well as the kind of sacrifice required. In Hebrews 9:26 we read, "Then Christ would have had to suffer many times since the creation of the world. But now he has appeared once for all at the end of the ages to do away with sin by the sacrifice of himself." Hebrews 10:10 tells us, "And by that will, we have been made holy through the sacrifice of the body of Jesus Christ once for all."

Simple definition # 11: **Freedom**
Psalm 142:7

Do we really understand what freedom is? Even though we hear this word in our society, I doubt whether we really understand what it means to be free. More than likely, you have never been physically enslaved! Jesus had a hard time explaining freedom to the Jewish leaders for this very reason (John 8:31-47). The Jewish leaders did not realize that they were prisoners (8:33). The Jews did know freedom was the opposite of slavery, but they did not know that they needed to be freed (John 8:33). The word "pardon" might be linked with freedom. The word means to release from further punishment; or to cancel or not exact punishment (2 Chr 30:18; Isa 55:7; Joel 3:21).

Forgiveness is freedom from the vertical consequences of sin — the ones between God and man. Isaiah 59:2 gives some of these consequences: "But your iniquities have separated you from your God; your sins have hidden his face from you, so that he will not hear." Forgiveness is freedom from the past and its control. Forgiveness is freedom from the chains that keep us from being what God intends. Freedom is the butterfly being released from the cocoon.

Forgiveness by God can (but not always) erase the horizontal consequences of sin — the ones between man to man; as well as the physical consequences caused by their sin. The horizontal consequences may be fines ordered to be paid, or imprisonment. The physical consequences may be physical scars, maiming, etc.

Here are a few verses that describe man's condition before forgiveness:

2 Peter 2:19; Romans 6:6, 14, 16-17 — We are a slave to what has mastered us.

Romans 7:23 — We are a prisoner of sin.

Romans 6:12; Psalm 66:18 — Sin reigns in our mortal bodies.

Many verses in the Bible discuss the issue of freedom. Some of them are:

Galatians 5:1: "It is for freedom that Christ has set us free. Stand firm, then, and do not let yourselves be burdened again by a yoke of slavery."

John 8:36: "So if the Son sets you free, you will be free indeed."

Romans 8:21: I love the word Paul chooses to describe freedom: He says it is glorious freedom. He also states we are brought into this freedom.

Galatians 2:4: Paul writes there were some who were trying to spy on this freedom and trying to make him a slave again.

James 1:25; 2:12: says the law gives freedom.

Psalm 142:7: David asks to be set free from his prison.

Psalm 146:7: David wrote that the Lord sets prisoners free.

Ezekiel 46:17: There was a year of freedom commanded in the Old Testament.

Jeremiah 34:17: God proclaims a strange freedom to those who did not obey him. God says these people have freedom to fall by the sword, plague and famine. How many people in the world are making this kind of choice today?

Freedom is never free. Someone had to pay the price for the freedom we experience. 1 Corinthians 6:20 tells us that, "You were bought at a price." The price was the death of Jesus. To free us from sin, God had to make the perfect sacrifice available to man. According to the law, the sacrifice had to be without blemish and defect (Lev 22:21-22; Num 19:2). In the Old Testament, animal sacrifice was an annual event. In Hebrews 10:3-4 we read, "But those sacrifices are an annual reminder of sins, because it is impossible for the blood of bulls and goats to take away sins." God had to come up with the perfect sacrifice for sin. He did; it was his only Son. In what way did Jesus meet the criteria for sacrifice? 1 Peter 1:18-19 gives us the answer. "For you know that it was not with perishable things such as silver or gold that you were redeemed from the empty way of life handed down to you from your forefathers, but with the precious blood of Christ, a lamb without blemish or defect. Exodus 12:5 describes how the lamb that was selected to be sacrificed had to be without defect. Its blood was then put on the doorframes to protect the house from the angel of death.

The forgiveness God has for man was almost impossible for God to give. It took such a drastic step as sending his own Son to die on a cross. This was a death without any dignity! Deuteronomy 21:23 states, "...anyone who is hung on a tree is under God's curse." Jesus became our curse so we could become clean in the sight of God. Jesus died so that he could present a "radiant church, without stain or wrinkle or any other blemish, but holy and blameless" to God (Eph 5:27). Because of Jesus' sacrifice we are holy and without blemish and free of accusation in the sight of God (Col 1:22). Christ has set Christians free from the law of sin and death (Rom 8:2).

If you take John 14:6 and combine it with John 8:32, you will have this statement: "If you know me as your Lord and Savior you shall be free." For one to proclaim freedom there must be authority. Jesus has the authority. In Matthew 9:6 (Mark 2:10; Luke 5:24) we find, "But so that you may know that the Son of Man has authority on earth to forgive sins..." This verse shows us that Jesus has authority to free us from the bondage of sin. If you take the first six letters of the word "authority" you get "author." Jesus and God are the authors of the forgiveness plan, so who better to carry it out? Matthew 9:8 tells us that when the crowd saw the authority God had given to this man (Jesus) they were filled with awe and praised God. Wouldn't it be nice if our churches today were filled with awe when a person repents and accepts God as Savior?

Jesus frees Christians from:
> The consequences of sin (Rom 6:23).
> Guilt that is the result of sin (Heb 10:2).

Hell (Rev 1:18).

The power of the devil (1 John 4:4).

Shame of past sins (2 Pet 1:9).

Now that you have read about the eleven simple definitions of forgiveness, let's look at single verse definitions of forgiveness. Following are some verses that provide short definitions of one or more aspects of forgiveness. The verses draw a "visual" definition that is easy to remember and teach. Let's look at an acrostic using the word "forgiveness":

F ellowship
O pportunity
R eadily
G iven
I n
V ictorious
E ncounters
N urturing
E very
S inful
S oul

Fellowship: God wants to restore our relationship.

Opportunity: A point in time when something good can happen.

Readily Given: God does this voluntarily.

In Victorious Encounters: In successful engagements with us.

Nurturing: Causing something to grow.

Every Sinful Soul: God makes salvation available for everyone.

Some Old Testament visual verses on forgiveness

Job 14:16-17 — not keeping track of sin; offenses sealed in a bag; covering over of sin.

Psalm 32:1 — blessing; sins are covered. R. A. Torrey said, "I am ready to meet God face to face tonight and look into those eyes of infinite holiness, for all my sins are covered by the atoning blood."

Psalm 32:2 — blessed; God not counting man's sins against him.

Psalm 51:2 — washing away of iniquity (guilt, sin); cleansing from sin. The Greek word for clean is **katharos** meaning to free from impurity (John 13:10-11; Lev 16:30).

Psalm 103:12 — removal of our transgressions as far as the east is from the west. Have you ever tried to figure out how far God removes your sins from you? It is immeasurable!

Isaiah 1:18 — sins being made white as snow; sins being made as white as wool.

Isaiah 4:4 — washing away the filth; cleansing the blood stain.

Isaiah 6:7 — guilt taken away; sins atoned for (Ps 65:3).

Isaiah 38:17 — God puts our sins behind his back; keeping me from the pit of destruction; love. (Remember that once God forgives us, he never looks back at our sins again!) See Psalms 40:2 and 103:12.

Isaiah 43:25 — forgiven for his sake; God not remembering our sins, which are blotted out and forgotten. This idea of God not remembering our past forgiven sins is mentioned several times in the Bible (Ezek 8:22; 31:34; Ps 25:11; 79:9; Heb 8:12; 10:17). This is an interesting verse because it shows that God gains something when he forgives us and we are forgiven. What could he gain? He gains or regains a relationship with us when he forgives us.

Remember that sin has put a barrier between us and God (Isa 59:2). Forgiveness restores the relationship that sin separated!

A short poem will help to convey the idea of God forgetting sin.

> Constantly remembering things I should forget.
> Constantly hearing, seeing, feeling deep within
>   things I want to forget.
> Constantly sad, sorry, feeling always guilty about
>   things I won't forget.
> Constantly waiting, wanting, feeling tormented,
>   punished for things I don't forget.
> Lord — come be my constant memory.
> Help me hear you, see you, feel you,
> Lord — come take away my guilt and sit with me
>   while I wait... Comfort me.
> Lord — help me remember that you forget.
>   H.C.

Isaiah 44:22 — sins are swept away like clouds and morning mist; being redeemed (Ps 130:7). It is almost like God has a "Magna Doodle™," and when we make a mistake, he sweeps it away as if it never existed. It is important to realize that your sins were erased by love and God's grace.

Isaiah 61:1 — bind the broken hearted; free the captives; release the prisoners.

Micah 7:19 — treading our sins under foot; hurling our sins into the depths of the sea; compassion.

Zechariah 3:4 — removing the filthy clothes; taking away of sin; putting on rich garments (Col 3:10, 12).

Zechariah 13:1 — cleansing from sin and impurity (Ezek 36:25).

Some New Testament visual verses on forgiveness

Luke 1:77 (KJV) – remission of sins.

John 5:24 – eternal life; no condemnation; crossing over from death to life. The Greek word for condemnation in this passage is *krisis*, meaning a passing of judgment upon.

John 8:32, 36 – freedom (see Rom 8:2). The Greek word for freedom used here is *eleutheroo*: meaning deliverance from sin.

Acts 3:19 – sins being wiped out; a time of refreshing from the Lord.

Romans 5:1 – peace with God. The Greek word used here is *eirene*. It means to have a harmonious relationship with.

Romans 6:6 – old self is crucified; sin rendered powerless.

Romans 6:18 – set free from sin; becoming a slave to righteousness (Rev 1:5).

Romans 6:23 – a gift of eternal life in Christ Jesus.

Romans 8:1 – no condemnation.

1 Corinthians 6:10 – inheritance into the kingdom.

1 Corinthians 6:11 – washing; justified; sanctified.

1 Corinthians 15:57 – victory through Christ.

2 Corinthians 5:19 – not counting our sins against us; reconciling the world to himself.

2 Corinthians 5:21 – becoming the righteousness of God.

Galatians 1:4 – rescued from the present evil age; the will of God.

Galatians 2:20 – Christ living in us; God giving himself up for us.

Galatians 2:21 – grace of God; can't be earned.

Galatians 3:14 – redemption; receiving the promise of the Spirit.

Galatians 5:1 — being set free by Christ.

Ephesians 1:7 — riches of his grace; redeemed by his blood.

Ephesians 2:6 — being raised up with Christ; seated with him in the heavenly realms.

Ephesians 2:8 — grace; gift of God (a gift can be rejected).

Ephesians 2:9 — something that can't be earned.

Ephesians 2:13 — brought near to God through the blood of Jesus.

Ephesians 2:14 — peace; making the two one; destroying the wall of hostility.

Colossians 1:12 — qualified to share in the inheritance of the saints.

Colossians 1:13 — brought out of darkness; rescued us from the dominion of darkness; being brought into the kingdom of God.

Colossians 1:14 — redemption; bought back. The Greek word *exagorazo* is the word "redeemed". It means to buy out, to purchase a slave with the view of freeing him, to release upon the receipt of ransom, or to deliver from physical torture.

Colossians 1:20 — peace through blood shed on the cross; reconciliation.

Colossians 2:13 — alive with Christ.

Colossians 2:14 — canceling the written code; nailing the law to the cross.

Hebrews 1:3 — Jesus Christ providing purification from sin.

Hebrews 9:15 — eternal inheritance; being set free from sin.

Hebrews 10:18 — no longer any need for sacrifices.

Hebrews 10:22 — cleansed from a guilty conscience; having our bodies washed with pure water (Ezek 36:33).

1 Peter 2:24 — healed; dead to sin; alive to righteousness.

We have just over fifty single verse ideas of forgiveness. They are easy to understand and teach because they use words that we can comprehend. They use words non-Christians can comprehend. This being true, what makes understanding forgiveness so difficult? Below are seven possible reasons.

1. The person's past experiences.

One problem in understanding forgiveness comes from the past. People tend to draw a comparison between the people in their lives and God. This comparison is usually based on a father or other significant male in the person's life. This is one of the reasons people have to struggle to understand the idea of a loving God. If they have not been loved by their earthly father, they are going to have a difficult time understanding and accepting love from their heavenly Father! I see this problem frequently. If you have not been forgiven by the significant people in your past, you are going to have a difficult time believing that God forgives. You may think, "If the imperfect people in my life have not forgiven me how can God, who is perfect, forgive me?" If the people in your past have forgiven you, but occasionally bring the event back to memory and use it as a weapon, you will expect God to do the same thing. Many times I hear the statement, "I can forgive, but I cannot forget." When this statement is heard frequently, we expect God to do the same thing. This statement means I forgive you for what you have done, but I have permission to bring it up to you over and over again. How can God forgive you when you don't forgive yourself?

2. Making forgiveness a feeling.

Another problem with understanding forgiveness is that people frequently attempt to make it a feeling. For-

232

giveness is **NOT** a feeling! Being forgiven has nothing to do with how you feel. This is one of Satan's favorite deceptions. God's forgiveness is full, free, and finished (John 19:30), but it is not a feeling.

People want to make it a feeling because they are trying to put a measurement on it, to guarantee it is there. Notice that in the above verses about forgiveness, there is nothing about its being a feeling. Forgiveness for a Christian is a spiritual fact. People ask me all the time what forgiveness feels like. I don't know what it feels like because it is not a feeling! Forgiveness based on feeling will never last and will cause spiritual confusion and frustration. In all my years as a Christian counselor I have never had anyone satisfactorily tell me what forgiveness feels like. Jesus tells us in Matthew 9:2, "Your sins are forgiven." He did **not** say you will **feel** forgiven!

There are two basic problems with making forgiveness a feeling:

1. *Feelings change very rapidly*. You can read the front page of the newspaper and be depressed and then turn to the comics and laugh.

2. *Making forgiveness a feeling greatly cheapens what forgiveness really is*. It takes away the reason Jesus died. Jesus did not feel like dying for mankind. No, he chose to die for mankind!

3. Low self-esteem.

Another major problem with understanding, accepting, and offering forgiveness is low self-esteem. I work with a lot of folks who believe they are not worthy of being forgiven (Ps 77:2). It is God who designated the value of man on the cross at Calvary. God is the one who makes people worthy of forgiveness, through what his Son did at Calvary. Yet, low self-esteem is one of the reasons people do not forgive themselves. They don't believe that they deserve it. It is true that no one deserves forgiveness. Instead, God allows forgiveness because of what he has done. Earnie Larsen in *From Anger to Forgiveness* writes, "In a very real sense, healthy self-esteem is the seedbed of truly healing forgiveness."[3]

Low self-esteem is one of the major factors in the failure of relationships. Low self-esteem also puts a big block in our relationship with God. It hinders our prayers and interferes with fellowship.

Low self-esteem is not a good witness. Picture this: when people are explaining to you about becoming a Christian and you ask them if they like themselves, they answer that they are totally worthless and they don't like themselves. I seriously doubt you would run down to the front of the church and accept Christ because of their attitudes about themselves. For more information about self-esteem, see chapter five in this book on the 24 steps of healing from bitterness, and look up step number 7.

4. The awkwardness of receiving gifts.

Another problem with understanding and accepting forgiveness is that adults are terrible at receiving gifts and compliments. Forgiveness is the ultimate gift and compliment from God (Eph 2:8). Gifts to adults make them think, "What does he want?" or "What has he done now?" (This usually does not hold true during the three major gift days — birthday, anniversary and Christmas.) If people are terrible receivers of simple gifts, how are they going to accept the greatest gift of all — Jesus as the Lamb of God?

Many people have a difficult time receiving compliments. Watch how uncomfortable people are when you tell them that they look nice. If they cannot receive so simple a compliment, how are they going to be able to receive the greatest compliment of all — Jesus dying on a cross to save them from their sins and from themselves?

5. Lack of knowledge of the need for forgiveness, and the effects of sin.

People often do not accept forgiveness because they do not realize they need it. They don't recognize the consequences of sin: it has caused man to be under a curse. Jesus dealt with people like this all of the time. In John 8:31-41 Jesus is talking to the Jews who believed in him, telling them that the truth shall make them free. The problem they had with this was they did not know they were in bondage and in need of forgiveness.

Satan tells people lies about the need to be forgiven. He says if people live good lives and hurt no one, God will forgive them, allowing them to go to heaven. There are going to be many good people who will not end up in heaven because that is all they are — they are good people and not Christian. Jesus said in John 14:6 he was the only way to get to heaven. People believe that since their parents are Christian and since they go to church on an occasional Sunday, probably Christmas and Easter, they are going to heaven. This belief in a promise of heaven without commitment is not scriptural. Jesus said that if you want to get into heaven there is a cost associated with it (Matt 10:37-38; 16:24; Mark 8:34; Luke 9:23; 14:27).

What are the consequences of sin of which man might be unaware? Lamentations 3:39 asks why any living man should complain when he is punished for his sins! Ezekiel 18:30 indicates sin can be our downfall. Below you will find a summary of what sin has caused for man. In reading these verses you can understand why it took such a drastic step as Jesus coming to the earth and dying on a cross to forgive sin! Just how seriously does God take sin? Sin was the only thing that caused Jesus to be crucified on Calvary.

Sin has done a variety of things to man:

It has caused man to be kicked out of the garden of Eden (Gen 3:23).

It has caused women to experience increased pain in child-birth (Gen 3:15). I am assuming the physical pain all people experience is one of the consequences of sin.

It has caused woman to be ruled over by man (Gen 3:16).

It has caused man to work very hard for the things he needs to live (Gen 3:18).

It has caused people to experience death (Gen 3:19; Rom 6:23; Gen 7:21-23; Rom 5:12).

It has put a separation between man and God (Isa 59:2).

It has caused God to hide his face from man. It has stopped him from hearing prayers (Deut 1:45; 31:17-18; Isa 57:17; 59:2).

It greatly displeases God (Isa 59:15).

It greatly angers God (Gen 32:9-10; Isa 57:17; Jer 17:4).

It causes the world to be under a curse (Deut 28:15-68).

It causes the world to become a prisoner (2 Pet 2:19).

It causes people not to prosper (2 Chr 24:20).

It has destroyed whole nations (Jer 12:17).

It has destroyed cities (Gen 19:12-13, 23-25).

It can deprive people of many good things (Jer 5:25).

It has made man and Satan mortal enemies (Gen 3:15).

It testifies against people (Isa 59:12).

It stops people from having peace (Isa 59:8).

It is a burden to God and wearies him (Isa 43:24).

Even if it is unknowingly committed, there is still guilt (Lev 4:13-15 & Num 15:22-29).

It makes people slaves (John 8:34).

It causes people to be punished (Isa 26:21; 57:17).

It puts people away from God (Eph 2:13).

It ensnares and holds people fast (Prov 5:22).

It will find people out (Num 32:23).

It is engraved on the heart (Jer 17:1).

It will cause people to lose their wealth (Jer 17:3).

It will cause people to lose their inheritance (Jer 17:4).

It will enslave people to their enemies (Jer 17:4).

It will kindle God's anger (Jer 17:4).

It will cause people to be destroyed (Ps 37:38).

It causes man to have a mind hostile to God (Rom 6:7).

A sinful mind is death (Rom 6:6).

Sin desires to master people (Gen 4:7).

Sin has bound people like a yoke (Lam 1:14).

It causes bitterness and hardships (Lam 3:5).

It weighs people down (Lam 3:7).

It brings disaster upon people (Isa 3:9).

God hates sin (Isa 61:8).

Sin will ruin and destroy (Mic 6:13).

Appetite will never be satisfied (Mic 6:14).

People will store things up for themselves, but not be able to save because of sin (Mic 6:14).

People will plant but not harvest (Mic 6:15).

People will press olives but not use the oil (Mic 6:15).

People will press grapes but not drink the wine (Mic 6:15).

Misfortune pursues the sinner (Prov 13:21).

Sinners will be destroyed (Ps 37:38).

People are snared by sin (Prov 29:6).

People are in bondage and are slaves to sin (2 Pet 2:19).

People are captive to sin (Acts 8:23).

A sinner's wealth is stored for the righteous (Prov 13:22).

Being cursed is one of the consequences of sin. Deuteronomy chapter 27 lists some of the things that will cause man to be under the curse of sin; verses are in parentheses.

(15) Cursed is the man who carves an image or idol.
(16) Cursed is the man who dishonors his father.
(17) Cursed is the man who moves his neighbor's boundary stone.
(18) Cursed is the man who leads the blind astray.
(19) Cursed is the one who withholds justice.
(20) Cursed is the man who sleeps with his father's wife.
(21) Cursed is the one who has sexual relationships with animals.
(22) Cursed is the man who sleeps with his sister.
(23) Cursed is the man who sleeps with his mother-in-law.
(24) Cursed is the one who kills his neighbor.
(25) Cursed is the one who accepts a bribe to kill.
(26) Cursed is the man who does not uphold the law.

God requires what punishment or penalty for sin? Leviticus 20:9-17 itemizes some of these:

(9) Cursing your parents: death (Deut 21:18-21).
(10) Adultery: both are put to death (Deut 22:22).
(11) Incest: both son and stepmother shall be put to death.
(12) sexual relations between father-in-law and daughter-in-law: both shall be put to death.
(13) male homosexuals shall be put to death.
(14) man marrying both mother and daughter: all shall be put to death.
(15) man having sexual relationships with an animal: both shall be put to death.
(16) woman having sexual relationships with an animal: both shall be put to death.

You may be thinking, "Those laws were valid only in the Old Testament" — remember what Jesus said, "Do not think that I have come to abolish the Law or the Prophets;

I have not come to abolish them but to fulfill them" (Matt 5:17). These laws still define sins.

6. Believing the cost of being forgiven is too great for what is gained.

Some people believe the cost is too great. They might say, "I don't want to give up all the fun that I am having here on earth for the Christian non-fun life." Jesus dealt with a man just like this in Luke 18:18-30. This man came asking about forgiveness — "What must I do to inherit eternal life?" The problem with this man was that he was looking for what he could do, and not at what God could do. I believe this is one of the major reasons people develop burnout from religion. They do all they can to be religious, but because they are not perfect, they soon quit. Jesus, in Matthew 16:24-26 asks, "What can a man give in exchange for his soul?" People ask the same question today, but they are afraid of the answer — so they don't listen to Jesus for his reply.

7. Difference in thought patterns between God and man.

People try to relate forgiveness to their own level instead of God's. In Isaiah 55:8 we read, "For my thoughts are not your thoughts, neither are your ways my ways." Micah 4:12 comments, "But they do not know the thoughts of the LORD; they do not understand his plan, he who gathers them like sheaves to the threshing floor" (Ps 92:5, 94:11; Ezek 18:29; Dan 4:37; Hos 14:9).

This difference in thinking pattern causes confusion. People always seem to have more questions about forgiveness than there are answers. The most frequently asked question is, "Why do I need to be forgiven?" This is the problem Jesus faced in John 3:1-15. Nicodemus comes at night to question Jesus about gaining eternal life. Jesus tells

Nicodemus he must be born again. Nicodemus automatically thinks of a physical birth and says "Surely I cannot enter a second time into my mother's womb to be born!" Jesus remarks in verse 12, "I have spoken to you of earthly things and you do not believe; how then will you believe if I speak of heavenly things?"

Paul communicates the same idea in 1 Corinthians 1:18-19 when he writes, "The message of the cross is foolishness to those who are perishing, but to us who are being saved it is the power of God." Paul later said "For the foolishness of God is wiser than man's wisdom, and the weakness of God is stronger than man's strength" (1 Cor 1:25).

Can you understand why Satan would like to take advantage of these problems in understanding forgiveness? He loves confusion. 2 Corinthians 4:4 tells us that "The god of this age (Satan) has blinded the minds of unbelievers, so that they cannot see the light of the gospel of the glory of Christ." Satan will try anything he possibly can to keep people away from the forgiving blood of Jesus. One of the things Satan does is to make forgiveness seem so complicated that people eventually give up and walk away. Forgiveness is a very simple concept, but with man's wisdom it becomes very cloudy. Jesus taught forgiveness to ordinary, unschooled men (Acts 4:13). These men are the reason you are a Christian! Being educated might make understanding forgiveness more difficult (Jer 6:10).

To show how simple forgiveness is to understand, let's look at two points:

1. Jesus taught forgiveness to children and they came to him. They receive gifts better (Mark 10:14-16).

2. Tax collectors and prostitutes accepted the way of righteousness before the chief priests and elders of the people did. Because of the awareness of their needs, they received the gift of forgiveness gratefully (Matt 21:31-32).

Theology, at times, seems to have created more questions then it has answered when it comes to God, the Bible and forgiveness. The more educated one becomes in theology the more difficult it makes the Jewish Carpenter's concepts.

Source Notes

1. Kenneth Kaunda, *The Riddle of Violence* (San Francisco: Harper and Row, 1980), p. 180.

2. Walter Wangerin, *As For Me and My House* (Nashville: Thomas Nelson Publishing, 1990), p. 79.

3. Earnie Larsen and Carol Larsen Hegarty, *From Anger to Forgiveness*, p. 134.

9

God's Steps to Forgiveness

"Forgiveness is the answer to the child's dream of a miracle by which
what is broken is made whole again, what is soiled is again made clean."
Dag Hammarskjold[1]

Love is the motivation that should compel you to forgive. Love for God
and his commands, and love for yourself (2 Cor 5:14; Matt 5:44; 1 Pet
4:8).

What makes forgiving so difficult? There are several
ways to answer this question. I believe there are at least
seven answers to this question.

1. *Because you are believing at least one of the twelve lies
Satan tells about forgiveness* (John 8:44). This is the leading reason people have a difficult time forgiving.

2. *Because you want the person who hurt you to suffer*.
When you want this, you are prolonging your suffering and
healing. Most people are unaware of this.

3. *Because you do not understand forgiveness from God's
point of view*. Too many people attempt to make forgiveness a feeling and not a spiritual fact. When you make for-

giveness a feeling, you take it out of God's hands and put it in your emotions. This is very dangerous.

Just because you remember your sins does not mean that they still exist. Remembering past forgiven sins often causes Christians to ask God to forgive them too many times for the same sin. They want to "feel" forgiven! They want to know by their emotions they are forgiven.

Acts 2:38 tell us what needs to be done to receive salvation: "Repent and be baptized, everyone of you, in the name of Jesus Christ for the forgiveness of your sins. And you will receive the gift of the Holy Spirit." (See Mark 16:15-16; Matt 28:19-20.) The Greek word for baptized there is **baptizo** meaning to dip, like for the dyeing of a garment. Baptism is essential for the forgiveness of sins between God and man. Paul in Romans 6:1-10 gives a beautiful description of what baptism is. He uses the phrases "buried with him through baptism"; "old self crucified"; and "died with Christ." Baptism will not make you **feel** different—it makes you different.

If you make forgiveness a feeling, you will constantly struggle with guilt and be insecure in your relationship with God. It is a fact that Christians are forgiven! T. Roland Philips said, "A Christian is not one who is seeking God's favor and forgiveness—he is one who has found them." Realize that when God gives his word he keeps it! (1 John 1:9). The reason this is so difficult to understand is because it is so simple. When a Christian sins, all he has to do is to confess it to God, and it is forgiven. Jesus taught this forgiveness concept to ordinary men and it changed the world (Acts 4:13). Jesus said that ordinary sinners would accept this concept before religious, educated sinners (Matt 21:31-32). What does God forgive? According to Jeremiah 31:34, God forgives wickedness. According to Exodus 34:7, God forgives wickedness, rebellion and sin. According to Psalm 32:5, God forgives guilt.

244

*4. Because you are still experiencing pain from what hap-
pened.* You probably don't want to forgive until all the
pain is relieved. It is important for you to understand that
forgiveness will help the pain go away!

*5. Because the person that hurt you has not asked for for-
giveness.* You believe that until they ask, you cannot possibly forgive. If they never ask, tell God that you forgive
them, and ask him to help you learn what forgiveness actually is. This is for your benefit. This will prevent bitterness.

6. Because you are being "self-protective." This is probably
one of the most common reasons for lack of forgiveness.
You see forgiveness as making yourself vulnerable to being
hurt again.

*7. Because forgiveness goes 100% against our human
nature.* Genesis 6:5 and 8:21 tell us that our nature is evil.
The nature of man is sinful (Eph 2:3). When a person has
been hurt their evil nature wants to get even. Forgiveness
to our human evil nature seems like spiritual stupidity.

As children grow up, they establish in their minds what
God is like. This is one of the reasons being a father is such
a difficult task; your children will compare God to you. If
the father is a good forgiver, then the child will be more
likely to accept forgiveness from the heavenly Father. It is
also during childhood that people learn what forgiveness
is. A professional basketball player made a commercial that
said, "I'm not a role model." What role models from
Scripture can be used to learn about forgiveness? Who can
people imitate? Ephesians 5:1 gives us these answers; the
best role model we can follow in his example of forgiveness is Jesus.

Two of the best earthly forgivers I have ever read about
are Jasper and Kathy Becker. Jasper Becker, a stepfather
whose daughter, Loren, was killed in an automobile acci-

dent said, "When you forgive someone, it isn't only a gift to that person. It's a gift to yourself. You forgive them for your own benefit. To heal your own wounds."

After Jorge had been arrested for the accident, Kathy, Loren's mom, "heard almost offhandedly that when Jorge was being questioned by police, he sat on the floor in a fetal position, rocking back and forth, while whispering that he wished he could give his own life for the one he took."

"'My heart just broke and softened when I heard that,' Kathy says. 'It was a spiritual, transcendent experience. I told the police to tell Jorge I love him. Suddenly a huge burden came out of my body. I felt lighter, better. I became happy again. I started to heal in that instant. It was contagious. My son, Jasper, Jorge, and Jorge's parents all began to heal. We became like an extended family.'"

"Once the Beckers forgave Jorge, and they saw how their burden had lifted, they wanted to share what they had learned about forgiveness with others. So, on November 2, 1991, they opened The Loren Quinn Institute (LQI) in an office park in Winter Park." This is a prime example of how the Lord would like to turn bad events into positive ministries.

"The Beckers attended Jorge's trial. They pleaded with the judge to show Jorge leniency. The judge was so impressed with their repeated appeals, he shortened Jorge's sentence to only six and a half months in jail. Kathy visited him there often. When he was released, he became like a beloved friend. 'He's studying to counsel children,' she says. 'He's very gentle. Handsome. He's just a beautiful child. Loren would have loved him.'"

"More than a year after LQI was founded, Kathy Becker and Jorge DeJesus appeared on the Maury Povich television show. They sat side by side, holding hands. Povich was aghast."

"'But, he killed your daughter!' he said."

"Kathy, a beautiful woman with short, brown hair, turned and looked at Jorge, a handsome youth with sad eyes, and said, 'I feel well because I forgave Jorge. Being hateful and unforgiving prevents healing.'"

"'It's a miracle,' said Jorge in an emotionless voice. 'Still, I wake up hurting inside. I thought I'd go to prison for life. I was terrified. Then she reached out to me.'"

"Povich stared in disbelief at the couple holding hands. 'I don't get it," he said. 'You hold his hand and he killed your daughter?' He shook his head. 'You're something else.'"

"'No, I'm not,' said Kathy Becker. 'I'm just another person.'"[2]

David is a good example of forgiveness:

❖ **1 Samuel 24:3-13:** David had a great chance to kill King Saul. He knew what the Lord wanted him to do, and he did it.

❖ **1 Samuel 26:12-25:** David again had a chance to kill Saul. He could have chosen to seek revenge on Saul, but he refrained.

❖ **2 Samuel 18:33:** David wished he would have died instead of his rebellious son Absalom.

Other good "forgivers":

❖ **Elisha** could have killed the men who were seeking to kill him (2 Kings 6:1-23).

❖ **Shadrach, Meshach** and **Abednego** could have been very angry at Nebuchadnezzar for throwing them into the fiery furnace, but they were not (Dan 3:1-30).

❖ The words **Stephen** said before his death, "Lord Jesus, receive my spirit. Lord, do not hold this sin against them," sound just like the words of Jesus while he was on the cross. Jesus said, "Father, forgive them, for they do not know what they are doing. Father, into your hands I commit my spirit" (Acts 6:8-15, 7:59-60; cf. Luke 23:34, 46).

❖ **Paul** is one of the best writers able to explain forgiveness. He understood it from a personal point of view. Paul was a murderer of Christians, who constantly had to face people that reminded him of his past (Acts 9:1-2; 2 Cor 11: 24-28). I believe that it was the guilt from his past that was his thorn in the flesh (2 Cor 12:8-9). Paul realized that God forgave him. He learned this on the road to Damascus (Acts 9).

❖ When **Joseph** met his brothers when they came asking for food, Joseph could have sent them away empty handed. Instead, he gave them forgiveness and food. He forgave his brothers when they did not even ask (Gen 37:1-36; 42:25-26; 45:14-15, 21-28). Joseph, like Daniel, is a good example of forgiveness. Daniel 2:13 and 6:16 tell about Daniel being unjustly persecuted. He was still very forgiving.

❖ Two interesting forgivers are **Moses** and **Paul**. Look at what Moses prays to God about his forgiving Israel's sin: "So Moses went back to the Lord and said, 'Oh, what a great sin these people have committed! They have made themselves gods of gold. But now, please forgive their sin – but if not, then blot me out of the book you have written'" (Exod 32:31-32). Paul writes, "For I could wish that I myself were cursed and cut off from Christ for the sake of my brothers, those of my own race, the people of Israel" (Rom 9:3-4). It appears that both of these people are willing to die so that their nation can go to heaven. Both of these people have traits similar to Jesus.

❖ **Barnabas** is a good example of forgiveness and a mediator in conflicts! Barnabas forgave Paul, encouraged him, and introduced him to the Church in Jerusalem (Acts 9:26-27). Saul and Barnabas went on missionary trips together (Acts 13:15).

Later on Barnabas and Paul got into a argument about taking John Mark on a missionary trip. Paul refused to forgive John Mark. Barnabas split with Paul and took John and sailed to Cyprus (Acts 15:36-41). Later Paul and John Mark were reconciled (2 Tim 4:9-13).

❖ Another good teacher of forgiveness is the **Samaritan woman** that Jesus met at the well (John 4). Many people believed in Jesus because of what she had told them. In John 4:42 we read, "They said to the woman, 'We no longer believe just because of what you said; now we have heard for ourselves, and we know that this man really is the Savior of the world.'" Forgiveness in this case is contagious. She had to tell others what she had seen, heard and received. This is the way it should be in all cases of forgiveness (Ps 51:13; 89:1; 107:2).

❖ **Esau** is an example of a bitter person who learned to forgive. What painful events took place in Esau's life? Jacob took Esau's birthright for a cup of soup (Gen 25:29-34). Jacob deceived Isaac and took Esau's blessing (Gen 27:14-29). At whom might Esau have been bitter?
- ❖ His father (Gen 27:33, 39-40)
- ❖ His mother (Gen 27:5-13)
- ❖ Jacob (Gen 25:29-34; 27:14-29)

Because of these events Esau:
- ❖ was furious and bitter (Gen 27:34).
- ❖ held a grudge (Gen 27:41).
- ❖ wanted to kill Jacob (Gen 27:42).

This is why Jacob fled to Laban, his uncle (Gen 27:43-45). Jacob spent at least 20 years with Laban (Gen 31:38). He had to work 7 years for each of his two wives. He had 12 children by these two wives and their two maidservants.

When Jacob prepared to meet Esau he expected the worst (Gen 32:7-8). Jacob prepared a "parade of gifts" to give to Esau as a way of appeasing him. The last thing Jacob remembered about Esau was his gaining comfort with the idea of killing Jacob after Jacob stole his blessing. Esau came to meet Jacob with 400 men. When Jacob saw these men coming, he separated his children with their mothers and went on ahead of them. When he approached Esau, he bowed down to the ground seven times (Gen 33:1-4). Esau ran to Jacob, embraced him, kissed him and they wept. This was not the response for which Jacob had prepared (Gen 33:5). Esau did not want to take the gifts Jacob had presented to him. Jacob begged him to take them. Esau told Jacob he had plenty of animals (Gen 33:9-11).

❖ **Jesus** is the ultimate example of forgiveness (Luke 23:34). It should have been impossible for God to forgive man. It took such a drastic step as sending his own Son to die the cruelest and most inhumane death known to man. Jesus was the only perfect sacrifice that could remove sin completely. In Hebrews 9:22 we read, "In fact, the law requires that nearly everything be cleansed with blood, and without the shedding of blood there is no forgiveness." (See Leviticus 14:14, 17-19, 25, 28, 31.) In Hebrews 10:3-4 we read, "But those [Old Testament] sacrifices are an annual reminder of sins, because it is impossible for the blood of bulls and goats to take away sins." It was impossible for the blood of bulls and goats, but not impossible for the blood of Jesus. Ephesians 1:7 tells us that "In him we have redemption through his blood, the forgiveness of sins, in accordance with the riches of God's grace." When was the first sacrifice for forgiveness? It was back in the garden of Eden when God killed some animals and made clothing for Adam and Eve (Gen 3:21).

Jesus was willing to forgive others without being verbally asked. Jesus could look into hearts and know that they were asking for forgiveness (Matt 9:4; Mark 2:8). Some of the people Jesus forgave without being verbally asked are:

Luke 7:36-48 — sinful woman
John 8:1-11 — woman caught in adultery
John 21:15:25; Mark 16:7 — Peter
Matthew 9:1-8; Mark 2:1-12; Luke 5:17-26 — paralyzed
    man
John 5:1-9 — paralyzed man at the pool
John 4:7-26 — woman at the well
Luke 23:34 — soldiers who crucified him
Luke 23:40-43 — criminal on the cross next to Jesus

What we learn about Jesus in these verses is:

How readily he forgives.
How he does not make people beg or plead for forgiveness.

They had several things in common:

They all came to Jesus.
They all had sinned.
They all felt the effects of guilt.

It seems that the whole world has these things in
common! I am not saying here that Jesus forgives everybody. He only forgives those who ask him! Today, the only
way to be saved is to hear the word of God (Rom 10:13-
17); believe (John 3:16-18; 6:40; Acts 8:8, 12-13, 36-38;
16:30-33); repent (Luke 13:2-5; Acts 2:36-41; 17:30; 2 Cor
7:10; 2 Pet 3:9); confess (Matt 10:32-33; Mark 8:38; Rom
10:9-11; 1 John 4:13-16); and be baptized by immersion
(Matt 28:18-20; Mark 16:15-16; John 3:5; Acts 2:36-41; 8:36-
38; 16:30-33; Rom 6:3-6; Col 2:11-12; 1 Pet 3:18-22).

Examples of contemporary forgivers:

❖ Some years ago, Coach Joe Paterno and his Penn State
football team were playing for the national championship
against Alabama in the Sugar Bowl. They probably would
have won, but they had a touchdown called back because

there was a twelfth man on the field. After the game, Paterno was asked to identify the man: "It's only a game," he said. "I have no intention of ever identifying the boy. He just made a mistake."

❖ In the summer of 1986 the *Columbus Dispatch* carried a story about a couple from Hopkinsville, KY whose son was killed by a drunk driver. For more than two years, the parents Frank and Elizabeth Morris dedicated their lives to punishing the drunken driver who killed their only child. Driven by hatred, they monitored his every court appearance, followed him to the jail to make sure he was serving his weekend sentence and watched his apartment to try and catch him violating his probation. "We wanted him in prison," Mrs. Morris said. "We wanted him dead."

Tommy Pigage, the young man who caused the fatal crash, still gets a lot of attention from the Morrises. They drive him to church twice a week and often set a place for him at their dinner table. Unable to find satisfaction through revenge, the couple recently decided to forgive Pigage and try to rebuild his life along with their own. "The hate and bitterness I was feeling was destroying me," Mrs. Morris said, "I needed to forgive Tommy to save myself." Since the Morrises made their decision to befriend him, Pigage, 26, has joined their church, quit drinking and become an active lecturer for Mothers Against Drunk Drivers.[3]

Before we begin looking at how to forgive, it is important to have an understanding of what the Bible teaches about forgiving people, and what needs to be forgiven. Forgiveness is:

❖ Commanded by Jesus (Mark 11:25)
❖ Commanded by Paul (Rom 12:19)
❖ To be unlimited (Matt 18:22; Luke 17:4)
❖ A characteristic of saints (Ps 7:4)

Forgiveness has companions such as:

- ❖ Patience (Col 3:13)
- ❖ Acts of kindness (Rom 12:20; Matt 5:38-42)
- ❖ Love (Matt 5:44-46)
- ❖ Prayer (Matt 5:44)

The victim of a loss, injustice, or betrayal must accept the fact that **God wants them to forgive** (Eph 5:1). It is God's solution – not man's (Exod 34:6-8). Forgiveness goes against human nature. This is why Christians are the only ones who can really forgive, because they have the Spirit of God that encourages forgiveness. In *Forgive and Forget* Lewis B. Smedes writes, "Nobody seems to be born with much talent for forgiving. We all need to learn from scratch, and the learning almost always runs against the grain."[4]

Before a person can forgive, knowledge of several biblical ideas are needed.

All sin is the same in the eyes of God (Rom 6:23). In the Sermon on the Mount Jesus taught that murder and anger carry the same spiritual consequence (Matt 5:21-22). He also taught that adultery and looking at a woman lustfully have the same spiritual consequence (Matt 5:27-28).

You may still suffer consequences of the person's sin, but you must still forgive (Acts 7:60). You might be suffering the effects of someone else's behavior. A good example of this would be the priests at Nob who were killed because of King Saul's bitterness towards David and God and because David lied to them (1 Sam 22:18-19).

All people are equal in the sight of God (Matt 20:12). The Bible teaches that no matter what you do in life or accomplish in life, the grave awaits all people.

Man has some traits of wickedness (Ps 36:1). Genesis 6:5 explains, "The Lord saw how great man's wickedness on the earth had become, and that every inclination of the thoughts of his heart was only evil all the time." In Genesis 8:21 we find, "The Lord smelled the pleasing aroma and said in his heart: 'Never again will I curse the ground because of man, even though every inclination of his heart is evil from childhood. And never again will I destroy all living creatures, as I have done.'"

One of the most fascinating questions I am asked about forgiveness is, "What must I forgive?" At times my answer surprises people. I believe there are several things (people) that need to be forgiven:

There appear to be at least five people who need to be forgiven:

The first person who needs to be forgiven might surprise you. It is **God**. Frequently when a person goes through loss, injustice or betrayal, the first person who gets blamed is God. Naomi blamed God for her losses. She tells people in Bethlehem, "Call me Mara [Bitter], because the Almighty has made my life very bitter. I went away full, but the LORD has brought me back empty. Why call me Naomi [Pleasant]? The LORD has afflicted me; the Almighty has brought misfortune upon me" (Ruth 1:20-21).

Job also blamed God for what happened in his life. Job said, "He throws me into the mud, and I am reduced to dust and ashes. I cry out to you, O God, but you do not answer; I stand up, but you merely look at me. You turn on me ruthlessly; with the might of your hand you attack me. You snatch me up and drive me before the wind; you toss me about in the storm" (Job 30:19-22).

Jeremiah in Lamentations 3:33 gives people a clear picture of God, "For he [God] does not willingly bring affliction or grief to the children of men." In Isaiah 54:15 God says, "If anyone does attack you, it will not be my doing; whoever attacks you will surrender to you." LeRoy

Lawson wrote, "When I say we must forgive God, I mean we must cleanse our minds and hearts from any tendency to blame him who is blameless."[5]

If you are like Naomi and Job and blame God for the event(s) that caused you grief, you might want to do a written assignment in which you are a reporter and you are interviewing God. What questions would you like to ask him? What answers do you believe he would give? I have had some clients do this, and they found great relief in what they wrote. Some of the best questions I have seen from this assignment are:

What were you feeling when I was hurt?

How do you feel about my being angry at you?

How come you did not protect me?

Why should I praise you for this event?

Why did you allow this event to happen to me?

What are you going to do to the person that hurt me?

Do I blame you for this event?

Do you still love me?

Was this a form of punishment?

Remember that you are going to answer these questions as God would answer them!

There are four other people who need to be forgiven:

The second person whom you need to forgive probably is going to surprise you as well. You need to forgive **yourself** next. If you have sinned, it is imperative for this to be done. Satan will continually attack you with sins in your past that you have done, for which you have not forgiven yourself. Why is it harder to forgive yourself than others? There are several answers to this question.

One of the major reasons people cannot forgive themselves for what they have done in the past is because they knew what they did was wrong before they did it. People tell me all the time, "I can't forgive myself, because I knew what I did was wrong." Probably the hardest thing to forgive yourself for is a sexual sin. 1 Corinthians 6:18 tells us to, "Flee from sexual immorality. All other sins a man commits are outside his body, but he who sins sexually sins against his own body." Because sexual sins are against the body, anytime a person sees his body, he can be reminded of the sin. This has got to be a great delight to Satan.

Another reason it is hard to forgive yourself is because you give everyone else more room for "errors" than you give yourself. You are harder on yourself than others. You have higher expectations for your behavior than you have for other people.

Another reason it is hard to forgive yourself is because you know yourself better than anyone else does. You are probably analyzing your motives and making yourself feel worthless. You probably have become very self-critical and have rationalized that you are not worthy of being forgiven.

Another reason it is hard to forgive yourself is because you want to keep yourself in bondage. You have gotten used to the idea of not forgiving yourself (Gen 47:19, 25; Exod 6:9; Ezra 9:8-9; Isa 14:3; Jer 30:8; 34:9-10; Rom 8:21; Hos 10:10). As stated before, people frequently don't forgive themselves as a form of insurance against future similar sin. This bondage is also a great way of punishing yourself for your past!

Another reason people have a difficult time forgiving themselves is because they have sinned against another person. They feel that they cannot forgive themselves until the person they hurt forgives them. This is a very dangerous belief. If you are the cause of a painful event, why do you need to forgive yourself? When God forgives you, but you don't forgive yourself—you will still go to heaven, but you will literally make a hell on earth. Forgiving yourself gets rid of one of Satan's strongholds.

If you are the victim of a painful event, you need to forgive yourself:

For blaming yourself originally for the behavior of another person. This crossed responsibility creates a lot of guilt and self-hatred. In working with victims of abuse I have come across very few of them who actually blame the perpetrator for what has happened to them. One of the reasons they blame themselves is simply that "they were there." This is not a reason for blaming yourself! For example, let's say you are in a bank and it is robbed. You walk up to the security guard and you tell him you are to blame because you were there when it occurred. Does he arrest you? Of course not! He will ask you what you did to cause the robbery. Your only answer is you were in the bank when it happened. I would also assume that the event occurred when you were alone with the perpetrator. In Deuteronomy 22:25-27 we read, "But if out in the country a man happens to meet a girl pledged to be married and rapes her, only the man who has done this shall die. Do nothing to the girl; she has committed no sin deserving death. This case is like that of someone who attacks and murders his neighbor, for the man found the girl out in the country, and though the betrothed girl screamed, there was no one to rescue her." When I give this verse to victims of sexual abuse they frequently tell me, "I did not even know that verse was in the Bible." Understanding this verse gives the victim freedom from what the perpetrator did.

Another reason people blame themselves for what happened is that they believe they did not fight hard enough. They eventually gave up. If they had fought harder, the events could have been prevented. More likely than not, if you would have fought harder the events would still have occurred. It was not your lack of fight, but the perpetrator's desires and will that caused the event. You might have to accept the fact that the event occurred because the person who hurt you was stronger than you. For comparison, suppose you have been given money to keep an airplane from taking off at the local airport. You grab onto the back of the plane and hold onto it with all of your strength. The plane still taxis down the runway and takes off. Are you to blame because you did not hold on tight enough, or was the plane too much for you to handle?

For condemning yourself after the event happened. 1 John 3:20-21 says the heart of a person can condemn them. This is what frequently happens after a painful event. Many people, after they have been hurt, put themselves in a "prison" that might as well be physical, since they have withdrawn from all people, and deny their emotions, becoming almost like machines.

Victims of abuse (betrayal, injustice and loss) frequently have changed some definitions of words. Words that once were positive now are seen as negative. Words like love, trust, and commitment, which carry a positive definition, are now seen in a negative way. "Love" becomes defined as hurt and being left. "Trust" becomes defined as pain and rejection. "Commitment" becomes defined as fear and a guarantee of rejection. Abused people believe this new dictionary and vocabulary list as a way of protecting themselves from getting hurt again. The only problem with this is it does not work. These new definitions actually create more pain and hurt.

For thinking you have to be perfect. Satan will use Scripture to make a Christian feel guilty when they are not perfect and fail (Lev 11:44-45; 19:2; Eph 5:1). Jesus accepted failure (Peter fell into the water); do you accept your failures? Failure is not sin. You do not have to confess

258

your failures to God. David wrote in Psalm 19:12 that God forgives hidden faults.

Failure is often due to expectations which are too high. This type of failure is not a sin and does not need to be confessed. Confessing that you are not perfect is not necessary. If it were, imagine how long it would take to confess to God for all your imperfections. This type of confession would become ritualistic and a meaningless process after a while.

The third person you need to forgive is **parents**. Frequently abuse victims will tell their parents about the abuse and the parents refuse to do anything about it. This may be due to the fact that they don't know what to do. But it also may be because the parents don't believe what the child is saying. If you have told your parents about an abusive situation and they did not do anything about it, forgive them. If you don't, Satan will hide in this area successfully destroying your family.

The most obvious person that needs to be forgiven is **the person (people) that hurt you**. It is also important that you forgive the penalty the person deserves. Forgiveness can be described as giving up your right to seek revenge. Forgiveness is canceling the debt. It is the forgiveness of injuries that is the most difficult. Jesus is the prime example of someone forgiving injuries (Luke 23:34).

George Bernard Shaw said, "I am ready to admit after contemplating the world and human nature for sixty years that I see no way out of the world's misery but by the way which would be found by Christ's will." What steps, found in Scripture, are God's way out of the misery of unforgiveness? Consider this quote about forgiving people who abused you by Rich Buhler:

> For you, the victim, one important goal of a successful season of recovery is ultimately to adopt an attitude of for-

giveness toward those who have been involved in causing your pain. Anything less than that will keep the pain alive and throbbing and will not accomplish anything productive for you or for the person who hurt you.

For many victims, the thought of forgiving those who caused their pain seems absurd and even impossible. Certainly forgiveness is contrary to the "get even" attitude of our society. It is an important step toward a more complete healing, however, which is one reason forgiveness was so paramount in the teachings of Jesus Christ.[6]

According to Matthew 18:22, Jesus said we should forgive our brother seventy-seven times (or seventy times seven). It is Christ's will that you forgive. It is God's solution to bitterness, not man's. Forgiveness is a choice, just as bitterness is!

Forgiveness is a process, not a one-time event. It is important to do the "steps to forgiveness" in order. These steps make forgiveness a process that will greatly aid your healing. These steps can be done mentally without any contact with the person who caused the injury, if you believe going to them face to face will create more pain for you.

If you are working with people on the issue of forgiveness, before helping a person to forgive it is important that you:

1) Understand and discuss with them what the loss, injustice, or betrayal was.
2) Understand and discuss with them what the relationship was between the victim and perpetrator.
3) Understand and discuss with them the lies they believe about forgiveness.
4) Help them understand what forgiveness is from God's point of view.

If you don't work through these four things first, when you bring up the idea of forgiving the person that hurt them it will be rejected totally!

Step # 1: **Pronounce a VERDICT**

Hold the person accountable and 100% responsible for their actions. In other words, blame the person who hurt you for what they have done. Leviticus 5:17 is one of the strong teachings about God holding a person responsible for their behavior. It reads, "If a person sins and does what is forbidden in any of the Lord's commands, even though he does not know it, he is guilty and will be held responsible." God holds a person responsible for their behavior before he forgives them, we must do the same.

One of the statements that I frequently hear is, "Fool me once, shame on you. Fool me twice, shame on me." The reason I don't like this statement is because the person who is hurt is blaming themselves for what the perpetrator has done. When you blame yourself for another person's actions, this makes it impossible for you to forgive them. This is one of the major reasons Satan wants you to blame yourself.

The verdict being pronounced is the first step of forgiveness. David asked God to do this in Psalm 10:15, "... call him to account for his wickedness that would not be found out." Many verses in the Bible discuss the issue of man being held accountable and responsible for his behavior by God (Gen 43:9; 44:10, 32; 1 Sam 25:24; 2 Sam 14:9; Rom 9:19; 14:12; 1 Pet 4:5). Holding the person accountable means that you do not allow for excuses, rationalization, or shifting blame to others.

One of the problems with this step is that man does not like to take responsibility for his actions. Man likes to blame others or come up with some excuses for his behavior. Consider these biblical examples of people not taking responsibility for their actions:

❖ **Adam** (Gen 3:12-13): He blamed Eve and God for his actions. Look at what he told God, "The woman you put here...."

261

❖ **Eve** (Gen 3:13): She blamed the serpent for her actions.

❖ **Sarai** (Gen 16:2-5): She blamed her husband for having a child with Hagar, her Egyptian maidservant. It was Sarai's idea for Abram to do this because they did not have any children together. She told Abram, "You are responsible for the wrong I am suffering. I put my servant in your arms, and now that she knows she is pregnant, she despises me. May the Lord judge between you and me" (Gen 16:5).

❖ **Esau** (Gen 25:29-34): He blamed Jacob for the loss of his birthright. It was Esau's idea to sell his birthright for some bread and lentil stew because he was famished.

❖ **Aaron** (Exod 32:1-4, 22-24): He blamed the people of Israel for the golden calf. He told Moses, "Do not be angry, my lord. You know how prone these people are to evil. They said to me, 'Make us gods who will go before us. As for this fellow Moses who brought us up out of Egypt, we don't know what has happened to him.' So I told them, 'Whoever has any gold jewelry, take it off.' Then they gave me the gold, and I threw it into the fire, and out came this calf!" (Exod 32:22-24) This is totally a lie. You don't throw gold into a fire and get a calf out of it. What you get is liquid gold. The truth is Aaron took the liquid gold and "made it into an idol cast in the image of a calf, fashioning it with a tool" (Exod 32:4).

❖ **Saul** (1 Sam 15:15-28): Samuel had told Saul to completely destroy the Amalekites and take no plunder. Saul blamed the soldiers for taking the sheep and plunder (1 Sam 15:21). He later told Samuel the reason he did this was because he was afraid of the people (1 Sam 15:24). It was because of Saul's disobedience in this situation that God tore the kingdom from him and gave it to David (1 Sam 15:28). This made King Saul bitter at Samuel, God and David!

262

When people blame themselves for the actions of others, I frequently have them to present their case as in court. I ask them to give me all the evidence and proof for the reason why they are blaming themselves. This works wonderfully with victims of molestation and rape. I tell them that if they have no proof or evidence, then they cannot be guilty. I will frequently bring in another Christian who will become the jury or judge who will hear their evidence. I have done this at many retreats and seminars. There are usually a lot of healing tears when this activity is done. For the first time they might realize that they were not to blame for the activity that occurred.

This step is very important; until it is done, there can be no forgiveness. One of the hardest things to convince abuse victims of is that the person who hurt them plotted what they were going to do. They not only plotted what they were going to do, they plotted when, where and how (Ps 36:1-4). It is very difficult for victims to realize that the person who hurt them did this because they were evil (Gen 6:6; 8:21). It is equally difficult for victims to recognize that the person who hurt them gained pleasure from what they did (Prov 9:17; 10:23).

Blaming the one who hurt you seems contrary to psychology which tends to make everyone a victim and teaches not to place blame. This step goes against the legal profession with its "no fault" philosophy. I found an interesting quote from a lawyer:

> As a lawyer my job is to see that people are treated fairly. But I am not to release them from the consequences of the acts...and the same is true as ministers of reconciliation. We are to help people, not remove them from accountability.[7]

Consider the following from Dr. James Dobson:

> If there is anything that an adulterer does not need, it is a guilt-ridden mate who understands his indiscretion and

assumes the blame for it. Such a person needs to be called to accountability, not excused by rationalization![8]

Jan Frank wrote:

Let me make a very bold, but factual, statement. A child victim is 100 percent free from any responsibility. The aggressor is always fully responsible. We have been duped often by society into thinking that the "seductive child" is merely getting what she asks for. This is false. I do not believe there is any such child walking around, but even if there were, the adult still holds complete responsibility for his behavior.[9]

Jan goes on to say:

My experience has taught me that a child who is behaving in a sexually precocious manner usually has been molested already. A victim of child molestation suffers from having her sexual arousal system activated prematurely. This causes confusion, misunderstanding and a sexual identity imbalance in the child. She is forced to deal with emotions and physiological responses that God did not intend for her to experience until the pubertal years. It is no wonder victims suffer difficulty in later years.[10]

This statement sounds like what Jesus taught, "But if anyone causes one of these little ones who believe in me to sin, it would be better for him to have a large millstone hung around his neck and to be drowned in the depths of the sea" (Matt 18:6).

A person who has been through an adulterous situation with a spouse is 100% free of any responsibility for the affair. I get very frustrated when I hear victims of adultery get blamed for what their prodigal spouse did. This 100% freedom from responsibility also goes for any sexual-crime victim. You will frequently hear people say things like, "She was dressed to be hurt," or "They should not have been in that place at that time." It is true that the victim of a rape situation may not have shown enough common sense, but this did not cause the crime to occur. What caused the crime to occur were the thoughts within the perpetrator's mind. By assigning responsibility for the painful event the proper party, you are giving yourself a chance to forgive them. When you recognize them as guilty, this allows the fruit of the Spirit to be manifested in your life again.

Many times the victim of an event becomes the accused. Sometimes this happens in the court system; but it usually occurs by the perpetrator or in the victim's mind. First John 3:21 reasons, "Dear friends, if our hearts do not condemn us, we have confidence before God." It is important you do not let your mind condemn you if God says you are innocent. God holds people accountable for their sins. If you are going to forgive the person who hurt you, it is vital that you hold them accountable! Do you think God would allow the verdict "guilty, but mentally ill?" Would God allow plea bargaining?

I am frequently asked how many victims of abuse blame themselves. My answer is 97% and the other 3% are lying about it. In other words I always assume that the victim of an event blames themselves, even when they tell me they don't blame themselves.

An assignment that I frequently give victims of sexual molestation and rape is to come up with a list of statements that begin with "you had no right..." I encourage them to come up with as many as 50. This will make them be very specific in the statement. The more specific the statement, the better the healing that occurs when the statement is made. This list is a great way of making the perpetrator responsible for his or her actions.

Psychology has aided people in not taking responsibility for their actions. At times psychology has helped to make excuses and created "illnesses" for people behaving sinfully. Crime has become a mental illness. *The Diagnostic and Statistical Manual of Mental Disorders* III-R lists these as "Impulse Control Disorders." The general description is "Failure to resist an impulse, drive or temptation to perform some act that is harmful to the person or others. There may or may not be conscious resistance to the impulse. The act may or may not be premeditated or planned."[11] Psychology has labeled crime a mental illness, thus allowing excuses and escape hatches. The DSM IV lists these "disorders":

Pyromania "disorder" — the irresistible impulse to set fire to people and their property.

Kleptomania "disorder" — the inability to restrain oneself from stealing.

Pedophilia "disorder" — the unstoppable urge to molest or rape children.

Intermittent Explosive "disorder" — the complete loss of one's temper, resulting in bodily assault or damage to property.

Sadistic Personality "disorder" — the persistent drive to be cruel, demeaning or aggressive towards others.

Consider the following two examples about people not taking responsibility for their actions.

In 1991 Michael Gilbert, a nationally known criminal psychiatrist was convicted of bribing a public official to set up a cocaine bust against a Miami lawyer. Gilbert argued that he was insane. His lawyer said in court that Gilbert was "crazy. He's short-circuiting in his brain. Short circuits, short circuits."[12]

A woman sued her therapist for unorthodox treatment with a patient. She said the therapist had sex with her and the therapist even invited the client to sleep with her husband. The therapist's defense was she could not remember anything about the psychotherapy she had given to this client because her silicone breast implants had leaked causing toxicity in her brain and conveniently, memory loss.[13]

Defense attorneys across America seem to be attempting to jump on the bandwagon and get rid of personal responsibility for criminals. Lawyers are becoming more creative in their defenses. Consider the next three newspaper articles about personal responsibility for crimes.

❖ The *South Bend Tribune* on Sunday, May 29, 1994, p. A-21, did a full page article called A LEGAL EXCUSE TO ATTACK OR KILL? DEFENDANTS POINTING INCREASINGLY TO ABUSE. It was written by Niko Price, an Associated Press Writer.

In the article Ryan Rainey, attorney for the National Center for the Prosecution of Child Abuse said, "You're going to a trend where you're saying, 'I can't take responsibility for my actions because of a bad upbringing.'" James Blatt, a Los Angeles attorney said, "Whether a lot of people like it or not, it may become an inherent part of American jurisprudence."

This article talked about several cases and some unique defenses and reasonings for crimes. For example:

Moosa Hanoukai's defense for killing his wife was because she made him sleep on the floor, called him names and paid him a nominal wage. James Blatt, his attorney argued that his wife, Manijeh, psychologically emasculated her husband. This caused him to lose all his self-esteem. Blatt argued his Persian Jewish background prevented him from seeking a divorce. He beat her to death with a wrench instead. I guess his background did not prevent murder. Hanoukai was sentenced to 11 years in prison for voluntary manslaughter. Blatt called this "a major victory" because he was acquitted of murder.

Kathleen Cady, the Deputy District Attorney, who prosecuted the Hanoukai case said, "Every single murderer has a reason to kill someone. I think it sends a very frightening message to the rest of society that all you have to do is come up with some kind of excuse when you commit a crime. Psychology and daytime programming on television have promoted this idea."

Daimion Osby received a mistrial in Fort Worth, Texas after gunning down two unarmed men. His lawyer argued that a racist country and an inner-city upbringing gave him "urban survival syndrome." This syndrome convinced him he had no alternative but to kill.

Colin Ferguson is accused of killing six and wounding 19 on a Long Island Railroad commuter train. His lawyers, Ronald L. Kuby and William Kunstler of New York say, "a racist society made a mentally unstable black man snap." They call this "black rage." David Rosenhan, a professor of law and psychology at Stanford University claims that such defense tactics show lawyers are becoming more creative in their use of abuse to explain crime.

Alan Dershowitz, a Harvard Law School Professor and author of the book *The Abuse Excuse* says, "They trivialize the defense. The history of abuse is not a license to kill."

There appears to be a defense against filing tax forms with the IRS. It is based on the idea that some traumatic experience in life has created an aversion to forms. This condition is called "failure to file syndrome."

Erik and Lyle Menendez shot their mother because (they claimed) they were abused by their father. The defense said the shooting, which took place in the living room of their parents mansion, was because of a lifetime of sexual and physical abuse which created fear. The juries were unable to decide either way.

Aurelia Macias is a Los Angeles woman who castrated her husband with scissors. She said her husband was trying to have sex with her while she gave milk to her baby. Prosecution said he was sleeping at the time of the attack. She was acquitted of mayhem and assault. A retrial on battery had the jury deadlocked. The couple at the time of this article had reconciled.

❖ The *LaPorte Herald-Argus* Thursday, May 26, 1994, p. 7. ADULT TEMPER TANTRUMS? MAYBE IT'S IN THE FAMILY'S GENES. Philadelphia (AP)

This article tells of a twin study dealing with anger, done by Dr. Emil Coccaro, who is the director of the Clinical Neuroscience Research Unit at the Medical College of Pennsylvania in Philadelphia. He presented his research at the annual meeting of the American Psychiatric Association on Tuesday, May 24, 1994. His "analysis suggested that indirect aggression, which basically means taking out one's anger on objects or throwing tantrums, had the strongest genetic influence. An estimated 40 percent of this trait was attributed to genes."

"Irritability was second with 38 percent, then direct aggression, which means hitting people, with 33 percent. Last was verbal aggression, which basically means screaming and cursing with 27 percent."

This study basically takes away responsibility for any aggressive act in at least one fourth of all cases, and as high as 40% in some cases. I wonder if this defense will work on judgment day before God. In Matthew 12:36-37 Jesus said, "But I tell you that men will have to give account on the day of judgment for every careless word they have spoken. For by your words you will be acquitted, and by your words you will be condemned." According to the above study, the new paraphrase of this verse would be that 73% of people will have to give an account on the day of judgment for every careless word they have spoken.

❖ BATTERED WOMEN SYNDROME *The Muncie Star*, Muncie, Indiana, June 12, 1994, pp. 1, 4. This paper did a whole series on Battered Women Syndrome (BWS). Does this theory legalize revenge and retaliation?

One of the stories told about a couple that had been

married for approximately three months. They had gotten into a fight outside a local cinema, and one hour later the woman stabbed her husband while he sat in a car. The woman claimed it was self-defense. She told authorities that she had been abused during their year of courtship and during the marriage. The attorney is going to claim self-defense.

The following quotes are taken from this article. Lori Spillane, deputy prosecutor said, "She can't get up the next day and shoot him because she's still mad. That's not self-defense; that's murder." Kelly Bryan, defense attorney said, "They might not have been in Vietnam, but a war zone can be a variety of places. For a woman, it can be her home."

Charles Colson in *A Dance With Deception* writes about Dan White who gunned down the mayor and city supervisor in San Francisco's City Hall. Dan pleaded temporary insanity. He said a steady diet of junk food raised his blood sugar and affected his brain. Colson also wrote that, "A woman was stopped recently by a Virginia police officer for erratic driving. She cursed, kicked, and scored above the legal limit on a breathalyzer test. Yet she successfully argued in court that she was not drunk, she was merely suffering from premenstrual syndrome, or PMS."[14]

One of the major difficulties in convincing the victim to blame the perpetrator is that the victim has become accustomed to blaming themselves. When a person has committed adultery, they will usually blame their spouse with a smorgasbord of reasons. Remember Adam blamed Eve and God; Eve blamed the serpent, and the serpent didn't have a leg to stand on!

The victim of adultery will usually believe these reasons, thinking why would my spouse lie about this? The reason the adulterous spouse is blaming the innocent spouse is that they don't want the guilt and responsibility for the affair. For years the innocent one will believe that a hurtful incident was their fault. This self-blaming becomes part of their personality. It is hard to break this pattern! Blaming oneself for the actions of others, or "crossed responsibility" makes forgiveness impossible. James Dobson said in the film, *Turn Your Heart Toward Home*, "You cannot take the total responsibility for the outcome of your children; for they do have a free will, and some are determined to exercise it."

How can you forgive if you don't place blame on the proper party? Yet, as I counsel many people who have been victimized by some tragic event in their lives, I find most victims blame themselves. People frequently tell me, "It's just easier to blame myself." I believe it takes two to have an affair—the adulterous man and adulterous woman!

I recently worked with some Christian parents whose son became prodigal. I asked them who they blamed for what their son was doing. Each of them blamed themselves, not their son. The mother said it was because she worked outside of the home, and this must have given her son the impression she did not love him. The father blamed himself because he had not been around his son as much as he thought he should have. But, if you are not in control of the situation that happened to you, you are not responsible for it!

I realize how difficult it is to blame someone for what they have done, but if you don't "blame" them, you will never be able to forgive them. This step might require that you see what has happened to you as a plot. Psalm 36:4 talks about a wicked man, "Even on his bed he plots evil; he commits his way to a sinful course and does not reject what is wrong." In Proverbs 6:14 we read, "...who plots evil with deceit in his heart — he always stirs up dissension." Psalm 73:7 tells us that, "From their callous hearts comes iniquity; the evil conceits of their minds know no limits."

271

The biblical fact is that man is responsible for his own actions whether psychology and the legal profession want to believe it or not. The truth here is that God holds people responsible for their sins. In Deuteronomy 24:16 we read that each person is responsible for his own sins. In Ezekiel 18:20 we learn that the soul who sins is the one who will die. Ezekiel 18:30 teaches that God will judge man for his ways. Ecclesiastes 12:14 says that God will bring every deed into judgment. This includes good and evil deeds, seen and unseen. Jesus taught that man will be held accountable for every careless word he has spoken (Matt 12:36). In Romans 14:12 Paul declares, "So then, each of us will give an account of himself to God." In Revelation 2:23 God says, "...I will repay each of you according to your deeds." Man is responsible to God for both his words and actions!

How many people did God hold responsible for their sin? A short list might help:

David and Bathsheba for their adultery (2 Sam 12:13-14).

Ananias and Sapphira for lying to the Holy Spirit about the amount of their gift (Acts 5:1-12).

Achan for taking plunder from Babylonia (Josh 7:20-26). In this case they not only stoned Achan to death, but also stoned to death his sons and daughters.

Sodom and Gomorrah for their sexual immorality (Gen 19:1-24).

Look at what God says about responsibility for sin in the following verses.

Genesis 3:14 — "because of what you have done...."

Genesis 3:17 — "because you listened and ate of the tree...."

Leviticus 5:1 — "He will be held responsible."

Leviticus 5:17 — "He is guilty and will be held responsible."

Leviticus 7:18 — "The person who eats any of it will be held responsible."

Leviticus 17:16 — "He will be held responsible."

Leviticus 19:8 — "Whoever eats it will be held responsible."

Leviticus 20:17 — "He will be held responsible."

Leviticus 20:19 — "Both will be held responsible."

Leviticus 20:20 — "They will be held responsible."

Leviticus 24:15 — "He will be held responsible."

Ezekiel chapter 18 is a debate on who is responsible for sin, a debate on personal accountability. I would encourage you to read this chapter and get a "God's-eye view" of responsibility for sin.

Step # 2: SENTENCE, DEBT, PENALTY

Realize that there is a sentence the offending party rightfully deserves. This penalty must be paid by him or by someone else. Paul wrote in Colossians 3:25, "Anyone who does wrong will be repaid for his wrong, and there is no favoritism." Many passages in the Bible teach about the sentence, debt and penalty (Num 5:31; 9:13; 18:22; Ezek 16:58; 23:35, 49; 44:10, 12; Hos 4:9; 12:2).

Neil T. Anderson writes in *The Bondage Breakers*, "Forgiveness is agreeing to live with the consequences of another person's sin. Forgiveness is costly; we pay the price of the evil we forgive. Yet you're going to live with those consequences whether you want to or not; your only choice is whether you will do so in bitterness of unforgiveness or the freedom of forgiveness. That's how Jesus forgave you—he took the consequences of your sin upon himself. All true forgiveness is substitutional, because no one really forgives without bearing the penalty of the other person's sin."[15]

There is always a penalty required to be paid for sin. In Romans 6:23 we read, "For the wages of sin is death...." There are many verses in the Bible that teach the idea that no one who does evil gets away "scot-free." In Job 4:8 we read, "As I have observed, those who plow evil and those who sow trouble reap it." In Proverbs 1:31 we read, "They will eat the fruit of their ways and be filled with the fruit of their schemes." Isaiah 3:11 teaches that, "Woe to the wicked! Disaster is upon them! They will be paid back for what their hands have done." Jeremiah 6:19 states, "Hear O earth: I am bringing disaster on this people, the fruit of their schemes, because they have not listened to my words and have rejected my law." Paul wrote in Galatians 6:7, "Do not be deceived: God cannot be mocked. A man reaps what he sows."

I do not believe that God is against the death penalty in certain cases of sin. Death was the payment for Sodom and Gomorrah (Gen 19), as well as people who lived during Noah's time (Gen 6). The Holy Spirit also killed Ananias and Sapphira for their sins (Acts 5:1-11). Romans 6:23 tells us the wages of sin is death. The word "wages" can be translated "payment." According to God, death is the payment needed for all sin (Deut 25:1-3; Prov 24:12; Num 5:7; Lev 5:5-7, 14-15, 6:6; Ps 62:12; Prov 11:21, 31; 14:14; 20:30).

Some of the capital punishment crimes in the Old Testament are:

- ❖ Striking and killing a man intentionally (Exod 21:12-14; Lev 24:17-22; Num 35:16-34).
- ❖ Attacking father or mother (Exod 21:15).
- ❖ Kidnapping (Exod 21:16; Deut 24:7).
- ❖ Cursing father or mother (Exod 21:17; Lev 20:9).
- ❖ Owning a bull that is known for goring people, and allowing the bull to kill someone (Exod 21:28-32).
- ❖ Killing a thief in the daylight (Exod 22:2-3).
- ❖ Sorcery (Exod 22:18).
- ❖ Sacrificing to other gods (Exod 22:20).
- ❖ Working on the Sabbath (Exod 31:14-15; 35:2).

- ❖ Taking advantage of strangers, widows or orphans (Exod 22:21-24).
- ❖ Sacrificing your children to Molech (Lev 20:2).
- ❖ Committing adultery {both are killed} (Lev 20:10; Deut 22:22-28).
- ❖ Sexual relations that are forbidden (Lev 20:12, 13, 14, 15, 16; Exod 22:19).
- ❖ Being a medium or spiritualist (Lev 20:27).
- ❖ A priest's daughter who becomes a prostitute (Lev 21:9).
- ❖ A priest who has contempt for God's requirements (Lev 22:9).
- ❖ Blaspheming the name of the Lord (Lev 24:13-16).
- ❖ Those who have been devoted to destruction (Lev 27:29).
- ❖ A non-Levite coming near the tabernacle while it is being set up (Num 1:55).
- ❖ Anyone who approaches the sanctuary besides Aaron and his sons (Num 3:10, 38).
- ❖ Kohathites going in to see the holy things (Num 4:20).
- ❖ Defiling the holy offering of the Israelites (Num 18:32).
- ❖ In cases of rape, only the man is guilty (Deut 22:25-26).

Are these sentences carried out in courtrooms today? No! Our society frequently rewards the perpetrators by putting them on daytime television, making them best selling authors and portraying them as victims. No sin goes unpunished by God (Exod 34:7; Num 14:18; Prov 11:21; 16:5; Jer 25:29; Nah 1:3; Isa 59:18).

In Genesis 3:14, 17 God says "because you have done this," and "...because you listened to your wife..." It is because of what each individual did that they were punished. Consider what the following verses say about punishment and restitution.

* Deuteronomy 25:1-3 — Punishment is given according to guilt.
* Numbers 5:7 — Restitution plus 20% was the sinner's penalty.
* Leviticus 5:6 — "As a penalty for his sin"... The animal offering was the penalty that needed to be paid.
* Leviticus 5:7 — "As a penalty for his sin"
* Leviticus 20:9-17 — Death was the penalty for sin.

* Satan's penalty for deceiving Eve was to crawl on his belly and eat dust (Gen 3:14-15).

* Eve's penalty for her sin was increased pain in childbirth (Gen 3:16).

* Adam's penalty for his sin was to have to work hard and sweat to get food (Gen 3:17-19).

What happens to the victim when they realize that God has a sentence for the person who hurt them? I encourage people who have been hurt to pray justice is done in their situation! For forgiveness to take place, justice is a vital step. The justice I am speaking of is not just God's justice, but also man's justice. I even encourage people to pray that the perpetrator will become aware of the wrath of God upon them, as the ultimate step in feeling that justice has been served.

Does God expect Christians to be like Jonah, and want God to give them (the people that hurt us) what they deserve? (Jonah 4:5) What vines and worms does God provide to teach people to have compassion on people who have hurt them? (Jonah 4:6-8) Many people tell me they believe it is unfair for God to "just forgive people for what they have done." Many people do not realize that just because you forgive someone for what they have done to you, this does not mean God forgives them. People need to understand the perpetrator will have to stand before God and give an account for everything he did to you (Rom

14:12). God will hold the person accountable for what they did to you. When you are forgiving someone you are not causing God to forgive them, but you are freeing yourself from the pain of the past.

I have worked with many people who have been forgiven by God, but they still have had to experience some kind of earthly punishment for what they have done. God's forgiveness does not mean you will not have to pay a penalty. It just means you will not have to pay an eternal penalty.

Step # 3: **REMEMBER**

"Don't try to forget what has happened to you." This is taught in Deuteronomy 25:17-19. If you make this one of your goals, you are going to be disappointed. Couples will remember the pain their spouse has caused them. The goal is not to forget what has happened to you but to forgive what has happened to you. Lewis B. Smedes writes in *Forgive and Forget*, "When we forgive someone, we do not forget the hurtful act, as if forgetting came along with the forgiveness package, the way strings come with a violin."[16]

There are times when it is better not to forget what has happened to you. Your painful past can create a ministry, a sweet ministry. Many times you can learn from what has happened. If you try to forget it, you may take away any teaching that might have occurred because of the event. This does not mean you should constantly bring the event up. But, if it comes up, it should not bother you as much emotionally as it once did. The challenge is to forgive, remember, but not use it as a weapon.

Forgetting the painful events of the past is not humanly possible. "Forgive and forget" is the cruelest advice anyone can give about the pain in your past. If you tell yourself to just forget the event, you won't. If someone tells you to think of anything except an elephant on roller skates going down a hill with a banana up its nose — you will think of the elephant (2 Cor 1:3-4; 9). The Bible teaches us that God has the ability to forget sin (Isa 43:25) Why did God not give us this ability? Lewis B. Smedes writes, "Forgetting, in fact, may be a dangerous way to escape the inner surgery of the heart that we call forgiving. There are two kinds of pain that we forget. We forget hurts too trivial to bother about. We forget pain too horrible for our memory to manage."[17]

In Isaiah 64:9 it says, "Do not remember our sins forever." Why did Isaiah write this? Could it be he believed there would be a time when God would remember the sins of people? Could it be that Isaiah had a hard time forgetting his sins, so he assumed God had the same problem? No where in Scripture can I find God telling people to forget the sins people have committed against them. Isaiah 43:18 advises us to "[f]orget the former things; do not dwell on the past."

God does not expect us to try to forget the events of the past, but he does not want us to dwell (live) in it. Something better is found in verse 19, where God exclaims, "See I am doing a new thing!... do you not perceive it?..." It is very dangerous to live in the past because you lose your present and future. I have been around many people who live in the "good ole days." One thing that is amazing is how good they actually make these days. It seems the flaws in the present tend to make people glorify the past.

There may be a time when you actually do forget what has happened to you. This is fine. The brain has a wonderful ability to "forget" the painful events of the past. I do not ask people to forget, or remember, all of the gory details of an event. Some things are better off forgotten. Some events are better to remember. At times it is God's will that we don't remember certain events. If a person remembers painful events, that is OK. I do not purposefully set out to have a person remember all of the events in the past.

This step is what I call the "pickles" step. While I was going to college, one of my summer jobs was working at a pickle factory. When I was first hired, they told me I could eat all of the pickles I wanted. To this very day, I cannot stand eating pickles. This factory allowed workers to eat all they wanted because they knew people would quickly tire of them. They were right. Our minds will remember the past, and gradually it will fade from view. And so will the effects! David Seamands writes, "The harder we try to keep bad memories out of conscious recall, the more powerful they become. Since they are not allowed to enter through the door of our minds directly, they come into our personalities (body, mind, and spirit), in disguised and destructive ways."[18]

Step # 4: CONFRONTATION

If it is possible, and profitable, confront the person that hurt you. Possible means that it can be done. Possible means that you are able to actually face the person. Profitable means that you think it will have a positive outcome. The word "confront" appears 13 times in the NIV Bible. "Confronted" appears 6 times and "confronting" appears 2 times. Confrontation is bold, spoken, assertive love. David Augsburger wrote, "Life without confrontation is directionless, aimless, and passive. When unchallenged, human beings tend to drift, to wander or to stagnate."[19]

Confrontation is not annihilation. It is not character assassination. It is important to confront only the offenses that really bother and affect you (Prov 19:11). It is important to confront events and not character. I would encourage you to fast and pray before the confrontation. Ask God to let you know what needs to be confronted and how to do it. Both Paul (Acts 9:9) and Esther fasted (4:15-16) when they were going through personal trials. Esther fasted in order to speak the proper words to the King. Fasting before confrontation may be one of the ways God gives the proper words to speak during the confrontation. If you decide to confront face to face, don't plan on what you are going to say — let God's Spirit speak through you (Isa 50:8; 51:16; 59:21).

What the person did to you needs to be confronted. Four types of offenses need to be addressed:

> A. What was said.
> B. What was done.
> C. What was not said.
> D. What was not done.

People tend to confront A & B, but neglect to confront C & D. These last two offenses often cause more pain than the first two. It is frequently in these last two offenses that bitterness hides the most. How often have you ever told a person they need to forgive someone for what they did not do? It is frequently in the omission of a desired behavior where Satan will hide and attack the most. What type of things can a person neglect to do that will cause pain? Many times people are hurt by a compliment not given. People are often hurt when support and encouragement are missing in situations.

Why confront others with what they have done to you? Because you care! A better word than confrontation would be "carefrontation." Other reasons to confront besides caring are:

❖ to edify (Eph 4:29; Col 3:16; 2 Cor 13:10).
❖ to bring them back to God (Matt 18:15; 2 Cor 2:5-11; 1 Cor 5).
❖ because of coming judgment (Rom 14:12; 1 Cor 5:12; Heb 9:27).
❖ to bring about change (Eph 4:20-24; John 8:2-11).

❖ to expose sin and ward off captivity (Lam 2:14).
❖ to expose false and misleading teachings (Lam 2:14).

Ask God to speak through you during the confrontation. He promises to do this! (This promise is found in Exod 4:12; Isa 50:4; Jer 1:9; Matt 10:19-20; Luke 12:11-12; 21:14-15; Mark 13:11). The Holy Spirit is very bold in its speaking (Acts 4:25, 31; 9:28; 13:9-11, 46; 14:3; 18:26; 19:8; 28:31; Exod 14:8; Num 33:3; Rom 10:20; 15:15; Mark 15:43). The Spirit does not give way to fear (2 Tim 1:7). It is hard to confront a person who has been both good and bad to you. I would encourage you to fast and pray before the confrontation and rely upon the Lord.

Confrontation is necessary to create healthy relationships. Webster's dictionary defines confronting as "bringing face-to-face." Jan Frank wrote, "Confrontation, then, is the actual placing of responsibility in the hands of its rightful owners. This enables the victim to unload a burden she has carried, which in reality was not hers to carry. She can unload the excess baggage and begin to be responsible for only what is hers."[20]

Confrontation, like the healing process, must be held up to God in constant prayer. Confrontation that is premature (meaning you have not done steps 1-3) is often very harmful and counterproductive. If it is possible and profitable, go to the person that hurt you. Confronting them is very difficult, but it can be very healing if done with godly motives. Tell the person how you were affected by what they did to you (Matt 5:23-25; Lev 19:17). You should confront all the people who have hurt you, but there is a priority list of confrontations:

1. People you see on a daily basis who have hurt you.
2. People you see on an occasional basis who have hurt you.
3. People from your past whom you don't see, who have hurt you. This one is like cleaning out the

281

closet. There may be years of junk needing to be thrown away.

Confrontation can be done in a face-to-face manner. In the NIV translation of the Bible the phrase "face to face" appears a number of times (2 Kgs 14:8; 2 Chr 25:17; Job 17:6; Ps 44:15; Jer 32:4; 34:3; Ezek 7:22). It is important to choose a safe, public place to confront someone face-to-face. Restaurants can be good places for confrontation unless you expect a loud argument. One of the benefits of this kind of place is that you can leave fairly easily if things don't go well. When you are confronting the person who hurt you:

1. The perpetrator will probably not agree that the events occurred as you remember them.
2. The perpetrator will probably try to blame you for what occurred, or will make excuses.
3. The perpetrator usually will **NOT** ask for forgiveness.
4. The perpetrator will probably not seek reconciliation.

Confrontation has to be done in an appropriate manner. Sometimes it is not wise to confront the person who hurt you face-to-face. You may have attempted to do this and were met with poor results. In cases like this, sit down and make a list of the things the person did to hurt you. Take some time in doing this. It is all right for you to pray that God reveal to you how you have been hurt by this person. After this list is done, write this person a letter. (**You are not going to mail this letter**!) This letter is designed to help you express how you have been hurt. In this letter it is important to express feelings of loss, injustice and betrayal. This letter is not supposed to be nice. It is designed to tell the person that hurt you exactly how you feel. I frequently tell people to write this letter and Q.B.N. (quit being nice). Express exactly how you feel with unfiltered emotions; that is, don't let the word "shouldn't" block the expression of any emotion. This word is a filter designed to delete or deny anger. This is not healthy. If you are the spouse or parent of someone who has been hurt in the past, you might want to write a letter telling the perpetrator how you feel about what they did. This is a great way to get rid of a lot of emotional baggage. You might feel guilt over what you have written if you are highly compassionate and sensitive. This guilt is due to the fact that you went against one of your values — not expressing anger. It feels strange to express it, and this creates guilt! Here are the four simple statements about letter confrontation:

> 1) Write it.
>
> 2) Read it out loud.
>
> 3) Burn it.
>
> 4) Bury it.

After reading this letter out loud, burn it and tell God "thank you" for what you have just gone through.

Imagine the person you are writing to is going to read this letter. One caution: this letter must be done in the same Christian manner as if you were confronting them face-to-face. You must write the truth in love, you must write in grace, and you must write with compassion and mercy (Eph 4:15; John 1:14; Jas 5:11). At the end of this letter, write that you choose to forgive them for what they have done to you. Tell them you do not seek revenge and they are forgiven by you. After this letter is written, read it out loud as if the person who hurt you were reading it. This may create some emotions for you. This is perfectly natural. Tears are:

T ransparency **T** otally
E xposing **E** ndangering
A nd **A** nd
R eleasing **R** eleasing
S elf **S** elf

Tears in these two definitions are "emotional stitches." The word "cry" is found 168 times in the NIV Bible. When a person is crying it could be seen as a prayer to God. David wrote a lot about this in Psalms (3:4; 5:2; 6:9; 9:12; 10:17; 17:1; 18:6; 22:2, 24; 28:2, 6; 29:9; 31:22; 34:15, 17; 39:12; 40:1; 55:17; 57:2; 61:1; 72:12; 84:2; 86:6; 88:1, 2, 13; 102:1; 106:44; 116:1; 119:147, 169; 130:1, 2; 140:6; 142:1, 5-6; 143:1; 144:14; 145:19). Weeping is a common theme found in Scripture.

Some people who wept in Scripture are: Hagar, Genesis 21:16; David, 2 Samuel 18:33; Rachel, Jeremiah 31:15; Sarah, Genesis 23:2; Ezra, Ezra 3:12; Michal, 2 Samuel 3:16; Nehemiah, Nehemiah 1:4; Esau, Genesis 27:38; the Jews, Esther 4:3; David and Jonathan, 1 Samuel 20:41; Hezekiah, 2 Kings 20:3; Hannah, 1 Samuel 1:7; Saul, 1 Samuel 24:16; Jeremiah, Jeremiah 9:1; Jacob, Genesis 27:35; Rachel, Genesis 29:11; Joseph, Genesis 42:24; Samson, Judges 14:16; Job, Job 2:12; Ezekiel, Ezekiel 8:14 and Jehoash, 2 Kings 13:14.

If you do decide to mail this letter it might not only be healing for you, but it might also free the person who has hurt you and has been carrying the guilt. This letter can bring your lives back together, and it will free you from the hurt, anger and bitterness. In this letter do not try to justify what the person did. Do not tell them what they did was no big deal. Another way of working out a confrontation without going face to face would be through a role play with some understanding person. Role plays are good because you are actually "talking" to the perpetrator.

Examples of three types of face-to-face biblical confrontation:

Story Confrontation: This is when you tell a story to a person about how their behavior hurt you. Then tell them how the story applies to what they have done to you.

One of the best scriptural examples of this type of confrontation is Nathan and David (2 Sam 12:1-14). When Nathan found out about David and Bathsheba, he went to David and told him a story about two men who had sheep. David was convicted by this story and repented.

Many of the parables that Jesus taught were very confrontive to the Pharisees. They knew Jesus was speaking to them. In Matthew 21:45 we read, "When the chief priests and Pharisees heard Jesus' parables, they knew he was talking about them."

Actual Fact Confrontation: This is confrontation just with the person's behavior and how it affected you. Examples of this kind of confrontation are:

Paul confronted sexual immorality within the Corinthian church (1 Cor 5:1-5).

Paul confronted the issue of being unequally yoked together with unbelievers (2 Cor 6:14-18).

Paul confronted Peter because he was being hypocritical (Gal 2:11-21).

Jesus confronted the rich ruler about which was more important to him, heaven or his possessions (Luke 18:18-30).

Jesus confronted the Pharisees about their "religious" behaviors (Matt 23:1-39).

Jesus confronted the temple merchants. This is when he drove them out of the temple (John 2:12-16).

Jesus confronted the woman at the well about her religious beliefs and her living conditions (John 4:7-18).

Question Confrontation: This is asking questions to get people to tell you their beliefs, or possibly confess a sin. There are a couple of examples of this in Scripture:

Jesus asks an interesting question to the Pharisees, "Have you never read in the Scriptures...?" (Matt 21:42).

Another such confrontation is when Jesus is at a Pharisee's house and he has his feet washed by a sinful women (Luke 7:36-48). This makes the Pharisee mad. Jesus said to him, "Two men owed money to a certain moneylender. One owed him five hundred denarii, and the other fifty. Neither of them had the money to pay him back, so he canceled the debts of both. Now which of them will love him more?"

The Bible teaches that verbal confrontation should be:

* ❖ Colossians 4:6 — seasoned with salt. Salt is often used to prevent spoilage, for healing and as a preservative.
* ❖ Ephesians 4:25 — truthful. (Prov 12:22)
* ❖ Galatians 6:1-2, 9-10 — gentle and supportive.
* ❖ Lamentations 2:14 — not said to tickle ears (2 Tim 4:3-4), in other words, not just saying what the listeners want to hear.
* ❖ Jeremiah 28:15 — spoken without telling lies.
* ❖ Leviticus 19:17 — frankly said and to the point.
* ❖ James 5:11 — said with compassion and mercy.
* ❖ John 1:14 — full of grace.

Biblical teachings about confrontation:

1. Examine your spiritual well being first (Matt 7:1-5).

2. Be willing to follow the pattern given by Jesus (Matt 5:23-24; 18:15-17).

3. Remember the goal is forgiveness. If repentance and reconciliation of fellowship occur, this is an added benefit! (Matt 5:24). The goal is to express to them how you feel so there can be a possible reunion. The purpose of speaking to the person is to create an atmosphere of healing. Both people benefit from this kind of confrontation. You benefit by unburdening your heart! They benefit because they can get rid of their guilt.

4. Confrontation should be done prayerfully. It is important that you pray not only for what to confront about, but also that the Spirit of God would speak through you (Luke 1:14-15). It also might be a good idea to have people praying for you during the time you are confronting the person who hurt you. This should give you confidence and a sense of peace about what you are doing.

What should you expect after confronting the person who hurt you?

Do not expect them to:

> tell you they are sorry for what they did.
> tell you they were wrong.
> ask for forgiveness.
> change their behavior.

Do expect them to:

> **reject you**. Actually when they reject you, they are rejecting the Lord (1 Thess 4:8).
> **attack** you personally by bring up your past.
> **be angry**.
> **be convicted** by the Holy Spirit (John 16:8).

If you expect the opposite of any of these things, when they do not occur, you will be more bitter and angry! If the person you confront has no Spiritual conviction, you have still unburdened your heart. So, the confrontation was still worthwhile and successful. In the book, *As For Me and My House*, this is called "giving notice." Walter Wangerin, Jr. writes:

> But forgiveness must at the same time be the clear communication to the sinner that she has sinned. It may seem saintly for the wounded party to suffer his pain in silence, and it is surely easier to keep that silence than risk opening wounds; but it does no good for the marriage, and it encourages no

change in the sinner. He, the one who was sinned against, must speak. "Giving notice" means that he will reveal to his spouse, as clearly as he can, what she has done. No, the purpose of this revelation is not to accuse: it is to impart information. Nor does he disclose the sin by acting out his hurt in front of her (that wants to punish her by increasing her guilt; but he has already separated her sin from his own hurt). With love and not with bitterness he explains both her act and its consequences, remembering always that this communication is for her sake, the sinner's sake, and showing always in his countenance a yearning love for her.[21]

To emphasize the importance of giving notice, consider how often the word "rebuke" or a form of it is found in Scripture. "Rebuke" is found 61 times; "rebuked" is found 32 times; "rebukes" is found 8 times; and "rebuking" is found 2 times in the New International Version. One of the words used for "rebuke" in the Old Testament is *ribh*, which is translated, "to contend with." One of the words used for "rebuke" in the New Testament is *elencho,* which is translated "to convict, refute, or reprove."

What makes confrontation so difficult to do? Many people feel that confrontation is judgmental and harmful. Many fears can surface when people think about confrontation. It is important that these fears be conquered and that confrontation still occur.

Step # 5: REMEMBER WHAT JESUS DID WITH YOUR SINS

"How can we gain a forgiving heart? Only by going to the cross and there seeing how much our Lord has forgiven us and at what cost. Then we shall see that the utmost we are called upon to forgive, compared to what we have been forgiven, is a very little thing" (Author Unknown).

Bob George writes, "Until you rest in the finality of the cross, you will never experience the reality of the resurrection."[22] The cross is what settled your account with Christ.

If you are a Christian, you are forgiven! Neil Strait said, "Christ on our cross is the way Calvary really reads. For he died for us—in our place. We, then, are debtors. Strange, that so often we act like we owe nothing."

Remember what God has done with your sin (Ps 106:13). Billy Graham said, "No man ever loved like Jesus, He taught the blind to see and the dumb to speak. He died on the cross to save us. He bore our sins. And now God says, 'Because he did, I can forgive you.'" Jesus paid the proper punishment, payment and penalty for our sins by his sacrifice at Calvary. Isaiah 53:5 states, "But he was pierced for our transgressions, he was crushed for our iniquities; the punishment that brought us peace was upon him, and by his wounds we are healed." Isaiah 53:10 reads, "Yet it was the LORD's will to crush him and cause him to suffer, and though the LORD makes his life a guilt offering, he will see his offspring and prolong his days, and the will of the LORD will prosper in his hand." In Jesus' place we were given the free gift of eternal life. In 2 Corinthians 5:21 we are told, "God made him who had no sin to be sin for us, so that in him we might become the righteousness of God." Only those who have been forgiven can actually understand what it means to be forgiven and to forgive others.

To refresh your memory about what God has done with your sins, it might be very helpful to read and memorize several verses. Isaiah 38:17, "Surely it was for my benefit that I suffered such anguish. In your love you have kept me from the pit of destruction; you have put all my sins behind your back." Isaiah 43:25, "I, even I, am he who blots out your transgressions, for my own sake, and remembers your sins no more." Isaiah 44:22, "I have swept away your offenses like a cloud, your sins like the morning mist. Return to me, for I have redeemed you." Micah 7:19, "You will again have compassion on us; you will tread our sins underfoot and hurl all our iniquities into the depths of the sea." Romans 6:23, "For the wages of sin is death, but the gift of God is eternal life in Christ Jesus our Lord."

This idea of remembering what Jesus did with our sins is very similar to Paul's teaching on communion found in 1 Corinthians 11:24-25: "and when he had given thanks, he broke it and said, 'This is my body, which is for you; do this in remembrance of me.' In the same way, after supper he took the cup, saying, 'This cup is the new covenant in my blood; do this, whenever you drink it, in remembrance of me.'" Jesus wanted the disciples to remember his death and why he was dying. By remembering what God did with your sins, this should provide the energy and willingness to forgive others. If you remember all that Jesus did for you, this should have a profound effect on how you treat enemies and your Christian brother. Consider this quote about what Jesus did for our sins:

> What God did makes sense. It makes sense that Jesus would be our sacrifice because a sacrifice was needed to justify man's presence before God. It makes sense that God would use the Old Law to tutor Israel on their need for grace. It makes sense that Jesus would be our High Priest. What God did makes sense. It can be taught, charted, and put in books on systematic theology.
>
> However, why God did it is absolutely absurd. When one leaves the method and examines the motive, the carefully stacked blocks of logic begin to tumble. That type of love isn't logical; it can't be neatly outlined in a sermon or explained in a term paper...
>
> Even after generations of people had spit in his face he still loved them. After a nation of chosen ones had stripped him naked and ripped his incarnated flesh, he still died for them. And even today, after billions have chosen to prostitute themselves before pimps of power, fame and wealth, he stills waits for them.

It is inexplicable. It doesn't have a drop of logic nor a thread of rationality. Bloodstained royalty. A God with tears. A creator with heart. God became earth's mockery to save his children. How absurd to think that such nobility would go to such poverty to share a treasure with such thankless souls.

But he did.[23]

Step # 6: OFFER FORGIVENESS TO THE PERSON THAT HURT YOU THE SAME WAY JESUS OFFERS IT TO YOU.

"Andrew Greeley has said that if a person forgave another person the way Jesus Christ forgives us all, we would say the forgiver was mad."[24] The last step of forgiveness is to have an "attitude" and willingness of forgiveness towards the person who hurt you. Your attitude of forgiveness must be like Jesus' (Phil 2:5). You must have an attitude that says in your mind, "If you would ask for forgiveness, I would give it to you." This attitude will help you to forgive the offending party the same way Jesus forgave you. Jesus forgave freely (Matt 10:8), completely (Col 2:13), and never brought the offense up again using it as a weapon to injure. Even if the people who hurt you don't ask for forgiveness, it still is important you have this attitude. It will prevent you from harboring bitterness in your heart! This attitude will improve all the relationships around you. This forgiveness is actually more than an "attitude." You can actually tell God or a friend that you forgive the person who hurt you, even though the offender is never aware of it.

There are at least two Scriptures that speak of forgiving the person who hurt you as Jesus forgave. Paul writes in Colossians 3:13, "Bear with each other and forgive whatever grievances you may have against one another. Forgive as the Lord forgave you." In Ephesians 4:32 Paul writes, "Be kind and compassionate to one another, forgiving each other, just as in Christ God forgave you." Paul must have thought this type of forgiveness possible or he would not have given this instruction. Jesus forgives, and helps immediately (Matt 14:31). Reluctance to forgive someone after they ask is a sure way to embitter someone. After they ask you to forgive them you might reply by saying, "I'll think about it." When Paul wrote about imitating God (Eph 5:1), he knew God is forgiving (Ps 130:4), and he does not harbor anger (Ps 103:9-10). These are two characteristics we need to have. I understand that forgiveness is not easy, but it is possible!

How can you forgive a person if they have never formally asked? If the person is not asking or behaving as if they are seeking forgiveness, you must still offer forgiveness to them. This means you have to be willing to forgive them in your heart, even if they don't ask (Matt 18:35). God offers forgiveness to the whole world, but not everyone accepts it. The same thing should happen with you (Eph 5:1). You have to offer it, but until the person accepts it, they won't be able to experience forgiveness, but you will.

Forgiveness is what people want, but they don't expect it (Exod 23:4-5). By forgiving the people who have hurt you, you become an example of Jesus to them! This is especially true when you forgive non-Christians. When a Christian forgives, this is the best witness in the world. They will question you on why you forgave them. This is your opportunity to tell them about your personal relationship with Jesus! YOUR FORGIVENESS WILL NEVER MATCH CALVARY, BUT CALVARY SHOULD BE THE REASON FOR FORGIVENESS (2 Cor 5:14).

After these six steps have been completed, it is important that you develop a good sense of humor. This is one of God's ways to deal with evil. In Psalm 37:13 we are assured, "But the Lord laughs at the wicked, for he knows their day is coming." Laughter is important because it protects the heart from becoming embittered. Laughter is especially important for people who are around the person who hurt them.

The hardest step to understand is # 2. The hardest step to do is # 4. People seem to think both these steps are mean. Nevertheless, both steps are important because if there is no debt owed, how can it be cancelled? Rendering a sentence is the debt that should be paid. You do not have to feel bad about this. God paid the penalty for sin at Calvary (1 Cor 6:20; 2 Cor 5:21). When you confront, you are telling the person the sentence that rightfully belongs to them.

For those situations where the person who hurt you might do it again, it is all right to avoid them. Paul writes in 2 Timothy 4:14-15, "Alexander the metalworker did me a great deal of harm. The Lord will repay him for what he has done. You too should be on your guard against him, because he strongly opposed our message." Jesus said in Matthew 5:39, "But I tell you, Do not resist an evil person. If someone strikes you on the right cheek, turn to him the other also." Jesus is telling Christians not to seek revenge or retaliation for what has been done to them. He is not giving people permission to abuse Christians! It must be emphasized that Jesus never allowed physical abuse unless it was part of the salvation plan (John 7:6; Matt 12:14-16; John 7:1; 8:58-59; 11:53-54; Luke 4:28-30).

How do you know for certain that you have forgiven the person that caused you loss, injustice and betrayal? You can tell you have forgiven a person when you remember what they have done, but you don't seek revenge. You know you have forgiven when you have a painful memory that does not create malice! You know you have forgiven when you can truthfully say to the person who has hurt you: "I wish you well, be happy and successful." "I seek no revenge or retaliation against you." "I wish you knew Jesus

Christ as your Lord and Savior." "I want you to go to heaven." Praying blessings for a person that hurt you is a good sign of forgiveness.

What should you not do about the past after it has been forgiven? It should never be brought up again as an illustration or in a fight. It should never be brought up again by a humorous remark. It is important that you do not jokingly bring up a person's past sin that you have forgiven. This will only make the person believe that you have not forgiven them and that your words can't be trusted. You may tell them that you were only kidding when you brought up this past sin, but they will not know if they can believe you or not (Prov 26:18-19).

It should not be brought up by innuendo. It should never be brought up again by your actions. Fathers, if you bring up a past forgiven sin of your child, you will make them think that you have not forgiven them. Doing this will also make it very difficult for your children to believe that God forgives them. They will "compare" your forgiveness style to God. Once you have forgiven a person, if you bring up the event to hurt the individual, *you have sinned*. You need to ask this person to forgive you for bringing up the past.

When you forgive the person who hurt you, you may be in a situation to offer them help. This is a very powerful witness. Look at the parable of the good Samaritan. He forgave the person who was on the road half-dead. (Oddly, I couldn't find a statement that the half-dead man was a Jew! I am assuming it, since Jesus was using this to teach a Jewish group. Luke 10:25-37). The good Samaritan had a reason, not a right, to be bitter. In spite of this he was very loving to a person who probably thought very little of him. Exodus 23:4-5 tells us what God wants Christians to do with enemies: "If you come across your enemy's ox or donkey wandering off, be sure to take it back to him. If you see the donkey of someone who hates you fallen down under its load, do not leave it there; be sure you help him with it." Make sure that you return the "donkey" in one piece and it's alive!

Forgiveness should occur:

1. As soon as possible (Eph 4:26-27).
2. As part of communion (1 Cor 11:27-28).
3. As part of our offering to God (Matt 5:23-24).
4. With all painful events, great and small (Col 3:13).

Psalm 32:8-11 is a useful help to forgiveness. It is a good devotion to read when working through forgiveness. Some of the verses say:

"*I will instruct you.*" Ask God to instruct you on reasons to forgive and how to forgive (8).

"*I will teach you the way you should go.*" Ask God to teach you what forgiveness is (8).

"*I will counsel you and watch over you.*" Ask God to teach you the proper steps of forgiveness (8).

"*Don't be like the mule or horse which have no understanding.*" Ask God to make your heart receptive to forgiving others (9).

"*Trust in the LORD.*" Ask God to teach you to trust in him more as you forgive others (10).

"*Rejoice in the LORD and be glad.*" Ask God to teach you to rejoice when you forgive, and also to rejoice because you are forgiven (11).

Why don't people ask God to forgive them?

1. Because they cannot believe what they did, and how it hurt others.

2. Because they want to punish themselves. Many people believe that after they have been punished for a certain time, God is more likely to forgive them. They may feel tremendous guilt for what they have done, and by punishing themselves they hope the guilt will go away (Ps 77:2).

3. Because they are not sure they can live up to God's standards after forgiveness. They probably believe if they ask God for forgiveness, he will expect them to be perfect.

4. Because they are sure they will do the sin again, and God will get angry when this happens.

5. Because they are using their past as "blackmail" to keep from repeating the same sin. As long as they remember what has been done, they believe they are not as likely to do it again. This is a form of insurance against future similar sin! Ironically, the opposite of this is true. The more they dwell on what they did, the more likely it is going to happen again.

In order for a Christian to be forgiven, all they have to do is confess their sin to God (1 John 1:9). **If you confess the same sin multiple times to God, you need to replace repeatedly asking God for forgiveness for that sin with thanksgiving that the sin is forgiven. You need to get away from the idea that forgiveness is an emotion. It is a biblical fact.** There are too many people who repeatedly confess to God the same sin over and over again. Instead of doing this, you need to learn to celebrate forgiveness from God. Instead of repeating the same confession, next time thank God that you are forgiven. There are three parables found in Luke 15 that deal with the idea of celebrating God's forgiveness. In the parable of the Lost Sheep, the man who found his lost sheep called his friends and neighbors to rejoice with him (Luke 15:6). In the parable of the lost coin, when she finds the coin that was lost the woman calls her friends and neighbors to rejoice with her (Luke 15:9). Jesus says this is what the angels do when a sinner repents (Luke 15:7, 10). In the parable of the Lost Son there is a celebration when the prodigal returns. It would be a wonderful thing if the Church celebrated more the forgiveness and grace of God!

6. They believe God will not forgive them, so why ask? They are sure God will only be more angry with them for asking him to forgive.

7. They believe they don't deserve to be forgiven and therefore won't accept it. Genesis 37:35 says, "All his sons and daughters came to comfort him, but he refused to be comforted." Jeremiah 31:15 says, "A voice is heard in Ramah, mourning and great weeping, Rachel weeping for her children and refusing to be comforted, because her children are no more." The reason for not accepting forgiveness and comfort may be a self-esteem problem, or extreme guilt. David wrote in Psalm 77:2, "When I was in distress, I sought the LORD; at night I stretched out untiring hands and my soul refused to be comforted." The reason for his soul refusing comfort was that David at times focused on the past (Ps 51:3), where all of his guilt and pain were stored (Ps 77:5-6). David recognized how close he had been to God at one time in his life. He also recognized to what depths he had fallen. This caused David a lot of pain (Ps 55:2).

8. Because they cannot take back what they have done.

How do you ask for forgiveness from someone you have hurt?

1. Go to the person you hurt (Matt 5:23).

2. Confess what you have done to them (Lev 5:5; 16:21-22; Num 5:7; Jas 5:16). Take 100% responsibility for your actions. Don't blame others for your actions. An acrostic definition for confession is:

C ompletely
O pen
N ecessitating
F reedom
E ncouraging
S piritual
S urvival
I ncluding
O ur
N urturing

When you confess what you have done to hurt them:

❖ **Be specific in your confession and apology.** A general confession of "I'm sorry for what I have done" is not as healing as a specific apology. It might be helpful for you to make a list of how you have hurt this person. Then confess each individual injury and ask for forgiveness for each individual injury.

❖ **Make no excuses** for your behavior.

❖ **Don't rationalize** your behavior.

❖ **Don't use the words "but," "only," or "just."** "But" means forget what I said before. If a person tells you, "I like your hair, but..." this means they really don't like your hair. The words "only" and "just" are minimizers.

What does the Bible teach about confession? Leviticus 5:5 (also see Num 5:6-7) tells us that confession of sin is a command from God and is a required part of the forgiveness process. Leviticus 16:21-22 teaches that confession was part of the scapegoat process of forgiving sin. The sins of the people were to be placed on the goat and the goat was then to be led into the wilderness and let go.

3. Make restitution if possible. This means that if you have stolen anything you must give it back. Restitution is a

necessary part of justice (Exod 22:3, 4, 5, 6, 11, 12, 14; Lev 5:16; 6:5; 22:14; 24:18, 21; Num 5:7, 8). Making restitution (payment) for sin is also in God's plan. Jesus was our payment or restitution!

4. Ask the person to forgive you (Matt 18:26, 29). Don't beg them to forgive you. Don't plead for their forgiveness. Only ask them to forgive you one time. Don't keep apologizing for what you have done. Don't demand that the person forgive you. Don't quote them Scripture about forgiveness and tell them that if they don't forgive they are sinning.

5. If the person does forgive you, don't expect the relationship to return to pre-sin behavior. There are still consequences for the sin even after forgiveness occurs. God forgave Adam and Eve, but they still suffered some results of their sin. God forgave them but still kicked them out of the garden.

It will take time for trust and respect to be developed again. The loss of respect and trust are two very common effects of sin. The restoration will not occur overnight. Respect and trust must be gained again by the person who sinned. This process may take a considerable amount of time. Getting angry because it may be a long process, only makes the situation worse.

If the person you have wronged chooses not to forgive you, move on; you have done everything you possibly can. You are not responsible for making the person you hurt forgive you. That is between them and the Lord. Don't beg or repeatedly ask the person to forgive you.

Asking for forgiveness from God when you are a Christian

It is important to see confession of sin as being like the breathing process: It has to be done on a regular basis. In Proverbs 28:13 we read, "He who conceals his sin does not prosper, but whoever confesses and renounces them finds mercy." What does God do with the confessed sins of a Christian?

> He keeps no record of confessed sin (Ps 130:3).
> He redeems fully (Ps 130:7).
> He forgives all sins (Ps 130:8).

How does this passage in Psalm 130 relate to 1 John 1:9? 1 John 1:9 tells us that confession to God about sins causes cleansing of all unrighteousness and forgiveness of sins. Confession is our responsibility towards God. Forgiveness is God's responsibility to a Christian after confession. God is faithful and will cleanse us from unrighteousness!

❖ In Leviticus 26:40-42 we read that confession causes God to remember his covenant he made with Jacob, Isaac and Abraham.

❖ Psalm 32:5 says confession takes away the guilt of sin. Confession can take away both true and false guilt. (That's a different topic.)

❖ Jeremiah 14:20 tells how the people acknowledged their sin and guilt before God.

❖ In Nehemiah 9:2-3 we read that confession was made part of worship.

❖ Jeremiah 3:12-14 specifies confession as part of the process of returning to God.

❖ Mark 1:5 says confession of sins came before baptism.

Do people need to confess all their sins to God in order for them to be forgiven? What if you have forgotten one or two sins; if you don't confess them, will you go to hell? This is where God's grace comes in. No one is able to remember all of their sins, and no one can confess all their sins to God. Could the Holy Spirit confess sins of a Christian and intercede for them? Romans 8:26-27 teaches that the Holy Spirit intercedes for Christians. I do believe that the Holy Spirit is repeatedly talking to God on our behalf.

I dearly love the story of the woman at the well, found in John 4:1-26. I especially like verses 16 and 17, where Jesus asks a question about the woman's husband because he is giving the woman a chance to confess her sins. When she does not tell Jesus the whole story about her husbands he fills in the blanks. This passage shows the compassion of our Lord.

One of my favorite verses in the Bible on forgiveness is 2 Chronicles 7:14. It reads, "[I]f my people, who are called by my name, will humble themselves and pray and seek my face and turn from their wicked ways, then will I hear from heaven and will forgive their sin and heal their land." This teaches that forgiveness is conditional because it contains the words "if" and "then." This verse applies to Christians only ("if my people, who are called by my name"). According to this passage there are four things that must be done for Christians to be forgiven.

1. Humble yourself before God. This is in agreement with James 4:10 which reads, "Humble yourselves before the Lord, and he will lift you up." Humbling ourselves to God is a command.

2. Prayer is the second step to a Christian receiving forgiveness from God. Paul writes in 1 Thessalonians 5:17 to "pray continually." This is another command.

3. Seeking God's face is the third step to a Christian receiving forgiveness. 1 Chronicles 16:11 reads, "Look to the LORD and his strength; seek his face always." This is another command that Christians must do.

4. Turning from evil ways is the last step for a Christian to receive forgiveness. In Isaiah 55:7 we read, "Let the wicked forsake his way and the evil man his thoughts. Let him turn to the Lord, and he will have mercy on him, and to our God, for he will freely pardon." This is another command for Christians and non-Christians alike to receive forgiveness.

Below is a 14-step approach to asking God to forgive you when you are a Christian. The first 12 steps are not necessarily in order. All of these steps are taken from Psalm 51. The number in parenthesis is a reference to the verse in this chapter.

(1) Ask God for mercy, not fairness. If you got what was fair, you would be dead and Jesus would be alive! (Luke 18:13-14)

(2) Ask God to wash and cleanse you (Isa 1:18).

(3) Admit to God you are always reminded of your sins. This constant reminder is called guilt (Ps 13:2).

(4) Admit to God you have sinned against him. This is what Joseph told Potiphar's wife when she approached him about having a sexual relationship with her. Joseph asked, "How then could I do such a wicked thing and sin against God? (Gen 39:9)

(5) Admit to God you are a sinner through and through.

(6) Be totally truthful and honest with God.

(7) Ask to be cleansed and washed.

(8) Ask to have your joy and gladness restored.

(9) Ask God to hide his face from your sins. Ask God to blot them out.

(10) Ask God to create in you a pure heart and to renew your spirit.

(11) Ask God not to leave you or to take his Spirit from you.

(12) Ask God to restore to you the joy of your salvation. Ask him to grant you a willing spirit to sustain you.

After you have done the above steps you will experience two consequences of being forgiven by God.

(13) You will seek to teach other people the ways of God. I believe God expects Christians to proclaim the mighty things he has done in their life. This includes telling people about being forgiven by God.

(14) Praises for God will come from your mouth. Psalm 107:1-2 tells us to "Give thanks to the LORD, for he is good; his love endures forever. Let the redeemed of the LORD say this — those he redeemed from the hand of the foe."

What should a Christian feel when he is forgiven? I am not a big fan of linking forgiveness with an emotion: when you make it a feeling, it can change so quickly! However, David in Psalm 126 gives us a couple of things a Christian should feel.

126:1 **When a person is forgiven, dreams and hopes should be restored**. You should have dreams, hope, laughter and joy restored to you (Ps 51:12). There should be a recognition of what God has done for you (Ps 107:2).

126:2 **Their mouths should be filled with laughter and songs of joy**. You should be proclaiming what the Lord has done.

126:3 **Recognize that the Lord has done great things for you**. You should be filled with joy.

Isaiah also addresses what a person should feel when they are forgiven. In Isaiah 32:17-18 he wrote that one of the fruits of righteousness should be peace. This same passage says the effects of peace should be quietness and confidence forever. Later the writer tells us that God's people will live in peaceful dwelling places and in secure homes that are places of undisturbed rest. Two of the best tranquilizers this world has ever known are not found in a bottle or given by a prescription from a doctor. They are: 1. a clear conscience; and 2. peace with God. It is reassuring to realize that both of these are found in forgiveness. God designed it that way!

Now that we are at the end of this material, it is important not only that you have read it, it is more important now that you apply it to your life. Obviously, I don't know if you need to forgive someone, or if you need to seek forgiveness from someone, but the application of this material in your life is a most important step. I am reminded of what the half brother of Jesus wrote, "Do not merely listen to the word, and so deceive yourselves. Do what it says. Anyone who listens to the word but does not do what it says is like a man who looks at his face in a mirror and, after looking at himself, goes away and immediately forgets what he looks like. But the man who looks intently into the perfect law that gives freedom, and continues to do this, not forgetting what he has heard, but doing it — he will be blessed in what he does" (Jas 1:22-25).

Source Notes

1. Dag Hammarskjold, *Markings* (New York: Alfred A. Knopf, 1964), p. 124.

2. Condensed from *American Way* magazine, 15 January 1994.

3. Source: *The Pastor's Story File* Number 18 — April, 1986.

4. Lewis B. Smedes, *Forgive and Forget* (Harper and Row, 1984), p. 118.

5. LeRoy Lawson, *Where Do We Grow from Here* (Cincinnati, OH: Standard, 1985), p. 13.

6. Rich Buhler, *Pain and Pretending* (Nashville: Nelson, 1988), p. 196.

7. John Edwards with John P. Boneck, *Reconciliation* (Minneapolis: Bethany House, 1984), p. 81.

8. Dr. James C. Dobson, *Love Must Be Tough* (Waco, TX: Word, 1983), p. 121.

9. Jan Frank, *A Door of Hope* (San Bernardino, CA: Here's Life Publishers, 1987), p.71.

10. Ibid.

11. *Diagnostic and Statistical Manual of Mental Disorders* III-R, p. 321.

12. Don Van Natta, Jr., "Defense Psychiatrist Who Claims Insanity Convicted of Bribery," *The Miami Herald*, 19 March 1991.

13. Sue Linday, "Trial Pits Live-in Patient against Therapist," *Rocky Mountain News*, 4 December 1994.

14. Charles Colson, *A Dance With Deception* (Dallas: Word, 1993), pp. 68, 69.

15. Neil T. Anderson,*The Bondage Breakers*, p. 195.

16. Lewis Smedes, *Forgive and Forget*, p. 38.

17. Ibid., p. 39.

18. David Seamands, *Healing of Memories* (Wheaton, IL: Victor Books, 1985), p. 39.

19. David Augsburger, *Caring Enough to Confront* (Ventura, CA: Regal Books, 1984), p. 50.

20. Jan Frank, *A Door of Hope,*, p. 109.

21. Walter Wangerin, Jr., *As For Me and My House* , p. 80.

22. Bob George, *Classic Christianity* (Eugene, OR: Harvest House, 1989), p. 56.

23. Max Lucado, *God Came Near* (Portland, OR: Multnomah Press, 1987).

24. Keith Miller, *The Scent of Love* (Carmel, NY: Guideposts, 1983), p. 192.

Appendix A

Questions about forgiveness

A follow up to Chapter 8

Read the passages below and answer the following questions:

Matthew 5:38-48

What does Jesus mean by "turn the other cheek"?

What does Jesus say we should do with people who persecute us?

Whom should we love? Why is this difficult?

How does this teaching relate to Paul's in Romans 12:20-21?

What type of enemies do you have? How did they become your enemies?

According to Matthew 5:39-41 what should we do when mistreated? How would doing this be a witness? What does the second mile represent?

According to Matthew 5:42 we should give. What should we expect in return?

What did Jesus say about "an eye for an eye"? How did Jesus change this teaching from the Old Testament? (Exod 21:23-25; Lev 24:17-20; Deut 19:21)

Matthew 5:23-26

What is more important than offerings to God according to Jesus?

What does God do with a gift given from an unforgiving heart?

What adjective does God use to describe how we should handle matters? (25) What happens if we don't handle matters in this way?

How does James 4:17 relate to this passage?

What is the warning at the end of this teaching?

Matthew 18:15-17

What should you do with a brother who has sinned against you?

Why is this confrontation so difficult?

Can you think of any times in the Old Testament where someone confronted sin? What about David and Nathan? (2 Sam 12)

What are some New Testament examples of confrontation of sin?

What are the biblical steps to correct a situation with a brother? What step(s) are overlooked most of the time?

Matthew 18:21-35

What was Jesus' response when asked how many times to forgive?

Why did Jesus tell a parable about forgiveness to Peter?

To which person in the parable do you relate the most?

What finally happens to the unmerciful servant? (v. 34).

How does this relate to Jesus' teaching in Matthew 6:14-15?

Do you think most people are aware of the importance of forgiving others? Why or why not?

Why do you think people have a hard time forgiving

others? Could it be that they want them to suffer for what they have done?

What does God expect people to do once they have been forgiven?

What does it mean to forgive someone from your heart? (v. 35).

What was the master's emotional response to the servant's lack of forgiveness? (v. 34).

Is it easier for God or man to forgive? Why?

What is the similarity in the two servants' pleas for forgiveness?

What did Jesus call the unforgiving person? (v. 32).

To what does Jesus compare forgiveness? (vv. 27, 32). How does this relate to Deuteronomy 15:1-13?

What was Jesus' response to the man's lack of forgiveness? How does Hebrews 13:8 and Malachi 3:6 bring this verse into modern life?

Who brought the servant to the master? (v. 24).

Who brings us to God?

Who cancels the debt(s) of sin?

Why do you think the servant did not come on his own to the master? Could it have been because of the size of the debt or because of fear of the master? How does this relate to why people may not ask God to forgive them?

According to Hebrews 4:16; 10:35-36 how should God be approached?

Luke 7:36-50

Why did Simon think Jesus was not a prophet?

What was the question Jesus asked in the parable? Why was it asked?

What two things did Jesus link with forgiveness in verse 42?

What were some of the acts of kindness the woman did for Jesus?

Did this woman ask for Jesus' forgiveness?

Was Jesus ready to forgive her?

In verse 50 what two things does Jesus link with forgiveness?

How is this encounter different from the healing of the paralytic? (Mark 2:1-12).

Why did this woman come to Jesus? How does this relate to what Jesus said in Matthew 21:31-32?

Was she surprised Jesus let her touch him? Would the Pharisees have done the same? Why was Jesus more popular with people?

Why did Jesus say, "Go in peace"? How does this relate to Isaiah 32:17?

Read Luke 18:9-14 and answer the following questions.

1. What was the difference in these two men?
2. What was different in their prayers?
3. What was the Pharisee's belief about himself?
4. Why did the tax collector stand at a distance?
5. About whom did the Pharisee pray?
6. Why did the tax collector not even look up to heaven?
7. Why was the tax collector justified before God?
8. How did the tax collector confess his sins?
9. Did the Pharisee confess any of his sins?
10. Why did Jesus tell this parable?
11. At whom was this parable directed?

Answer these questions on Acts 13:38-39

1. In what way is Jesus' forgiveness complete?
2. What must be believed to be justified?
3. What is the word linked with justified?

What are the two words linked with justification in 1 Corinthians 6:11?

What are two consequences if we are justified by grace? (Titus 3:7)

Select Bibliography

American Way 1/15/94

Anderson, Neil T. *The Bondage Breakers*. Eugene, OR: Harvest House, 1990.

Arterburn, Stephen F., M.Ed. and David A. Stoop, Ph.D. *When Someone You Love Is Someone You Hate*. Waco, TX: Word, 1988.

Augsburger, David. *Caring Enough to Confront*. Ventura, CA: Regal Books, 1984.

Backus, William, Ph.D. *Telling the Truth to Troubled People*. Minneapolis: Bethany, 1985.

Barna, George. *The Barna Report: What Americans Believe*. Ventura, CA: Regal Books, 1991.

Bass, Ellen and Laura Davis. *Courage to Heal*. New York: Harper & Row, 1988.

Benson, Dr. Herbert W. "Does Prayer Heal?" *Reader's Digest*, March, 1996.

Buhler, Rich. *Pain and Pretending*. Nashville: Nelson, 1988.

Carrington, W.L. *Psychology, Religion, and Human Need*. Great Neck, NY: Channel Press, 1957.

Colson, Charles. *A Dance With Deception*. Dallas: Word, 1993.

Dobson, Dr. James C. *Love Must Be Tough*. Waco, TX: Word, 1983.

Edwards, John with John P. Boneck, *Reconciliation*. Minneapolis: Bethany House, 1984.

Hickey, Neil. "How Much Violence on TV?" *Ethics: Easier Said Than Done. TV Guide.* Issue 21, 1993.

Frank, Jan. *A Door of Hope*. San Bernardino, CA: Here's Life Publishers, 1987.

Friedman, M.D. and Rosenman, M.D. *Type A Behavior and Your Heart*. New York: A Fawcett Crest Book.

Fromm, Erich. *Art of Loving*. New York: Colophon Books, Harper & Row, 1956.

George, Bob. *Classic Christianity*. Eugene, OR: Harvest House, 1989.

Graham, Billy. *Answers to Life's Problems*. Minneapolis: Grason, 1988.

_____. *Hope for the Troubled Heart*. Minneapolis: Grason, 1991.

Greenberg, Jerald. *Journal of Applied Psychology*, October 1992

Hammarskjold, Dag. *Markings*. New York: Alfred A. Knopf, 1964.

Hargrave, Terry D. *Families and Forgiveness*. New York: Brunner/Mazel, 1994.

Hemfelt, Minirth, and Meier. *We Are Driven*. Nashville: Nelson, 1989.

Hoffman, Martin. "The Role of the Father in Moral Internalization," in *The Role of the Father in Child Development*, Michael E. Lamb, ed. New York: John Wiley and Sons, 1981.

Hyers, Conrad. *Comic Vision and the Christian Faith*. New York: Pilgrim Press, 1981.

Kaunda, Kenneth. *The Riddle of Violence*. San Francisco: Harper & Row, 1980.

Keller, W. Philip. *A Gardener Looks at the Fruits of the Spirit.* Waco, TX: Word, 1979.

Klein, Allen. *The Healing Power of Humor.* Los Angeles: Jeremy P. Tarcher, 1989.

Larsen, Earnie and Carol Larsen Hegarty. *From Anger to Forgiveness.* New York: A Hazelden Book, 1992.

Lawson, LeRoy. *Where Do We Grow from Here.* Cincinnati: Standard, 1985.

Lerner, Harriet Goldhor, Ph.D. *The Dance of Anger.* New York: Harper & Row, 1985.

Lewis, C.S. *Mere Christianity.* New York: Macmillan, Collier Books, 1952.

_____. *The Problem with Pain.* London: Fontana, 1961.

Lucado, Max. *God Came Near.* Portland, OR: Multnomah, 1987.

Mallory, James D., Jr., M.D. *The Kink and I.* Wheaton, IL: Victor Books, 1974.

McDowell, Josh and Bill Jones. *The Teenage Q/A Book.* Dallas: Word, 1990.

McGinnis, Alan L. *Bringing Out the Best in People.* Minneapolis: Augsburg, 1985.

Miller, Keith. *The Scent of Love.* Carmel, NY: Guideposts, 1983.

Morley, Patrick M. *Walking with Christ in the Details of Life.* Nashville: Nelson, 1992.

Peck, M. Scott. *People of the Lie.* New York: Simon & Schuster, 1983.

Pittman, Frank. *Private Lies: Infidelity and the Betrayal of Intimacy.* New York: W.W. Norton, 1989.

Polson, Dan. *Living without Losing.* Eugene, OR: Harvest House, 1975.

Proto, Louis. *Be Your Own Best Friend.* New York, Berkley Books, 1994.

Seamands, David. *Healing of Memories.* Wheaton, IL: Victor Books, 1985.

Siegel, Bernie, M.D. *Love, Medicine and Miracles.* New York: Harper & Row, 1990.

_____. *Peace, Love, and Healing.* New York: Harper & Row, 1989.

Simonton, O. Carl, Stephanie Matthews-Simonton, James Creighton. *Getting Well Again.* Los Angeles: Jeremy P. Tarcher, Inc., 1978.

Smalley, Gary and John Trent. *Love Is a Decision.* Dallas: Word, 1989.

Smedes, Lewis B. *Forgive and Forget.* San Francisco: Harper and Row, 1984.

Spurgeon, C.H. *Day by Day with C.H. Spurgeon.* Grand Rapids: Kregel, 1992.

Talley, Jim. *Reconcilable Differences.* Nashville: Nelson, 1991.

Tillich, Paul. *The Eternal Now.* New York: Scribner's, 1963.

"The Pastor's Story File" Number 18—April, 1986.

Veninga, Robert L. *A Gift of Hope.* Boston: Little, Brown, 1985.

Walter Wangerin, Jr., *As For Me and My House.* Nashville: Nelson, 1990.

Worthington, Everett L., Jr. *Marriage Counseling: A Christian Approach to Counseling Couples.* Downers Grove: InterVarsity Press, 1989.

Wright, H. Norman *Making Peace with Your Past.* Old Tappan, NJ: Revell, 1985.

Youthworker Update, March 1993. El Cajon, CA: Youth Specialties, Inc.

About the Author

Charles Gerber, MA, is the founder and executive director of Christian Counseling Services in Muncie, Indiana. He has authored three other books for College Press (the latest, *Mirror of the Heart*, released in August, 2001) and is a popular national speaker.

Charley speaks nationally on the topic of forgiveness as well as other topics related to Christian counseling. He presents seminars and workshops at churches and conventions on a variety of mental health-related subjects.

Charley lives in Muncie with his wife, Janelle, and his two children, Joshua and Caitlyn. He is an elder at University Christian Church in Muncie, IN.

Contact Information

Christian Counseling Services
1804 North Wheeling Ave.
Muncie, Indiana 47303

(765) 289-1631

email: CCSCharley@aol.com

Printed in the United States
74857LV00003B/1-24